Lecture Notes
in Economics and
Mathematical Systems

Managing Editors: M. Beckmann and W. Krelle

298

Chew Soo Hong
Zheng Quan

Integral Global Optimization

Theory, Implementation and Applications

Springer-Verlag
Berlin Heidelberg New York London Paris Tokyo

Authors

CHEW Soo Hong
Department of Economics, Johns Hopkins University
Charles & 34th Streets, Baltimore, Maryland 21218, USA

ZHENG Quan
Department of Mathematics, Shanghai University of Science and Technology
Shanghai, China

ISBN 3-540-18772-3 Springer-Verlag Berlin Heidelberg New York
ISBN 0-387-18772-3 Springer-Verlag New York Berlin Heidelberg

Printed in Germany

Printing and binding: Druckhaus Beltz, Hemsbach/Bergstr.
2142/3140-543210

ACKNOWLEDGMENTS

We are grateful to Richard Auster, Kevin McCabe, Mike Ransom, Stan Reynolds and especially Fernando Saldanha for helpful comments and suggestions during a series of lectures, which paralleled the writing of this monograph, in the Spring semester of 1983 at the University of Arizona. (At the time, Chew was on the economics faculty there and Zheng was a visiting scholar.) We would also like to thank Jennifer Mao for her many useful suggestions and patience in reading earlier drafts of this monograph.

Contents

CHAPTER I

PRELIMINARY

§1 Introduction

1.1 Statement of the Problem

Suppose X is a Hausdorff topological space, f a real valued function on X and S a closed subset of X. The problem is to find the infimum of f over S:

$$\bar{c} = \inf_{x \in S} f(x) \tag{1.1}$$

and the set of global minima $\bar{c}$ that solve this problem. We begin with the following assumptions:

Assumption A1: f is continuous on S.

Assumption A2: There is a real number c such that the intersection of the level set

$$H_c = \{ x \mid f(x) \leq c \} \tag{1.2}$$

and S is nonempty and compact.

Consequently, the above problem is reduced to finding

$$\bar{c} = \min_{x \in S \cap H_c} f(x). \tag{1.3}$$

In this case, the set of global minima $\bar{H}$ is nonempty, i.e.,

$$\bar{H} = H_{\bar{c}} \cap S \neq \emptyset. \tag{1.4}$$

In what follows, we shall maintain Assumptions A1 and A2 except when we consider the noncontinuous case. Since the problem is referred to rather frequently, we restate it as follows:

Problem (P): Under Assumptions A1 and A2, find the global minimum value

$$\bar{c} = \min_{x \in S} f(x)$$

and the set of global minima

$$\bar{H} = \{ x \mid f(x) = \bar{c} \}.$$

1.2 Examples

The problem is stated in a general form so that the theory and methods discussed here can be applied to a wide class of optimization problems.

Example 1.1 (Mathematical Programming): Let $f : \mathbb{R}^n \to \mathbb{R}$, $g : \mathbb{R}^n \to \mathbb{R}^m$, and $\ell : \mathbb{R}^n \to \mathbb{R}^r$ be continuous. Mathematical programming deals with the problem of minimizing f subject to constraints

$$g(x) \leq 0, \quad \ell(x) = 0. \tag{1.5}$$

Here, we have $X = \mathbb{R}^n$, $S = \{x \mid g(x) \leq 0, \ \ell(x) = 0\}$. Clearly, this is a special case of (1.1).

Example 1.2 (Rational Approximation): Let $h_i : [0,1] \to \mathbb{R}$, $i = 1,\cdots,m$, and $g_j : [0,1] \to \mathbb{R}$, $j = 1,\cdots,r$, be continuous. The problem is to minimize the distance F between an upper-semi-continuous function f and a rational linear combination of h_i's and g_j's:

$$F(x) = \left\| f - \frac{\Sigma_{i=1}^m x_i h_i}{\Sigma_{j=1}^r x_{m+j} g_j} \right\| = \max_{0 \leq t \leq 1} \left| f(t) - \frac{\Sigma_{i=1}^m x_i h_i(t)}{\Sigma_{j=1}^r x_{m+j} g_j(t)} \right| \tag{1.6}$$

over all possible coefficient vectors $x = (x_1,\cdots,x_n) \in \mathbb{R}^n = X$, where $n = m+r$. Sometimes (for instance, in optimal design of networks), the variable x is restricted to a set S. For example, $S = \{x \mid a^i \leq x^i \leq b^i, \ i = 1,\cdots,n\}$. Note that function f need not be differentiable or convex.

Example 1.3 (Integer Programming): Let $X = \{x_1, x_2, \cdots\}$ and let each subset of X be an open set. Then X is a topological space with the discrete topology.

Let f be a real-valued function on X, and S a subset of X. The function f is continuous because $\{x \mid f(x) \leq c\}$ or $\{x \mid f(x) < c\}$ is both open and closed for arbitrary real number c.

Example 1.4 (Calculus of Variations): The problem is to minimize

$$F(x) = \int_0^1 f(x(t),\dot{x}(t),t)dt + g(x(0),x(1)) \tag{1.7}$$

over the linear space $X = \mathcal{A}_m[0,1]$, consisting of absolutely continuous functions from $[0,1]$ to $\mathbb{R}^n$, where $\dot{x}$ denotes the derivative of x with respect to the time variable t, which can be represented by a measurable function whose values are uniquely determined except on a set of measure zero. The function $f(\cdot,\cdot,t)$ and g on $\mathbb{R}^n \times \mathbb{R}^n$ are assumed to be continuous. Clearly, $F(x)$ is well defined and continuous. Let $S \subset X = \mathcal{A}_m[0,1]$. Then the problem of calculus of variations becomes

$$\begin{array}{c} \text{minimize } F(x) \\ x \in S \end{array}$$

<u>Example 1.5</u> (Optimal Control): The problem considered here is to minimize

$$F(x,u) = \int_0^1 f_0(x(t),u(t),t)dt + g(x(0),x(1)) \tag{1.8}$$

over the set S consisting of function $x \in \mathcal{A}_m[0,1]$ and $u \in L_n^1[0,1]$ satisfying

$$\begin{aligned} &\dot{x}(t) = f(x(t),u(t),t) \quad \text{a.e.,} \quad t \in [0,1] \\ &f_i(x(t),u(t),t) \leq 0 \quad \text{a.e.,} \quad i = 1,\cdots,m \\ &\ell_j(x(0),x(1)) \quad \leq 0 \quad \text{a.e.,} \quad j = 1,\cdots,r \end{aligned} \tag{1.9}$$

where $X = \mathcal{A}_m[0,1] \times L_n^1[0,1]$. The function f is assumed to be Lipschitz such that the differential equation solution exists for each given control $u(t)$. The functions f_i and ℓ_j are continuous.

1.3 <u>Outline</u>

We provide, in this outline, a brief description of the organization and development of the material in the rest of the monograph. After discussing, in the next section, the concept of measure appropriate to our approach, called Q-measure, we are ready to derive, in the following chapter, various integral characterizations of global optimality corresponding to a continuous function f on a topological space X with respect to a Q-measure μ.

In Section 1 of Chapter II, the concept of mean value of f over level sets in X is defined. The mean value for the minimal level set is obtained via a limiting process. Necessary and sufficient conditions for global optimality in terms of the behavior of the above mean value are then derived. In the next section, we extend our mean value definition to the case of variance as well as higher moments of f, and obtain the corresponding characterizations of global optimality for these cases. Section 3 examines the constrained cases using the rejection method and the reduction method. The latter is illustrated in the context of linear equality constraints. Our modification of the penalty method for the mean value as well as variance and higher-moment characterizations are discussed in Section 4. Section 5 applies our global optimization theory to the case of convex functions incorporating a brief discussion of Clarke's generalized gradients. The relation between our approach and the standard, derivative-based Kuhn-Tucker theory is explored in Section 6. Section 7 concerns integer and mixed programming with a suitable definition of continuity with respect to the discrete topology. Section 8 treats a class of discontinuous functions with "accessible" global minima.

Theoretical algorithms based on the various characterizations of global optimality in Chapter II are developed in Chapter III. Section 1 describes the mean value level set method and proves its convergence (which does not depend on the choice of the initial data) and the limited influence of error propagation. The corresponding rejection and reduction algorithms are discussed in Section 2. The global versions of the sequential and nonsequential penalty methods are treated in Sections 3 and 4, respectively. A theoretical strategy to improve computational efficiency by adaptively changing search domains is the subject of the next section. Section 6 considers the issue of stability of the global minimum value and the set of global minima. Finally, we demonstrate in Section 7 that the global minimum value of a lower dimensional "approximating" problem always converges to the global minimum value for the original problem.

In Chapter IV, we are ready to apply the understanding gained thus far to the question of computer implementation of the theoretical algorithms discussed. Except near the end of Section 4 where we comment on the possibility of multiple solutions, we shall consider only the case of a unique global minimum, admitting the possibility of numerous (countably infinite, in the test problem) local minima. Section 1 describes a simple Monte Carlo model with the unique global optimum in the initial search domain. Statistical analysis of this model is provided in Section 2 where we show that the growth in the amount of computation in relation to the degree of precision is slower than its square. A refinement, partly adopting the change-of-domain strategy discussed in Section 5 of Chapter III, is presented in the next section to reduce the realized skew rate. Observations about the implementability of the other theoretical algorithms -- the rejection method, the reduction method, and the integer and mixed programming -- are described in Section 4. We end Chapter IV by examining and comparing the performance of our implemented algorithms with respect to several numerical test problems.

To illustrate the usefulness of the integral approach to global optimization, examples on implementation are discussed in Chapter V in terms of the specific methods used.

The numbering of expressions, definitions, examples, propositions, lemmas, theorems and corollaries is section-specific. For example, "Definition 2.4" is the forth definition to appear in Section 2 of the current chapter. When an expression, definition, etc. from a different chapter is referred to, the corresponding number is prefixed with a Roman numeral indicating the chapter. Lemmas, propositions, theorems and corollaries are numbered in the same sequence. For instance, we have Propositions 1.1 - 1.6, Lemma 1.7 and Theorem 1.8 in Chapter II.

§2 An Appropriate Concept of Measure

2.1 Q-Measure

Let X be a Hausdorff topological space, Ω a σ-field of subsets of X, and μ a measure on Ω. The triple (X,Ω,μ) is called a measure space. Consider the following additional requirements which are compatible with the topological properties of X:

(i) Ω is a Borel field, i.e., each open set of X is in Ω.

(ii) Any nonempty open set has positive measure.

(iii) The measure of a compact set in X is bounded.

A measure space which has all these properties (properties (i) and (ii)) is said to be a Q-measure space (Q_1-measure space). A measure space (X,Ω,μ_0) is said to be a Q_0-measure space if $\mu_0 = \lim_{n\to\infty} \mu_n$ and $\{(X,\Omega,\mu_n)\}$ is a sequence of Q-measure spaces.

Example 2.1: The Lebesque measure space in the Euclidean space of dimension n, $(\mathbb{R}^n,\mathcal{B},\mu)$, is a Q-measure space.

Example 2.2: The Lebesque measure space on a manifold L of dimension m in $\mathbb{R}^n$, $(L,\mathcal{B}_L,\mu_L)$, is also a Q-measure space.

Example 2.3: The nondegenerate Gaussian measure on a separable Hilbert space H, (H,Ω,μ), is also a Q-measure space.

Example 2.4: (X,Ω,μ), where

$$\mu(A) = \begin{cases} 1 & \text{if } x_0 \in A \\ 0 & \text{if } x_0 \notin A, \end{cases}$$

is not a Q-measure space but is a Q_0-measure space for $X = \mathbb{R}^n$.

In our framework, we will deal with a variety of Q-measure space tailored to the specific contexts of the optimization problems. How can we establish the connection between measure theory and global optimization? The following lemmas yield a sufficient global optimality condition which plays an important role in the subsequent development.

2.2 Lemmata

Definition 2.1: A subset G of a topological space X is said to be robust if $cl(intG) = clG$.

Lemma 2.1: Let (X,Ω,μ) be a Q_1-measure space and G be a robust subset of X. Suppose the intersection of level set $H_c = \{x \mid f(x) \leq c\}$ and G is nonempty. If $\mu(H_c \cap G) = 0$, then c is the global minimum value of f over G and $H_c \cap G$ is the set of global minima.

Proof: Let us first establish the following intermediate result. Suppose E is an open set and G is a robust set. If $E \cap G \neq \emptyset$, then there exists a nonempty open set B contained in $E \cap G$. Let $x \in E \cap G$. Since E is an open set, there is an open set B_1 such that $x \in B_1 \subset E$. On the other hand, $x \in G \subset clG = cl(intG)$. Therefore, $B_1 \cap (intG) \neq \emptyset$ so that there is an open set $B \subset B_1 \cap (intG) \subset E \cap G$.

Suppose c is not the global minimum value of f over G whereas $\hat{c}$ is. Then

$$c - \hat{c} \triangleq 2\eta > 0.$$

Let $E = \{x \mid f(x) < c-\eta\}$ which is nonempty and open since f is continuous and $c-\eta > \hat{c}$. We have that

$$\emptyset \neq H_{\hat{c}} \cap G \subset E \cap G \subset H_c \cap G.$$

Therefore, there is an open set B such that

$$B \subset E \cap G \subset H_c \cap G.$$

However,

$$0 < \mu(B) \leq \mu(H_c \cap G)$$

because μ is a Q_1-measure. We have a contradiction with respect to the condition $\mu(H_c \cap G) = 0$. ∎

Note that the condition $\mu(H_c \cap G) = 0$ is not necessary (see the following counter example).

Example 2.5: Let $f(x) = 0$ for $0 \leq x \leq 1$. Here, $X = \mathbb{R}^1$, and the Lebesque measure space on $\mathbb{R}^1$ is used as a Q-measure space. $G = [0,1] \subset \mathbb{R}^1$, and $c = 0$ is the global minimum value of f over G. But $\mu(H_c \cap G) = 1 \neq 0$.

In the following discussion we always assume that the measure space (X,Ω,μ) is a Q-measure space.

We restate Lemma 2.1 below in an opposite way.

Lemma 2.2: Let (X,Ω,μ) be a Q-measure space and G a robust set. If $c > \bar{c}$ (i.e., $\bar{c}$ is the global minimum value of f over G), then

$$\mu(H_c \cap G) > 0.$$

CHAPTER II

INTEGRAL CHARACTERIZATIONS OF GLOBAL OPTIMALITY

Optimality conditions, i.e. the conditions by which one can determine if a point x is a candidate for a minimum, play an important role in the theory of optimization. There have been numerous studies of how to characterize the optimal value of a nonlinear function in a constrained set. However, almost all such attempts are of a local nature. Even then, they have tended to require several levels of differentiability unless some convexity hypotheses are imposed. The search for necessary and sufficient conditions for global optimality without requiring any convexity is an important and needed endeavor.

Our approach differs from the traditional, derivative-based ones by appealing to the theory of measure and integration. In this chapter we introduce the concepts of mean value, variance and higher moments of a function over level sets to characterize the global optimality of a function with and without constraints. For convex or differentiable functions, these conditions reduce to the standard ones. In the last section of this chapter, we obtain the optimality conditions for a class of not necessarily continuous functions called robust functions.

§1 Mean Value Conditions

In this section, the concept of mean value of a function over its level sets will be introduced. This concept is useful in considering the global optimality conditions and global algorithm. In Subsection 1.3, we prove the mean value condition theorem, which gives us two sufficient and necessary conditions for global optimality.

1.1 Mean Value over Level Sets

Let X be a Hausdorff topological space, f be a real-valued function on X, and (X,Ω,μ) be a Q-measure space. Suppose Assumptions A1 and A2 in Chapter I hold.

Definition 1.1: Suppose $c > \bar{c} = \min f(x)$. We define

$$M(f,c) = \frac{1}{\mu(H_c)}\int_{H_c} f(x)d\mu \tag{1.1}$$

to be the mean value of the function f over its level set

$$H_c = \{ x \mid f(x) \le c \}. \tag{1.2}$$

According to Lemma I.2.2, $\mu(H_c) > 0$ for $c > \bar{c}$. Consequently, mean value (1.1) is well defined given the continuity of f.

The following are properties of our mean value.

Proposition 1.0: For $c > \bar{c}$,

$$M(f,c) \le c. \tag{1.3}$$

Proof: By definition, $f(x) \le c$ for $x \in H_c$ so that

$$M(f,c) = \frac{1}{\mu(H_c)}\int_{H_c} f(x)d\mu \le \frac{1}{\mu(H_c)}\int_{H_c} cd\mu = \frac{1}{\mu(H_c)}\cdot c\cdot\mu(H_c) = c. \quad \blacksquare$$

Proposition 1.1: If $c_2 \ge c_1 > \bar{c}$, then

$$M(f,c_2) \ge M(f,c_1). \tag{1.4}$$

Proof: Applying Proposition 1.0 and known properties of integration, we have

$$M(f,c_2) = \frac{1}{\mu(H_{c_2})}\int_{H_{c_2}} f(x)d\mu$$

$$= \frac{1}{\mu(H_{c_2})}\left[\int_{H_{c_1}} f(x)d\mu + \int_{H_{c_2}\setminus H_{c_1}} f(x)d\mu\right]$$

$$\geq \frac{1}{\mu(H_{c_2})}\int_{H_{c_1}} f(x)d\mu + \frac{\mu(H_{c_2})-\mu(H_{c_1})}{\mu(H_{c_2})} c_1$$

$$\geq \frac{1}{\mu(H_{c_2})}\int_{H_{c_1}} f(x)d\mu + \frac{\mu(H_{c_2})-\mu(H_{c_1})}{\mu(H_{c_2})} \frac{1}{\mu(H_{c_1})}\int_{H_{c_1}} f(x)d\mu$$

$$= \frac{\mu(H_{c_1})+\mu(H_{c_2})-\mu(H_{c_1})}{\mu(H_{c_1})\mu(H_{c_2})}\int_{H_{c_1}} f(x)d\mu$$

$$= \frac{1}{\mu(H_{c_1})}\int_{H_{c_1}} f(x)d\mu = M(f,c_1). \quad \blacksquare$$

Lemma 1.2: Suppose $\{c_k\}$ is a decreasing sequence which tends to $c \geq \bar{c} = \min f(x)$ as $k \to \infty$. Then,

$$H_c = \bigcap_{k=1}^{\infty} H_{c_k} = \lim_{k\to\infty} H_{c_k}$$

and

$$\lim_{k\to\infty} \mu(H_{c_k}) = \mu(H_c).$$

Proof: According to the definition of level sets, we have

$$H_c \subset H_{c_k} \subset H_{c_{k-1}}, \quad k = 1,2,\cdots.$$

Hence, $\lim_{k\to\infty} H_{c_k} = \bigcap_{k=1}^{\infty} H_{c_k}$. If $x \in \bigcap_{k=1}^{\infty} H_{c_k}$, then $f(x) \leq c_k$ for all $k = 1,2,\cdots$. Hence, $f(x) \leq c$; i.e., $x \in H_c$. The conclusion follows immediately from the continuity of the measure. $\blacksquare$

Proposition 1.3: Suppose $\{c_k\}$ is a decreasing sequence whose limit is $c > \bar{c}$. Then

$$M(f,c) = \lim_{c_k \downarrow c} M(f,c_k). \tag{1.5}$$

Proof: According to Proposition 1.1, the sequence $\{M(f,c_k)\}$ is decreasing and $M(f,c_k) \geq M(f,c)$ for $k = 1,2,\cdots$, so that the limit (1.5) exists. Moreover,

$$0 \leq \frac{1}{\mu(H_{c_k})}\int_{H_{c_k}} f(x)d\mu - \frac{1}{\mu(H_c)}\int_{H_c} f(x)d\mu$$

$$\leq \left|\frac{1}{\mu(H_{c_k})}\int_{H_{c_k}} f(x)d\mu - \frac{1}{\mu(H_c)}\int_{H_{c_k}} f(x)d\mu\right|$$

$$+ \left|\frac{1}{\mu(H_c)}\int_{H_{c_k}} f(x)d\mu - \frac{1}{\mu(H_c)}\int_{H_c} f(x)d\mu\right|$$

$$\leq \left|\left[\frac{1}{\mu(H_{c_k})} - \frac{1}{\mu(H_c)}\right]\int_{H_{c_k}} f(x)d\mu\right| + \frac{1}{\mu(H_c)}\left|\int_{H_{c_k}\setminus H_c} f(x)d\mu\right|.$$

The latter two terms will tend to zero as c_k goes to c because of the continuity of μ and the absolute continuity of the integral of a bounded measurable function f. ∎

Proposition 1.4: The mean value of a function over its level sets has the following properties:

(1) Constancy: $M(\lambda,c) = \lambda$ for a constant $\lambda \geq c$. (1.6)

(2) Homogeneity: $M(\lambda f,\lambda c) = \lambda M(f,c)$ for constants $\lambda > 0$ and $c > \bar{c}$. (1.7)

(3) Translation: $M(f+\lambda,c+\lambda) = M(f,c) + \lambda$ for constants $\lambda > 0$ and $c > \bar{c}$. (1.8)

Proof: (1) is obvious.

(2): Since $\{x \mid \lambda f(x) \leq \lambda c\} = \{x \mid f(x) \leq c\} = H_c$ for $\lambda > 0$, we have

$$M(\lambda f,\lambda c) = \frac{1}{\mu(H_c)}\int_{H_c} \lambda f(x)d\mu = \lambda M(f,c).$$

(3): We have $\{x \mid f(x)+\lambda \leq c+\lambda\} = \{x \mid f(x) \leq c\}$ for each λ. Hence,

$$M(f+\lambda,c+\lambda) = \frac{1}{\mu(H_c)}\int_{H_c} [f(x)+\lambda]d\mu = M(f,c) + \lambda.$$ ∎

The appropriate definition of differentiability for our mean value is given below:

Definition 1.2: We define the limit

$$\partial_\mu M(f,c) = \lim_{\Delta c\to 0} \frac{M(f,c+\Delta c)-M(f,c)}{\mu(H_{c+\Delta c})-\mu(H_c)} \tag{1.9}$$

to be the μ-derivative of $M(f,c)$ with respect to the measure $\mu(H_c)$ of level set H_c, if it exists.

Suppose $\Delta c > 0$. In order to investigate the existence of the limit (1.9), denote by ΔH_c the difference $H_{c+\Delta c}-H_c$. We have

$$\frac{M(f,c+\Delta c)-M(f,c)}{\mu(\Delta H_c)} = \frac{1}{\mu(H_{\Delta c})}\left[\frac{1}{\mu(H_{c+\Delta c})}\int_{H_{c+\Delta c}} f(x)d\mu - \frac{1}{\mu(H_c)}\int_{H_c} f(x)d\mu\right]$$

$$= \frac{1}{\mu(\Delta H_c)}\left[\frac{1}{\mu(H_{c+\Delta c})}\int_{H_{\Delta c}} f(x)d\mu + \left[\frac{1}{\mu(H_{c+\Delta c})} - \frac{1}{\mu(H_c)}\right]\int_{H_c} f(x)d\mu\right].$$

Hence,

$$\partial_\mu M(f,c) = \lim_{\Delta c\downarrow 0}\left[\frac{1}{\mu(H_{c+\Delta c})}\frac{1}{\mu(\Delta H_c)}\int_{\Delta H_c} f(x)d\mu - \frac{1}{\mu(H_{c+\Delta c})\mu(H_c)}\int_{H_c} f(x)d\mu\right] = \frac{c-M(f,c)}{\mu(H_c)}.$$

When $\Delta c < 0$, we can prove that

$$\lim_{\Delta c\uparrow 0} \frac{M(f,c+\Delta c)-M(f,c)}{\mu(H_{c+\Delta c})-\mu(H_c)} = \frac{c-M(f,c^-)}{\mu(H_c)} .$$

Therefore, we have proved:

<u>Proposition 1.5</u>: If $\lim_{\Delta c\to 0} \mu(H_{c+\Delta c}) = \mu(H_c)$, then

$$\partial_\mu M(f,c) = \frac{c-M(f,c)}{\mu(H_c)}, \qquad c > \bar{c}. \tag{1.10}$$

But the right-hand and left-hand derivatives always exist:

$$\partial_\mu^+ M(f,c) = \lim_{\Delta c\to 0^+} \frac{M(f,c+\Delta c)-M(f,c)}{\mu(\Delta H_c)} = \frac{c-M(f,c)}{\mu(H_c)} = \partial_\mu M(f,c), \qquad c > \bar{c}; \tag{1.11}$$

$$\partial_\mu^- M(f,c) = \lim_{\Delta c\to 0^-} \frac{M(f,c+\Delta c)-M(f,c)}{\mu(\Delta H_c)} = \frac{c-M(f,c^-)}{\mu(H_c)}, \qquad c > \bar{c}. \tag{1.12}$$

As an increasing function of c ($> \bar{c}$), $\chi(c) = \mu(H_c)$ is differentiable almost everywhere. If it is differentiable at c, then

$$\frac{dM(f,c)}{dc} = \lim_{\Delta c\to 0} \frac{M(f,c+\Delta c)-M(f,c)}{\Delta c}$$

$$= \lim_{\Delta c\to 0} \frac{\mu(\Delta H_c)}{\Delta c}\frac{M(f,c+\Delta c)-M(f,c)}{\mu(\Delta H_c)} = \frac{\chi'(c)}{\chi(c)}\left[c-M(f,c)\right].$$

<u>Proposition 1.6</u>: If $\chi(c) = \mu(H_c)$ is differentiable at $c > \bar{c}$, then

$$\frac{dM(f,c)}{dc} = \frac{\chi'(c)}{\chi(c)}\left[c-M(f,c)\right]. \tag{1.13}$$

1.2 A Limit-Based Definition

We have defined the concept of mean value for $c > \bar{c}$. What happens at $\bar{c}$? When $c = \bar{c}$, the measure $\mu(H_c)$ may vanish, in which case Definition (1.1) would not make sense. The following definition circumvents the above difficulty.

Definition 1.3: Let $c \geq \bar{c}$ and let $\{c_k\}$ be a decreasing sequence whose limit is c. The mean value M(f,c) is defined to be:

$$M(f,c) = \lim_{c_k \downarrow c} \frac{1}{\mu(H_{c_k})}\int_{H_{c_k}} f(x)d\mu. \tag{1.14}$$

The above limit is well defined since $\{M(f,c_k)\}$ is a decreasing bounded sequence. Moreover, this limit does not depend on the choice of the decreasing sequence. Suppose we take another decreasing sequence $\{b_k\}$ which tends to c as $k \to \infty$. Combining the two sequences $\{c_k\}$ and $\{b_k\}$ and reordering them, we obtain a new decreasing sequence $\{d_k\}$ which still tends to c. Now, we have a new bounded decreasing sequence $\{\frac{1}{\mu(H_{d_m})}\int_{H_{d_m}} f(x)d\mu\}$ whose limit exists. Therefore, as two subsequences of the same sequence, the following limits exist and are equal:

$$\lim_{k\to\infty} \frac{1}{\mu(H_{c_k})}\int_{H_{c_k}} f(x)d\mu = \lim_{k\to\infty} \frac{1}{\mu(H_{b_k})}\int_{H_{b_k}} f(x)d\mu.$$

By Proposition 1.3, it is clear that Definition 1.3 extends Definition 1.1 to the case of $c \geq \bar{c}$. By the same token, Propositions 1.0, 1.1, 1.3 and 1.4 remain valid for $c \geq \bar{c}$.

An alternative equivalent definition of mean value in terms of a right-hand limit process is given by:

Definition 1.4: Let $c \geq \bar{c}$, the mean value M(f,c) is defined to be the limit

$$M(f,c) = \lim_{\substack{d\to c \\ d>c}} \frac{1}{\mu(H_d)}\int_{H_d} f(x)d\mu. \tag{1.15}$$

The equivalence between the definitions of (1.14) and (1.15) follows immediately from Lemma 1.7 below.

Lemma 1.7: Suppose g is a real-valued function on $\mathbb{R}$. Then

$$\lim_{t \to t_o^+} g(t) = A \tag{1.16}$$

exists if and only if for each decreasing sequence $\{t_n\}$ whose limit is t_o:

$$\lim_{n\to\infty} g(t_n) = A. \tag{1.17}$$

Proof: Since condition (1.17) is obviously necessary, it suffices to prove its sufficiency. Suppose, under condition (1.17), that there is a sequence $y_n \to t_o$, $y_n > t_o$ such that (i) $\lim_{n\to\infty} g(y_n) \neq A$ or (ii) the limit does not exist.

Under case (i), we can find a decreasing subsequence $\{y_{n_k}\}$ of $\{y_n\}$ such that $y_{n_k} \downarrow t_o$ as $n_k \to \infty$. Condition (1.17) implies that $\lim_{n_k\to\infty} g(y_{n_k}) = A$, which is a contradiction.

Under case (ii), $\{g(y_n)\}$ may be unbounded. In this case, we can find a subsequence $\{g(y_{n_k})\}$ which tends to infinity. We then extract from $\{y_{n_k}\}$ a decreasing subsequence $\{y_{n_k'}\}$ which tends to t_o. Again, condition (1.17) requires that $\lim_{n_k'\to\infty} g(y_{n_k'}) = A$, which gives rise to a contradiction. If $\{g(y_n)\}$ is bounded, then we can find a subsequence $\{g(y_{n_k})\}$ which tends to some limit $B \neq A$ and we are back to case (i).

Finally, we should show that it is possible to find a decreasing subsequence $\{y_{n_k}\}$ from each sequence $\{y_n\}$ $(y_n \to t_o,\ y_n > t_o)$. Take y_1 as y_{n_1}. There are infinitely many terms of sequence $\{y_n\}$ within the interval $(t_o, (t_o+y_{n_1})/2)$ since $y_{n_1} > t_o$. Take any one of them and call it y_{n_2} $(n_2 > n_1)$. We have $t_o < y_{n_2} < (t_o+y_{n_1})/2 < y_{n_1}$. There are again infinitely many terms of the sequence $\{y_n\}$ within the interval $(t_o,(t_o+y_{n_2})/2)$. Repeating the process to obtain y_{n_3} such that $n_3 > n_2 > \cdots$, we obtain a subsequence $\{y_{n_k}\}$ such that $n_1 < n_2 < \cdots < n_k < \cdots$ and $y_{n_2} - t_o < (y_{n_1}-t_o)/2;\ \cdots;\ (y_{n_k}-t_o)/2 < \cdots < \frac{1}{2^{k-1}}(y_{n_1}-t_o)$. Therefore, $y_{n_k} \downarrow t_o$ as $n_k \to \infty$. ∎

1.3 Mean Value Conditions

We are now ready to prove our mean value characterization of global optimality.

Theorem 1.8 (Mean Value Conditions): For Problem (P), the following are equivalent:

a. a point $\bar{x}$ is a global minimum with $\bar{c} = f(\bar{x})$ as the corresponding global minimum value;

b.
$$M(f,c) \geq \bar{c} \quad \text{for } c > \bar{c} \tag{1.18}$$

c.
$$M(f,\bar{c}) = \bar{c}. \tag{1.19}$$

Proof: Suppose $\bar{c}$ is not the global minimum value of f and $\hat{c}$ is. Then $\bar{c}-\hat{c} = 2\eta > 0$. According to Lemma I.2.2, $\mu(H_{\hat{c}+\eta}) > 0$ and $\mu(H_{\bar{c}}) > 0$. We have

$$M(f,\bar{c}) = \frac{1}{\mu(H_{\bar{c}})}\int_{H_{\bar{c}}} f(x)d\mu = \frac{1}{\mu(H_{\bar{c}})}\left[\int_{H_{\bar{c}}\setminus H_{\hat{c}+\eta}} f(x)d\mu + \int_{H_{\hat{c}+\eta}} f(x)d\mu\right]$$

$$\leq \frac{\bar{c}}{\mu(H_{\bar{c}})}\left[\mu(H_{\bar{c}})-\mu(H_{\hat{c}+\eta})\right] + \frac{\hat{c}+\eta}{\mu(H_{\bar{c}})}\mu(H_{\hat{c}+\eta}) = \bar{c} - \beta,$$

where

$$\beta = \eta\frac{\mu(H_{\hat{c}+\eta})}{\mu(H_{\bar{c}})} > 0. \tag{1.20}$$

This establishes the sufficiency of (1.18) or (1.19).

To demonstrate the necessity of (1.18) and (1.19), suppose $\bar{c}$ is the global minimum value of f. Then $f(x) \geq \bar{c}$ for all x. So, for $c > \bar{c}$, we have

$$M(f,c) = \frac{1}{\mu(H_c)}\int_{H_c} f(x)d\mu \geq \frac{1}{\mu(H_c)}\int_{H_c} \bar{c}d\mu = \bar{c},$$

which is (1.18). Take a decreasing sequence $\{c_k\}$ such that $\lim_{k\to\infty} c_k = \bar{c}$. From (1.18) we have

$$\lim_{c_k \downarrow \bar{c}} M(f,c_k) \geq \bar{c},$$

i.e., $M(f,\bar{c}) \geq \bar{c}$. But $M(f,c) \leq c$ for $c > \bar{c}$, so that $M(f,\bar{c}) \leq \bar{c}$. Therefore,

$$M(f,\bar{c}) = \bar{c}.$$

∎

Let us take a look at an example.

Example 1.1: Minimize f(x), where $f(x) = |x|^\alpha$, $\alpha > 0$. For $c > 0$,

$$H_c = \{ x \mid |x|^\alpha \le c \} = [-c^{1/\alpha}, c^{1/\alpha}],$$

$$M(f,c) = \frac{1}{2c^{1/\alpha}} \int_{-c^{1/\alpha}}^{c^{1/\alpha}} |x|^\alpha dx = \frac{1}{c^{1/\alpha}} \int_0^{c^{1/\alpha}} x^\alpha dx = \frac{1}{1+\alpha} c.$$

Here, we consider the Lebesque measure μ. Let $\bar{c}$ be the global minimum value. Then

$$M(f,\bar{c}) = \frac{1}{1+\alpha} \bar{c} = \bar{c}.$$

Hence

$$\bar{c} = 0 \quad \text{and} \quad H_{\bar{c}} = \{0\}.$$

Remark: A point $\bar{x}$ is a global minimum point if and only if it is a global minimum point of f+a and αf, $\alpha > 0$.

In fact, let $\bar{c} = f(\bar{x})$. According to Proposition 1.4,

$$M(f+a, \bar{c}+a) = M(f,\bar{c}) + a = \bar{c} + a,$$

$$M(\alpha f, \alpha\bar{c}) = \alpha M(f,\bar{c}) = \alpha\bar{c}.$$

Hence $\bar{c}+a$ and $\alpha\bar{c}$ are the global minimum values and $\bar{x}$ is a global minimum for f+a and αf, respectively.

§2 Variance and Higher Moment Conditions

In this section we will further introduce the concepts of variance and higher moments to prove the corresponding global optimality conditions. In doing so, we shall retain all the relevant assumptions in the proceeding section.

2.1 Variance over Level Sets

Definition 2.1: Suppose $c > \bar{c} = \min f(x)$. We define

$$V(f,c) = \frac{1}{\mu(H_c)}\int_{H_c} [f(x)-M(f,c)]^2 d\mu \tag{2.1}$$

and

$$V_1(f,c) = \frac{1}{\mu(H_c)}\int_{H_c} [f(x)-c]^2 d\mu \tag{2.2}$$

to be the variance and the modified variance, respectively, of the function f over its level set H_c.

Obviously, both variance (2.1) and modified variance (2.2) are well defined. They have the following properties:

Proposition 2.0: For $c > \bar{c}$, we have

$$V(f,c) = M_2(f,c;0) - [M(f,c)]^2, \tag{2.3}$$

where

$$M_2(f,c;0) = \frac{1}{\mu(H_c)}\int_{H_c} [f(x)]^2 d\mu.$$

Proof:

$$\begin{aligned} V(f,c) &= \frac{1}{\mu(H_c)}\int_{H_c} [f(x)-M(f,c)]^2 d\mu \\ &= \frac{1}{\mu(H_c)}\int_{H_c} \{[f(x)]^2 - 2M(f,c)f(x) + [M(f,c)]^2\} d\mu \\ &= \frac{1}{\mu(H_c)}\int_{H_c} [f(x)]^2 d\mu - \frac{2M(f,c)}{\mu(H_c)}\int_{H_c} f(x) d\mu + [M(f,c)]^2 \\ &= M_2(f,c;0) - [M(f,c)]^2. \quad \blacksquare \end{aligned}$$

Proposition 2.1: The variance of a function over its level set has the following properties:

(1) Positivity: $V(f,c) \geq 0 \quad \text{for } c > \bar{c};$ (2.4)

(2) $V(\lambda,c) = 0 \quad \text{for a constant } \lambda \geq c;$ (2.5)

(3) Second-Degree Homogeneity:

$$V(\lambda f,\lambda c) = \lambda^2 V(f,c) \quad \text{for } \lambda > 0 \text{ and } c > \bar{c}; \tag{2.6}$$

(4) Cancellation: $V(f+\lambda, c+\lambda) = V(f,c)$ for $c > \bar{c}$. (2.7)

Proof: (1) and (2) are obvious.

(3): Since $\{x \mid \lambda f(x) \leq \lambda c\} = \{x \mid f(x) \leq c\} = H_c$ for $c > \bar{c}$ and $\lambda > 0$, we have

$$V(\lambda f, \lambda c) = \frac{1}{\mu(H_c)} \int_{H_c} \left[\lambda f(x) - M(\lambda f, \lambda c)\right]^2 d\mu$$

$$= \frac{1}{\mu(H_c)} \int_{H_c} \left[\lambda f(x) - \lambda M(f,c)\right]^2 d\mu$$

$$= \frac{\lambda^2}{\mu(H_c)} \int_{H_c} \left[f(x) - M(f,c)\right]^2 d\mu = \lambda^2 V(f,c).$$

(4): We have $\{x \mid f(x)+\lambda \leq c+\lambda\} = \{x \mid f(x) \leq c\} = H_c$. Hence,

$$V(f+\lambda, c+\lambda) = \frac{1}{\mu(H_c)} \int_{H_c} \left[f(x)+\lambda - M(f+\lambda, c+\lambda)\right]^2 d\mu$$

$$= \frac{1}{\mu(H_c)} \int_{H_c} \left[f(x)+\lambda - M(f,c) - \lambda\right]^2 d\mu = V(f,c). \quad \blacksquare$$

Since $V(f,c)$ is not generally monotone in c, the following lemma is needed in the proof of Proposition 2.3.

Lemma 2.2:

$$\frac{1}{\mu(H_c)} \int_{H_c} \left[f(x)+\lambda\right]^2 d\mu$$

is nondecreasing in c for $c > \bar{c}$ if $f+\lambda \geq 0$.

Proof: Suppose $c_1 \geq c_2 > \bar{c}$. Then

$$\frac{1}{\mu(H_{c_1})} \int_{H_{c_1}} \left[f(x)+\lambda\right]^2 d\mu$$

$$= \frac{1}{\mu(H_{c_1})} \int_{H_{c_1} \setminus H_{c_2}} \left[f(x)+\lambda\right]^2 d\mu + \frac{1}{\mu(H_{c_1})} \int_{H_{c_2}} \left[f(x)+\lambda\right]^2 d\mu$$

$$\geq (c_2+\lambda)^2 \frac{\mu(H_{c_1}) - \mu(H_{c_2})}{\mu(H_{c_1})} + \frac{1}{\mu(H_{c_1})} \int_{H_{c_2}} \left[f(x)+\lambda\right]^2 d\mu$$

$$\geq \frac{\mu(H_{c_1}) - \mu(H_{c_2})}{\mu(H_{c_1})} \frac{1}{\mu(H_{c_2})} \int_{H_{c_2}} \left[f(x)+\lambda\right]^2 d\mu + \frac{1}{\mu(H_{c_1})} \int_{H_{c_2}} \left[f(x)+\lambda\right]^2 d\mu$$

$$= \frac{1}{\mu(H_{c_2})}\int_{H_{c_2}} \left[f(x)+\lambda\right]^2 d\mu.$$

Hence, $\frac{1}{\mu(H_c)}\int_{H_c} [f(x)+\lambda]^2 d\mu$ is nondecreasing in c for $c > \bar{c}$. ∎

Suppose $\{c_k\}$ is a decreasing sequence which tends to c as $k \to \infty$. Then $\{\frac{1}{\mu(H_{c_k})}\int_{H_{c_k}} [f(x)+\lambda]^2 d\mu\}$ is also a decreasing sequence.

<u>Proposition 2.3</u>: Suppose $\{c_k\}$ is a decreasing sequence which tends to $c > \bar{c}$. Then

$$V(f,c) = \lim_{c_k \downarrow c} V(f,c_k). \tag{2.8}$$

<u>Proof</u>: Since the sequence $\{\frac{1}{\mu(H_{c_k})}\int_{H_{c_k}} [f(x)+\lambda]^2 d\mu\}$ is decreasing (Lemma 2.2), bounded from below by $\frac{1}{\mu(H_c)}\int_{H_c} [f(x)+\lambda]^2 d\mu$,

$$\lim_{c_k \downarrow c} \frac{1}{\mu(H_{c_k})}\int_{H_{c_k}} [f(x)+\lambda]^2 d\mu \tag{2.9}$$

exists. Moreover,

$$\begin{aligned}
0 &\le \frac{1}{\mu(H_{c_k})}\int_{H_{c_k}} [f(x)+\lambda]^2 d\mu - \frac{1}{\mu(H_c)}\int_{H_c} [f(x)+\lambda]^2 d\mu \\
&\le \left|\frac{1}{\mu(H_{c_k})}\int_{H_{c_k}} [f(x)+\lambda]^2 d\mu - \frac{1}{\mu(H_c)}\int_{H_{c_k}} [f(x)+\lambda]^2 d\mu\right| \\
&\qquad + \left|\frac{1}{\mu(H_c)}\int_{H_{c_k}} [f(x)+\lambda]^2 d\mu - \frac{1}{\mu(H_c)}\int_{H_c} [f(x)+\lambda]^2 d\mu\right| \\
&\le \left|\left(\frac{1}{\mu(H_{c_k})} - \frac{1}{\mu(H_c)}\right)\int_{H_{c_k}} [f(x)+\lambda]^2 d\mu\right| + \frac{1}{\mu(H_c)}\left|\int_{H_{c_k}\setminus H_c} [f(x)+\lambda]^2 d\mu\right|.
\end{aligned}$$

The continuity of measure and the absolute continuity of the integral of a bounded continuous function $[f(x)+\lambda]^2$ imply that each of the terms on the right hand side tends to zero. Furthermore, according to Proposition 1.4, we have

$$[M(f+\lambda,c+\lambda)]^2 = [M(f,c)+\lambda]^2 = \lim_{c_k \downarrow c} [M(f,c_k)+\lambda]^2 = \lim_{c_k \downarrow c} [M(f+\lambda,c_k+\lambda)]^2.$$

Hence, since $\{x \mid f(x)+\lambda \le c_k+\lambda\} = H_{c_k}$, we obtain

$$\lim_{c_k \downarrow c} V(f,c_k) = \lim_{c_k \downarrow c} V(f+\lambda, c_k+\lambda)$$

$$= \lim_{c_k \downarrow c} \{\frac{1}{\mu(H_{c_k})}\int_{H_{c_k}} [f(x)+\lambda]^2 d\mu - [M(f+\lambda, c_k+\lambda)]^2\}$$

$$= \frac{1}{\mu(H_c)}\int_{H_c} [f(x)+\lambda]^2 d\mu - [M(f+\lambda, c_k+\lambda)]^2$$

$$= V(f+\lambda, c+\lambda) = V(f,c). \quad \blacksquare$$

Next, we provide a definition of the derivative of V(f,c) with respect to changes in the measure of the level set H_c induced by changes in the level set parameter c.

<u>Definition 2.2</u>: For $c > \bar{c}$, we define

$$\partial_\mu V(f,c) = \lim_{c' \to c} \frac{V(f,c')-V(f,c)}{\mu(H_{c'})-\mu(H_c)},$$

if it exists, to be the level-set derivative of V(f,c) with respect to the measure μ.

<u>Proposition 2.4</u>: Suppose $\lim_{c' \to c} \mu(H_{c'}) = \mu(H_c)$, $c > \bar{c}$. Then

$$\partial_\mu V(f,c) = \frac{1}{\mu(H_c)}\Big[[c-M(f,c)]^2 - V(f,c)\Big]. \tag{2.10}$$

<u>Proof</u>: Suppose $c' > c$. Let $\Delta H_c = H_{c'} \backslash H_c$. Then

$$\frac{V(f,c')-V(f,c)}{\mu(\Delta H_c)}$$

$$= \frac{1}{\mu(\Delta H_c)}\Big[\frac{1}{\mu(H_{c'})}\int_{H_{c'}} [f(x)-M(f,c')]^2 d\mu - \frac{1}{\mu(H_c)}\int_{H_c} [f(x)-M(f,c)]^2 d\mu\Big]$$

$$= \frac{1}{\mu(\Delta H_c)}\Big[\frac{1}{\mu(H_{c'})}\int_{\Delta H_c} [f(x)-M(f,c')]^2 d\mu - \frac{1}{\mu(H_c)}\int_{H_c} [f(x)-M(f,c)]^2 d\mu$$

$$+ \frac{1}{\mu(H_{c'})}\int_{H_c} \{[f(x)-M(f,c)]^2 + 2[M(f,c)-M(f,c')][f(x)-M(f,c)]\}d\mu$$

$$+ \frac{\mu(H_c)}{\mu(H_{c'})}[M(f,c)-M(f,c')]^2\Big]$$

$$= \frac{1}{\mu(\Delta H_c)}\Big[\frac{1}{\mu(H_{c'})}\int_{\Delta H_c} [f(x)-M(f,c')]^2 d\mu + [\frac{1}{\mu(H_{c'})} - \frac{1}{\mu(H_c)}]\int_{H_c} [f(x)-M(f,c)]^2 d\mu$$

$$+ \frac{2[M(f,c)-M(f,c')]}{\mu(H_{c'})}\int_{H_c} [f(x)-M(f,c)]d\mu + \frac{\mu(H_c)}{\mu(H_{c'})}[M(f,c)-M(f,c')]^2\Big].$$

Suppose $\lim_{c' \to c} \mu(H_{c'}) = \mu(H_c)$. Then

$$\partial_\mu V(f,c) = \lim_{c' \to c} \frac{V(f,c')-V(f,c)}{\mu(H_{c'})-\mu(H_c)} = \frac{[c-M(f,c)]^2}{\mu(H_c)} - \frac{V(f,c)}{\mu(H_c)}$$

$$= \frac{1}{\mu(H_c)}\Big[[c-M(f,c)]^2 - V(f,c)\Big]. \blacksquare$$

Like the mean value case, the right-hand and left-hand derivatives of variance also always exist:

$$\partial_\mu^+ V(f,c) = \lim_{\Delta c \to 0^+} \frac{V(f,c+\Delta c)-V(f,c)}{\mu(H_{c+\Delta c})-\mu(H_c)} = \partial_\mu V(f,c) \tag{2.11}$$

$$\partial_\mu^- V(f,c) = \lim_{\Delta c \to 0^-} \frac{V(f,c+\Delta c)-V(f,c)}{\mu(H_{c+\Delta c})-\mu(H_c)}. \tag{2.12}$$

Again, we define the derivative of variance $V(f,c)$ with respect to c as follows:

$$\frac{dV(f,c)}{dc} = \lim_{c' \to c} \frac{V(f,c')-V(f,c)}{c'-c} \tag{2.13}$$

if the limit exists. Like the mean value case, we have:

<u>Proposition 2.5</u>: If $\chi(c) = \mu(H_c)$ is differentiable at $c > \bar{c}$, then

$$\frac{dV(f,c)}{dc} = \frac{\chi'(c)}{\chi(c)}\Big[[c-M(f,c)]^2 - V(f,c)\Big]. \tag{2.14}$$

The following proposition is useful in deriving properties of the modified variance from those of the variance.

<u>Proposition 2.6</u>: For $c > \bar{c}$, we have

$$V_1(f,c) = V(f,c) + [M(f,c)-c]^2. \tag{2.15}$$

<u>Proof</u>:

$$V_1(f,c) = \frac{1}{\mu(H_c)}\int_{H_c} [f(x)-c]^2 d\mu$$

$$= \frac{1}{\mu(H_c)}\int_{H_c} \Big[[f(x)-M(f,c)]^2 + 2[M(f,c)-c][f(x)-M(f,c)] + [M(f,c)-c]^2\Big] d\mu$$

$$= \frac{1}{\mu(H_c)}\int_{H_c} [f(x)-M(f,c)]^2 d\mu + \frac{2[M(f,c)-c]}{\mu(H_c)}\int_{H_c} [f(x)-M(f,c)] d\mu + [M(f,c)-c]^2$$

$$= V(f,c) + [M(f,c)-c]^2. \blacksquare$$

<u>Proposition 2.7</u>: The modified variance of a function over its level sets has the following properties:

(1) $$V_1(f,c) \geq V(f,c) \quad \text{for } c > \bar{c}; \tag{2.16}$$

(2) Suppose $\{c_k\}$ is a decreasing sequence which tends to $c > \bar{c}$. Then

$$\lim_{c_k \downarrow c} V_1(f,c_k) = V_1(f,c). \tag{2.17}$$

Proposition 2.8: Suppose $\chi(c) = \mu(H_c)$ is differentiable at $c > \bar{c}$. Then

$$\partial_\mu V_1(f,c) = \frac{2[c-M(f,c)]}{\chi'(c)} - \frac{V_1(f,c)}{\chi(c)}; \tag{2.18}$$

$$\frac{dV_1(f,c)}{dc} = 2[c-M(f,c)] - \frac{\chi'(c)}{\chi(c)} V_1(f,c). \tag{2.19}$$

Proof: If $\chi(c)$ is differentiable at c, then $\frac{dV(f,c)}{dc}$ exists and

$$\frac{dV_1(f,c)}{dc} = \frac{dV(f,c)}{dc} + 2[M(f,c)-c][\frac{dM(f,c)}{dc} - 1]$$

$$= \frac{\chi'(c)}{\chi(c)}\Big[[c-M(f,c)]^2 - V(f,c)\Big] + \frac{\chi'(c)}{\chi(c)} 2[M(f,c)-c][c-M(f,c)] + 2[c-M(f,c)]$$

$$= 2[c-M(f,c)] - \frac{\chi'(c)}{\chi(c)} V_1(f,c)$$

and

$$\partial_\mu V_1(f,c) = \frac{1}{\chi'(c)} \frac{dV_1(f,c)}{dc} = \frac{2[c-M(f,c)]}{\chi'(c)} - \frac{V_1(f,c)}{\chi(c)}. \qquad \blacksquare$$

2.2 A Limit-Based Definition

We can also define the variance $V(f,c)$ and the modified variance $V_1(f,c)$ of f over its level sets for all $c \geq \bar{c}$ by a limiting process.

Definition 2.3: Let $c \geq \bar{c} = \min f(x)$ and $\{c_k\}$ be a decreasing sequence which tends to c as $k \to \infty$. The limits

$$V(f,c) = \lim_{c_k \downarrow c} \frac{1}{\mu(H_{c_k})}\int_{H_{c_k}} [f(x)-M(f,c)]^2 d\mu \tag{2.20}$$

$$V_1(f,c) = \lim_{c_k \downarrow c} \frac{1}{\mu(H_{c_k})}\int_{H_{c_k}} [f(x)-c]^2 d\mu \tag{2.21}$$

are called the variance and the modified variance, respectively, of f over its level set H_c.

Both limits (2.20) and (2.21) exist by the proof of Proposition 2.3 and Proposition 2.7. Like the mean value case, these limits are independent of the choice of the decreasing sequences. Note that Definitions (2.20) and (2.21) are consistent with (2.1) and (2.2) by Propositions 2.3 and 2.7. Moreover, Propositions 2.0, 2.1, 2.3, 2.6 and 2.7 remain valid for $c \geq \bar{c}$ after applying a similar limit-based argument.

It is clear from Lemma 1.7 that Definitions (2.20) and (2.21) are equivalent to the following alternative definitions.

Definition 2.4: Let $c \geq \bar{c}$. The limits

$$V(f,c) = \lim_{\substack{d \to c \\ d > c}} \frac{1}{\mu(H_d)} \int_{H_d} [f(x) - M(f,c)]^2 d\mu \tag{2.22}$$

and

$$V_1(f,c) = \lim_{\substack{d \to c \\ d > c}} \frac{1}{\mu(H_d)} \int_{H_d} [f(x) - c]^2 d\mu \tag{2.23}$$

are called the variance and the modified variance of f over its level set H_c, respectively.

2.3 Variance Conditions

In this subsection, the variance condition and the modified variance conditions will be stated and proved.

Theorem 2.9 (Variance Conditions): For Problem (P), the following are equivalent:

a. a point $\bar{x}$ is a global minimum point with $\bar{c} = f(\bar{x})$ as the corresponding global minimum value of f;

b. $$V(f,\bar{c}) = 0 \tag{2.24}$$

c. $$V_1(f,\bar{c}) = 0. \tag{2.25}$$

Proof: To prove the sufficiency of condition (2.24) by contradiction, suppose $\bar{x}$ is not a global minimum point so that $\bar{c} = f(\bar{x})$ is not the global minimum value of f. Using Lemma I.2.2, we have $\mu(H_{\bar{c}}) > 0$. We shall show that $V(f,\bar{c}) > 0$. Suppose the contrary that

$$V(f,\bar{c}) = \frac{1}{\mu(H_{\bar{c}})}\int_{H_{\bar{c}}} [f(x)-M(f,\bar{c})]^2 d\mu = 0.$$

Then $f(x) = M(f,\bar{c})\ \forall\ x \in H_{\bar{c}}$ since f is a continuous function. But $\bar{x} \in H_{\bar{c}} = \{x \mid f(x) \le \bar{c}\}$. Therefore $\bar{c} = f(\bar{x}) = M(f,\bar{c})$; i.e., $\bar{x}$ is a global minimum of $f(x)$ by Theorem 1.8. This is a contradiction.

To prove the necessity of condition (2.24), suppose $\bar{x}$ is a global minimum point while $V(f,\bar{c}) = 2\eta > 0$ with $\bar{c} = f(\bar{x})$. Let $\{c_k\}$ be a decreasing sequence which tends to c as $k \to \infty$. Therefore there is a positive integer N such that

$$V(f,c_k) > \eta \quad \text{for } k > N. \tag{2.26}$$

This means (by Propositions 2.0 and 2.1) that

$$\frac{1}{\mu(H_{c_k})}\int_{H_{c_k}} [f(x)+\lambda]^2 d\mu > \left[\frac{1}{\mu(H_{c_k})}\int_{H_{c_k}} [f(x)+\lambda]d\mu\right]^2 + \eta, \tag{2.27}$$

where λ is a real number such that $f(x)+\lambda \ge 0$. Since $\bar{c} \le f(x) \le c_k$ for $x \in H_{c_k}$, we have from (2.27)

$$(c_k+\lambda)^2 > (\bar{c}+\lambda)^2 + \eta. \tag{2.28}$$

As k tends to ∞, (2.28) implies that

$$(\bar{c}+\lambda)^2 \ge (\bar{c}+\lambda)^2 + \eta,$$

which is a contradiction.

We now turn our attention to the modified variance condition. If $V_1(f,\bar{c}) = 0$, then $V(f,\bar{c}) = 0$ since $0 \le V(f,\bar{c}) \le V_1(f,\bar{c})$. Hence, $\bar{x}$ is a global minimum and $\bar{c}$ is the global minimum value of f.

Conversely, if $\bar{x}$ is a global minimum of f, then $M(f,\bar{c}) = \bar{c} = f(\bar{x})$. This means that $V_1(f,\bar{c}) = V(f,\bar{c})$. Therefore, $V_1(f,\bar{c}) = V(f,\bar{c}) = 0$. ∎

<u>Example 2.1</u>: Minimize $f(x) = |x|^\alpha$, with $\alpha > 0$.

For $c > 0$, $H_c = [-c^{1/\alpha}, c^{1/\alpha}]$.

$$V_1(f,c) = \frac{1}{2c^{1/\alpha}}\int_{-c^{1/\alpha}}^{c^{1/\alpha}} [|x|^\alpha - c]^2 dx$$

$$= \frac{1}{c^{1/\alpha}} \left[\int_0^{c^{1/\alpha}} x^{2\alpha} dx - 2c \int_0^{c^{1/\alpha}} x^{\alpha} dx \right] + c^2 = \frac{2\alpha^2}{(1+\alpha)(1+2\alpha)} c^2,$$

where we take the Lebesque measure μ. Let $\bar{c}$ be the global minimum value. Then

$$V_1(f,\bar{c}) = \frac{2\alpha^2}{(1+\alpha)(1+2\alpha)}(\bar{c})^2 = 0.$$

Hence,

$$\bar{c} = 0 \quad \text{and} \quad H_{\bar{c}} = \{0\}.$$

Example 2.2 (Simplex Method for Nonlinear Minimization (Nelder-Mead Method)): The criterion

$$\frac{1}{n} \Sigma_{i=1}^{n+1} [f(x_i) - f(x_c)]^2 < \epsilon \tag{2.29}$$

is suggested for the iterative process, where ϵ is a small positive number given in advance.

We can regard condition (2.29) as an approximation of the variance condition (2.24). If we take a small ball $B_\delta(\bar{x}) = \{x \mid \|x-\bar{x}\| \le \delta\}$ in X with the induced Euclidean topology, then the variance condition can be applied in the local case.

If, instead of (2.29), we use

$$\frac{1}{n+1} \Sigma_{i=1}^{n+1} [f(x_i) - f_{max}]^2 < \epsilon, \tag{2.30}$$

where

$$f_{max} = \max \{f(x_1, \cdots, f(x_{n+1})\}, \tag{2.31}$$

then it should be more sensitive. The condition (2.30) is an approximation form of the modified variance condition (2.25).

The variance as well as the modified variance conditions will be used in Chapters III and IV as criteria in the search algorithms for global minimum.

2.4 Higher Moments

Hereafter we shall denote by I^+ the set of all positive integers. Suppose

$c > \bar{c} = \min f(x)$. Then $\mu(H_c) > 0$.

Definition 2.5: Suppose $m \in I^+$ and $c > \bar{c}$. We define

$$M_m(f,c;a) = \frac{1}{\mu(H_c)}\int_{H_c} [f(x)-a]^m d\mu \tag{2.32}$$

to be the mth moment of f over its level set H_c centered at a.

This concept extends those of mean value, variance and modified variance. Specifically,

$$M(f,c) = M_1(f,c;0), \tag{2.33}$$

$$V(f,c) = M_2(f,c;M(f,c)), \tag{2.34}$$

and

$$V_1(f,c) = M_2(f,c;c). \tag{2.35}$$

Proposition 2.10: The mth moment of f over its level set has the following properties:

(1) mth degree positive homogeneity:

$$M_m(\lambda f,\lambda c;\lambda a) = \lambda^m M_m(f,c;a) \quad \text{for } c > \bar{c} \text{ and } \lambda \geq 0; \tag{2.36}$$

(2) cancellation:

$$M_m(f+\lambda,c+\lambda;a+\lambda) = M_m(f,c;a) = \Sigma_{i=0}^m(-1)^{m-i}\binom{m}{i}M([f+\lambda]^i,[c+\lambda]^i)\cdot[a+\lambda]^{m-i}, \tag{2.37}$$

for $c > \bar{c}$ and real λ,

where $\binom{m}{i} = \frac{m!}{i!(m-i)!}$.

Proof: (1): Since $\{x \mid \lambda f(x) \leq \lambda c\} = \{x \mid f(x) \leq c\} = H_c$ for $\lambda > 0$,

$$M_m(\lambda f,\lambda c;\lambda a) = \frac{1}{\mu(H_c)}\int_{H_c} [\lambda f(x)-\lambda a]^m d\mu = \frac{\lambda^m}{\mu(H_c)}\int_{H_c} [f(x)-a]^m d\mu = \lambda^m M_m(f,c;a).$$

(2): Since $\{x \mid f(x)+\lambda \leq c+\lambda\} = H_c$ for real number λ, we have

$$M_m(f+\lambda,c+\lambda;a+\lambda) = \frac{1}{\mu(H_c)}\int_{H_c} [f(x)+\lambda-(a+\lambda)]^m d\mu = M_m(f,c;a)$$

$$= \Sigma_{i=0}^m(-1)^{m-i}\binom{m}{i}\left[\frac{1}{\mu(H_c)}\int_{H_c} [f(x)+\lambda]^i d\mu\right][a+\lambda]^{m-i}$$

$$= \Sigma_{i=0}^m(-1)^{m-i}\binom{m}{i}M([f+\lambda]^i,[c+\lambda]^i)[a+\lambda]^{m-i}. \quad ∎$$

Like the mean value and the variance cases, $M_m(f,c;a)$ is right-hand continuous in c.

Proposition 2.11: Suppose $\{c_k\}$ is a decreasing sequence which tends to c as $k \to \infty$ and $c > \bar{c}$. Then

$$M_m(f,c;a) = \lim_{c_k \downarrow c} M_m(f,c_k;a) \quad \text{for } m \in I^+. \tag{2.38}$$

Proof: Take a real number λ such that $f(x)+\lambda \geq 0$ for $x \in H_{c_1}$. Now $\{(c_k+\lambda)^i\}$ is a decreasing sequence which tends to $(c+\lambda)^i$. By Proposition 2.10,

$$\lim_{c_k \downarrow c} M_m(f,c_k;a) = \lim_{c_k \downarrow c} \Sigma_{i=0}^{m}(-1)^{m-i}\binom{m}{i}M([f+\lambda]^i,[c_k+\lambda]^i)[a+\lambda]^{m-i}$$

$$= \Sigma_{i=0}^{m}(-1)^{m-i}\binom{m}{i}M([f+\lambda]^i,[c+\lambda]^i)[a+\lambda]^{m-i}$$

$$= M_m(f,c;a),$$

since

$$\lim_{c_k \downarrow c} M([f+\lambda]^i,[c_k+\lambda]^i) = M([f+\lambda]^i,[c+\lambda]^i) \tag{2.39}$$

applying Proposition 1.3. ∎

The following extends Definition 2.5 to allow for the possibility of $c = \bar{c}$.

Definition 2.6: Suppose $c \geq \bar{c}$ and $m \in I^+$. Then the mth moment of f over its level set H_c centered at a is defined to be

$$M_m(f,c;a) = \lim_{c_k \downarrow c} \frac{1}{\mu(H_{c_k})}\int_{H_{c_k}} [f(x)-a]^m d\mu. \tag{2.40}$$

The limit (2.39) exists for each i, so the definition (2.40), which does not depend on the choice of the decreasing sequence $\{c_k\}$, is well defined. Note that Definition 2.6 is consistent with Definition 2.5, and Propositions 2.10 and 2.11 are also valid for $c \geq \bar{c}$.

Applying Lemma 1.7 and Proposition 2.11, the following offers an equivalent alternative definition of $M_m(f,c;a)$.

Definition 2.7: Suppose $c \geq \bar{c}$ and $m \in I^+$. Then the mth moment of f over its level set H_c centered at a is defined to be

$$M_m(f,c;a) = \lim_{\substack{d \to c \\ d > c}} \frac{1}{\mu(H_d)}\int_{H_d} [f(x)-a]^m d\mu. \tag{2.41}$$

2.5 Higher Moment Conditions

We shall demonstrate that the mean value and variance conditions of the earlier subsections are special cases of the higher moment conditions developed in this subsection. In particular, they correspond to the odd and the even higher moments, respectively.

We provide the odd moment conditions first.

Theorem 2.12: For Problem (P), the following are equivalent:

a. a point $\bar{x}$ is a global minimum and $\bar{c} = f(\bar{x})$ is the corresponding minimum value of f;

b. $$M_{2m-1}(f,c;0) \geq (\bar{c})^{2m-1} \quad \text{for } c > \bar{c} \text{ and some } m \in I^+, \tag{2.42}$$

c. $$M_{2m-1}(f,\bar{c};0) = (\bar{c})^{2m-1} \quad \text{for some } m \in I^+. \tag{2.43}$$

Proof: Note that $\bar{c}$ is the global minimum value of f if and only if $(\bar{c})^{2m-1}$ is the global minimum value of f^{2m-1}. Also, the level set H_c induced by f is identical to the level set $H_{c^{2m-1}}$ induced by f^{2m-1}. Expressions (2.42) and (2.43) are simply restatements of the mean value conditions in Theorem 1.8 for f^{2m-1} over its level sets $H_{c^{2m-1}}$ parametrized by c^{2m-1}. ∎

Theorem 2.13: With respect to the above problem, a point $\bar{x}$ is a global minimum point and $\bar{c} = f(\bar{x})$ is the corresponding global minimum value if and only if

$$M_{2m}(f,\bar{c};M(f,\bar{c})) = 0 \quad \text{for some } m \in I^+. \tag{2.44}$$

Proof: Suppose condition (2.44) holds but $\bar{c} = f(\bar{x})$ is not the global minimum value of f. Then $\mu(H_{\bar{c}}) > 0$. We have

$$\frac{1}{\mu(H_{\bar{c}})}\int_{H_{\bar{c}}} [f(x)-M(f,\bar{c})]^{2m} d\mu = 0, \tag{2.45}$$

which implies that $f(x) = M(f,\bar{c})\ \forall\ x \in H_{\bar{c}}$ since f is continuous. It follows that

$$M(f,\bar{c}) = f(\bar{x}),$$

so that $\bar{x}$ is a global minimum point of f. This yields a contradiction.

Observe that $|f(x)| \leq L$ for $x \in H_{c_o}$, where $c_o > \bar{c}$ and $L = \max\{c_o, |\bar{c}|\}$. We have, for $x \in H_{c_o}$,

$$0 \leq [f(x)-M(f,c)]^{2m} \leq (2L)^{2m-2}[f(x)-M(f,c)]^2$$

so that

$$0 \leq M_{2m}(f,c;M(f,c)) \leq (2L)^{2m-2}V(f,c), \quad m \in I^+.$$

If $\bar{c} = f(\bar{x})$ is the global minimum value, then $V(f,\bar{c}) = 0$, which implies that

$$M_{2m}(f,\bar{c};M(f,\bar{c})) = 0.$$

This proves the necessity of (2.44). ∎

Conditions (2.42) and (2.43) are not extendable to the even moments; neither can condition (2.44) be extended to the odd moments. A more general form of higher-moment condition which applies to odd as well as even moments is given below:

<u>Theorem 2.14</u>: A point $\bar{x}$ is a global minimum point for the problem in Theorem 2.12, and $\bar{c} = f(\bar{x})$ is the corresponding global minimum value if and only if

$$M_m(f,\bar{c};\bar{c}) = 0 \quad \text{for some } m \in I^+. \tag{2.46}$$

<u>Proof</u>: (Necessity) Suppose $\bar{c} = f(\bar{x})$ is the global minimum value and m is odd. Then

$$M_m(f,c;c) \leq 0 \quad \text{for } c > \bar{c}$$

since $f(x)-c \leq 0$ for $x \in H_c$. But, for any decreasing sequence $\{c_k\}$ which tends to $\bar{c}$, we have

$$\begin{aligned} &\lim_{c_k \downarrow \bar{c}} M_m(f,c_k;c_k) \\ &= \lim_{c_k \downarrow \bar{c}} \Sigma_{i=0}^{m-1}(-1)^{m-i}\binom{m}{i}\frac{1}{\mu(H_{c_k})}\left[\int_{H_{c_k}} [f(x)-\bar{c}]^i d\mu\right][\bar{c}-c_k]^{m-i} \\ &+ \lim_{c_k \downarrow \bar{c}} \frac{1}{\mu(H_{c_k})}\int_{H_{c_k}} [f(x)-\bar{c}]^m d\mu \\ &= M_m(f,\bar{c};\bar{c}). \end{aligned} \tag{2.47}$$

Thus,

$$M_m(f,\bar{c};\bar{c}) \leq 0. \tag{2.48}$$

On the other hand, since $f(x)-\bar{c} \geq 0 \ \forall\, x$,

$$M_m(f,\bar{c};\bar{c}) = \lim_{c_k \downarrow \bar{c}} M_m(f,c_k;\bar{c}) = \lim_{c_k \downarrow \bar{c}} \frac{1}{\mu(H_{c_k})}\int_{H_{c_k}} [f(x)-\bar{c}]^m d\mu \geq 0. \tag{2.49}$$

Hence, from (2.48) and (2.49), we have

$$M_m(f,\bar{c};\bar{c}) = 0.$$

If m is even and $\bar{c} = f(\bar{x})$ is the global minimum value, then $M(f,\bar{c}) = \bar{c}$ so that (2.45) is equivalent to

$$M_m(f,\bar{c};\bar{c}) = 0.$$

(Sufficiency) If m is even and $M_m(f,\bar{c};\bar{c}) = 0$ but $\bar{c} = f(\bar{x})$ is not the global minimum value of f, then $\mu(H_{\bar{c}}) > 0$. We have

$$\frac{1}{\mu(H_{\bar{c}})}\int_{H_{\bar{c}}} [f(x)-\bar{c}]^m d\mu = 0,$$

which implies that $f(x) = \bar{c} \ \forall\, x \in H_{\bar{c}}$ since $f(x)$ is continuous. It follows that

$$M(f,\bar{c}) = \bar{c}.$$

Therefore, $\bar{c}$ is the global minimum value.

Suppose m is odd, $\bar{x}$ is not a global minimum and $\bar{c} = f(\bar{x})$ is not the global minimum value of f, while $\hat{c}$ is. Let $2\eta = \bar{c}-\hat{c} > 0$. We have $\mu(H_{\bar{c}})$ and $\mu(H_{\bar{c}-\eta})$ both positive. Meanwhile,

$$f(x) \leq \bar{c}-\eta \quad \text{for } x \in H_{\bar{c}-\eta}.$$

For m odd, we have

$$[f(x)-\bar{c}]^m \leq -\eta^m \quad \text{for } x \in H_{\bar{c}-\eta}$$

and

$$[f(x)-\bar{c}]^m \leq 0 \quad \text{for } x \in H_{\bar{c}}.$$

We now have

$$\begin{aligned} M_m(f,\bar{c};\bar{c}) &= \frac{1}{\mu(H_{\bar{c}})}\int_{H_{\bar{c}}} [f(x)-\bar{c}]^m d\mu \\ &= \frac{1}{\mu(H_{\bar{c}})}\int_{H_{\bar{c}} \setminus H_{\bar{c}-\eta}} [f(x)-\bar{c}]^m d\mu + \frac{1}{\mu(H_{\bar{c}})}\int_{H_{\bar{c}-\eta}} [f(x)-\bar{c}]^m d\mu \\ &\leq -\eta^m \left[\mu(H_{\bar{c}-\eta})/\mu(H_{\bar{c}})\right] < 0. \end{aligned}$$

This is a contradiction to condition (2.46). ∎

Example 2.3: The criterion

$$\frac{1}{n}\sum_{i=1}^{n+1}[f(x_i)-f_{max}]^m < \epsilon, \tag{2.50}$$

which resembles condition (2.46), may be used instead of conditions (2.29) and (2.30) in a nonlinear minimization problem.

§3 The Constrained Cases

This section parallels the development in the previous sections of the mean value, variance and higher-moment characterizations of global optimality for some constrained cases. Specifically, we treat the case of a robust feasible set, the case where the feasible set is a manifold, and the intersection of those two cases. An exposition in terms of a linear manifold in $\mathbb{R}^n$ corresponding to a set of linear equality constraints ends the section.

3.1 Rejection Conditions

Suppose the set $S \subset X$ is robust. Consider the problem of finding the global minimum value of a real-valued function f on X over S. As before, we assume that Assumptions A1 and A2 are satisfied.

Let (X,Ω,μ) be a Q-measure space. We can construct a derived Q-measure space $(X\cap S,\Omega_S,\mu_S)$ in the following manner. The set $O\cap S$ is regarded as an open set if set O is an open set in X. The family of sets $\Omega_S = \{S\cap B \mid B \in \Omega\}$ is a σ-field. The measure μ_S is defined by

$$\mu_S(A) = \mu(A\cap S) \quad \text{for } A \in \Omega. \tag{3.1}$$

A nonempty open set in $X\cap S$ is written as $O\cap S$ ($\neq \emptyset$). By the proof of Lemma

I.2.1, we have

$$\mu_S(O) = \mu(O \cap S) > 0.$$

Hence, $(X \cap S, \Omega_S, \mu_S)$ is a Q-measure space.

Definition 3.1: Suppose $S \subset X$ is a robust set. The measure space $(X \cap S, \Omega_S, \mu_S)$ is called a rejection measure space.

The rejection versions of mean value, variance and higher moments of a function over its level sets are defined below.

Definition 3.2: Suppose $\{c_k\}$ is a decreasing sequence which tends to $c \geq \bar{c} = \min_{x \in S} f(x)$. The limits

$$M(f,c;S) = \lim_{c_k \downarrow c} \frac{1}{\mu(H_{c_k} \cap S)} \int_{H_{c_k} \cap S} f(x) d\mu, \tag{3.2}$$

$$V(f,c;S) = \lim_{c_k \downarrow c} \frac{1}{\mu(H_{c_k} \cap S)} \int_{H_{c_k} \cap S} [f(x)-M(f,c;S)]^2 d\mu, \tag{3.3}$$

$$V_1(f,c;S) = \lim_{c_k \downarrow c} \frac{1}{\mu(H_{c_k} \cap S)} \int_{H_{c_k} \cap S} [f(x)-c]^2 d\mu, \tag{3.4}$$

and

$$M_m(f,c;a;S) = \lim_{c_k \downarrow c} \frac{1}{\mu(H_{c_k} \cap S)} \int_{H_{c_k} \cap S} [f(x)-a]^m d\mu, \quad m \in I^+, \tag{3.5}$$

are respectively called the rejection mean value, rejection variance, rejection modified variance and rejection mth moment of f over $H_c \cap S$.

Since a rejection measure derived from a Q-measure is also a Q-measure, the above definitions are well defined. Consequently, the rejection moments inherit all the properties of the moments of f over its level sets H_c developed in Sections 1 and 2. The corresponding rejection global optimality conditions are collected in Theorem 3.1 below.

Theorem 3.1: With respect to the constrained minimization problem (P) with a robust constrained set S, the following are equivalent:

a. $\bar{x} \in S$ is a global minimum and $\bar{c} = f(\bar{x})$ is the corresponding global minimum value;

b. $$M(f,c;S) \geq \bar{c} \quad \text{for } c > \bar{c}; \tag{3.6}$$

c. $$M(f,\bar{c};S) = \bar{c}; \tag{3.7}$$

d. $$V(f,\bar{c};S) = 0; \tag{3.8}$$

e. $$V_1(f,\bar{c};S) = 0; \tag{3.9}$$

f. $$M_{2m-1}(f,c;0;S) \geq (\bar{c})^{2m-1} \quad \text{for } c > \bar{c} \text{ and some } m \in I^+; \tag{3.10}$$

g. $$M_{2m-1}(f,\bar{c};0;S) = (\bar{c})^{2m-1} \quad \text{for some } m \in I^+; \tag{3.11}$$

h. $$M_{2m}(f,\bar{c};M(f,\bar{c};S);S) = 0 \quad \text{for some } m \in I^+; \tag{3.12}$$

i. $$M_m(f,\bar{c};\bar{c};S) = 0 \quad \text{for some } m \in I^+. \tag{3.13}$$

<u>Example 3.1</u>: Consider the problem of finding the minimum of $f(x) = x$ over the robust set $S = [1,2]$. For any c, the level set $H_c = \{x \mid x \leq c\} = (-\infty,c]$ so that

$$M(f,c;S) = \frac{1}{\mu(H_c \cap S)}\int_{H_c \cap S} f(x)d\mu = \frac{1}{c-1}\int_1^c x dx = \frac{1}{2(c-1)}(c^2-1) = \frac{c+1}{2}$$

for $c \geq 1$. Applying the mean value condition, we have

$$M(f,\bar{c};S) = \bar{c} = \frac{\bar{c}+1}{2}.$$

Hence, $\bar{c} = 1$ and $\bar{H} = \{1\}$.

3.2 Reduction Conditions

A manifold L in a Hausdorff space X is a Hausdorff topological subspace of X in which each point has an open neighborhood homeomorphic to a topological space Y. Sometimes the topological space Y is endowed with a special structure. For instance, $Y = \mathbb{R}^m$. In this case the manifold L is called a topological m-manifold. In this subsection we only consider a general case of manifold. In the next subsection, we will consider in detail a linear m-manifold in $X = \mathbb{R}^n$.

Suppose the constrained set L is a manifold in X. Then the minimization problem is restricted to the manifold L. In L, the open set has the form $L \cap O$, where O is an open set in X. Let $\Omega_L = \{L \cap B \mid B \in \Omega\}$, where Ω is a Borel field of subsets of X. We further suppose that there is a Q-measure μ_L on Ω_L. Thus we have a reduction Q-measure space (L,Ω_L,μ_L).

<u>Definition 3.3</u>: Suppose $L \subset X$ is a manifold. The Q-measure space (L,Ω_L,μ_L)

is called a reduction measure space.

We can also provide the reduction version of the moments of a function over its truncated level sets.

Definition 3.4: Suppose $\{c_k\}$ is a decreasing sequence which tends to $c \geq \bar{c} = \min_{x \in L} f(x)$ as $k \to \infty$. The limits

$$M(f,c;L) = \lim_{c_k \downarrow c} \frac{1}{\mu_L(H_{c_k} \cap L)} \int_{H_{c_k} \cap L} f(x) d\mu_L, \tag{3.14}$$

$$V(f,c;L) = \lim_{c_k \downarrow c} \frac{1}{\mu_L(H_{c_k} \cap L)} \int_{H_{c_k} \cap L} [f(x)-M(f,c;L)]^2 d\mu_L, \tag{3.15}$$

$$V_1(f,c;L) = \lim_{c_k \downarrow c} \frac{1}{\mu_L(H_{c_k} \cap L)} \int_{H_{c_k} \cap L} [f(x)-c]^2 d\mu_L, \tag{3.16}$$

and

$$M_m(f,c;a;L) = \lim_{c_k \downarrow c} \frac{1}{\mu_L(H_{c_k} \cap L)} \int_{H_{c_k} \cap L} [f(x)-a]^m d\mu_L, \quad m \in I^+, \tag{3.17}$$

are respectively the reduction mean value, reduction variance, reduction modified variance and reduction mth moment of f over $H_c \cap L$.

As in the rejection case, these limits are well defined and the useful properties of various moments of f over its level sets H_c treated in Sections 1 and 2 remain valid. The optimality conditions in terms of the reduction moments are given below.

Theorem 3.2: With respect to the constrained minimization problem (P) over a manifold $S = L \subset X$, the following are equivalent:

a. $\bar{x} \in L$ is a global minimum and $\bar{c} = f(\bar{x})$ is the corresponding global minimum value;

b. $$M(f,c;L) \geq \bar{c} \quad \text{for } c > \bar{c}; \tag{3.18}$$

c. $$M(f,\bar{c};L) = \bar{c}; \tag{3.19}$$

d. $$V(f,\bar{c};L) = 0; \tag{3.20}$$

e. $$V_1(f,\bar{c};L) = 0; \tag{3.21}$$

f. $$M_{2m-1}(f,c;0;L) \geq (\bar{c})^{2m-1} \quad \text{for } c > \bar{c} \text{ and some } m \in I^+; \tag{3.22}$$

g. $$M_{2m-1}(f,\bar{c};0;L) = \bar{c} \quad \text{for some } m \in I^+; \tag{3.23}$$

h. $$M_{2m}(f,\bar{c};M(f,\bar{c};L);L) = 0 \quad \text{for some } m \in I^+; \tag{3.24}$$

i. $$M_m(f,\bar{c};\bar{c};L) = 0 \quad \text{for some } m \in I^+. \tag{3.25}$$

Suppose (L,Ω_L,μ_L) is a Q-measure space, G is a robust set in X and $L\cap(\text{int}G) \neq \emptyset$. Then a rejection-reduction measure $\mu_{L\cap G}$ can also be introduced:

$$\mu_{L\cap G}(A) = \mu_L(A\cap G) \quad \text{for } A \in \Omega_L. \tag{3.26}$$

The following definitions and theorem are similar to those of the rejection and the reduction cases:

<u>Definition 3.5</u>: Suppose $\{c_k\}$ is a decreasing sequence which tends to $c \geq \bar{c} = \min_{x\in L\cap G} f(x)$ as $k \to \infty$. The limits

$$M(f,c;L\cap G) = \lim_{c_k \downarrow c} \frac{1}{\mu_L(H_{c_k}\cap L\cap G)} \int_{H_{c_k}\cap L\cap G} f(x)d\mu_L, \tag{3.27}$$

$$V(f,c;L\cap G) = \lim_{c_k \downarrow c} \frac{1}{\mu_L(H_{c_k}\cap L\cap G)} \int_{H_{c_k}\cap L\cap G} [f(x)-M(f,c;L\cap G)]^2 d\mu_L, \tag{3.28}$$

$$V_1(f,c;L\cap G) = \lim_{c_k \downarrow c} \frac{1}{\mu_L(H_{c_k}\cap L\cap G)} \int_{H_{c_k}\cap L\cap G} [f(x)-c]^2 d\mu_L, \tag{3.29}$$

$$M_m(f,c;a;L\cap G) = \lim_{c_k \downarrow c} \frac{1}{\mu_L(H_{c_k}\cap L\cap G)} \int_{H_{c_k}\cap L\cap G} [f(x)-a]^m d\mu_L, \quad m \in I^+, \tag{3.30}$$

are the <u>rejection-reduction</u> mean value, variance, modified variance and <u>mth</u> moment of f over $H_c\cap L\cap G$, respectively.

<u>Theorem 3.3</u>: With respect to the constrained minimization problem (P) over $S = L\cap G$, the following are equivalent:

a. $\bar{x} \in L\cap G$ is a global minimum and $\bar{c} = f(\bar{x})$ is the corresponding global minimum value;

b. $$M(f,c;L\cap G) \geq \bar{c} \quad \text{for } c > \bar{c}; \tag{3.31}$$

c. $$M(f,\bar{c};L\cap G) = \bar{c}; \tag{3.32}$$

d. $$V(f,\bar{c};L\cap G) = 0; \tag{3.33}$$

e. $$V_1(f,\bar{c};L\cap G) = 0; \tag{3.34}$$

f. $$M_{2m-1}(f,c;0;L\cap G) \geq (\bar{c})^{2m-1} \quad \text{for } c > \bar{c} \text{ and some } m \in I^+; \tag{3.35}$$

g. $$M_{2m-1}(f,\bar{c};0;L\cap G) = \bar{c} \quad \text{for some } m \in I^+; \tag{3.36}$$

h. $$M_{2m}(f,\bar{c};M(f,\bar{c};L\cap G);L\cap G) = 0 \quad \text{for some } m \in I^+; \tag{3.37}$$

i. $$M_m(f,\bar{c};\bar{c};L\cap G) = 0 \quad \text{for some } m \in I^+. \tag{3.38}$$

We observe that our constrained global optimality conditions share a unified form with those of the unconstrained case. The difference between them arises mainly in the definition of different Q-measure spaces. We can also use different Q-measure spaces for the same problem. In the next subsection, we treat the case of linear equality constraints in $\mathbb{R}^n$ as an example of the application of the reduction conditions.

3.3 Linear Equality Constraints

In this subsection, a linear equality constrained minimization problem will be dealt with. Let the constrained set L, which is a linear manifold, be given by

$$L = \{ x \mid \ell_i(x) = 0,\ i = 1,2,\cdots,r,\ x \in X = \mathbb{R}^n \} \tag{3.39}$$

where

$$\ell_i(x) = \Sigma_{j=1}^{n} a_{ij}x^j + b_i, \quad i = 1,2,\cdots,r, \tag{3.40}$$

$x = (x^1,x^2,\cdots,x^n) \in \mathbb{R}^n$, and a_{ij}, b_i $(i = 1,\cdots,r;\ j = 1,\cdots,n)$ are real numbers. Let

$$A = \begin{bmatrix} a_{11} & a_{12} & \cdots & a_{1n} \\ a_{21} & a_{22} & \cdots & a_{2n} \\ \cdots & \cdots & \cdots & \cdots \\ a_{r1} & a_{r2} & \cdots & a_{rn} \end{bmatrix} \tag{3.41}$$

and

$$\bar{A} = \begin{bmatrix} a_{11} & a_{12} & \cdots & a_{1n} & b_1 \\ a_{21} & a_{22} & \cdots & a_{2n} & b_2 \\ \cdots & \cdots & \cdots & \cdots & \cdots \\ a_{r1} & a_{r2} & \cdots & a_{rn} & b_r \end{bmatrix}. \tag{3.42}$$

If $\mathrm{rank}(A) < \mathrm{rank}(\bar{A}) \le r$, then the constraints are inconsistent and L would be empty so that the minimization problem

$$\min_{x \in L} f(x) \tag{3.43}$$

has no solution. If $\mathrm{rank}(A) = \mathrm{rank}(\bar{A}) < r$, the constraints are linearly dependent and a maximal linearly independent set can be derived from them. Therefore, without loss of generality, we always assume that

$$\operatorname{rank}(A) = \operatorname{rank}(\bar{A}) = r. \tag{3.44}$$

Reduction Method I

From (3.44), it follows that L is an affine manifold of n-r dimension, and has the form

$$L = x_o + L_o,$$

where $x_o \in \mathbb{R}^n$ is a fixed vector and L_o a linear subspace of n-r dimension. Therefore there exist n orthonormal vectors $v_1,\cdots,v_n$ such that the first n-r of them generate L_o and the others span the orthogonal complement $L_o^{\perp}$ of L_o. Consequently, each $x \in \mathbb{R}^n$ is a linear combination of $\{v_1,\cdots,v_n\}$ as well as $\{e_1,\cdots,e_n\}$, where the latter is the usual basis of $\mathbb{R}^n$. In other words,

$$\begin{aligned} x &= x^1e_1 + x^2e_2 + \cdots + x^ne_n \\ &= y^1v_1 + y^2v_2 + \cdots + y^{n-r}e_{n-r} + z^1v_{n-r+1} + \cdots + z^rv_{n.} \end{aligned}$$

In particular, one has

$$v_i = \alpha_{i1}e_1 + \alpha_{i2}e_2 + \cdots + \alpha_{in}e_n,$$

where $\alpha_{ij} = \langle v_i, e_j\rangle$ (i.e., the inner product of v_i and e_j), i, j = 1,2,$\cdots$,n. Consequently,

$$\begin{aligned} x^i &= \alpha_{1i}y^1 + \cdots + \alpha_{n-r,i}y^{n-r} + \alpha_{n-r+1,i}z^1 + \cdots + \alpha_{ni}z^r \\ &= \chi_o^i(y^1,\cdots,y^{n-r},z^1,\cdots,z^r) = \chi_o^i(y,z), \qquad i = 1,2,\cdots,n, \end{aligned}$$

which are linear functionals of $y^1,\cdots,y^{n-r}$, $z^1,\cdots,z^r$. In vector form, we have

$$x = (\chi_o^1(y,z),\cdots,\chi_o^n(y,z)) = \chi_o(y,z). \tag{3.45}$$

If we take x_o as the new origin and $\{v_1,\cdots,v_n\}$ as the corresponding orthonormal basis, then the new coordinates of x are

$$\chi^i(y,z) = \chi_o^i(y,z) + x_o^i, \qquad i = 1,2,\cdots,n$$

and

$$x = \chi(y,z) = (\chi^1(y,z),\cdots,\chi^n(y,z)). \tag{3.46}$$

It is easy to see that

$$L = \{ x \in \mathbb{R}^n \mid x^i = \chi^i(y,0),\ -\infty < y^j < \infty,\ i = 1,2,\cdots,n,\ j = 1,2,\cdots,n-r \}. \tag{3.47}$$

Expression (3.47) indicates that the characteristic of linear constrained set L, expressed by χ, is much easier to identify.

For convenience, we introduce a new n-dimensional Euclidean space $\mathbb{R}^n$, with basis $\{v_1,\cdots,v_n\}$. Let $J : \mathbb{R}_1^n \to \mathbb{R}^n$ be a mapping defined by

$$x = Ju = \chi(y,z),$$

where $u = (y,z)$ with $y \in \mathbb{R}_1^{n-r}$ and $z \in \mathbb{R}_1^r$.

Denoting $J^{-1} = T$, one has by (3.37),

$$T[L] = \{ (y,0) \in \mathbb{R}_1^n \mid (y,z) \in \mathbb{R}_1^n = \mathbb{R}_1^{n-r} \times \mathbb{R}_1^r \}.$$

Let P be the projection of $\mathbb{R}_1^n$ onto $\mathbb{R}_1^{n-r}$, i.e.,

$$P[(y,z)] = y \in \mathbb{R}_1^{n-r}. \tag{3.48}$$

Then

$$PT[L] = \mathbb{R}_1^{n-r}, \tag{3.49}$$

and PT is a one-to-one mapping from L onto $\mathbb{R}_1^{n-r}$.

Since J assigns the zero vector of $\mathbb{R}_1^n$ to x_o, T is not necessarily norm-preserving; but it is distance-preserving, i.e., it satisfies:

$$\|Tx_1 - Tx_2\|_{\mathbb{R}_1^n} = \|x_1 - x_2\|_{\mathbb{R}^n}, \quad \forall\, x_1,\ x_2 \in \mathbb{R}^n. \tag{3.50}$$

Since PT is a one-to-one transformation from L onto $\mathbb{R}_1^{n-r}$,

$$L = \{ x \mid Tx \in T[L] \} = \{ x \mid PTx \in PT[L] \}.$$

It follows from (3.40) that

$$\min_{x \in L} f(x) = \min_{PTx \in PT[L]} f(x) = \min_{y \in \mathbb{R}_1^{n-r}} f_1(y), \tag{3.51}$$

where

$$f_1(y) = f(\chi(y,0)). \tag{3.52}$$

We can therefore define the reduction measure

$$\mu_L(B) = \mu_{n-r}(PT[B]), \tag{3.53}$$

where μ_{n-r} is the Lebesque measure on $\mathbb{R}_1^{n-r}$.

Reduction Method II

The condition (3.44) implies that the matrix A has some nonsingular $r \times r$ submatrix which, one may assume without loss of generality, consists of all entries in the first r rows and columns of A. It is clear that in such cases $x^1, \cdots, x^r$ can be expressed as linear combinations of $x^{r+1}, \cdots, x^n$ as below:

$$x^i = \varphi^i(x^{r+1},\cdots,x^n), \quad i = 1,\cdots,r,$$

or

$$x = J_1(\varphi(x_{n-r}),x_{n-r}), \tag{3.54}$$

where $x_{n-r} = (x^{r+1},\cdots,x^n) \in \mathbb{R}^{n-r}$ and $\varphi(x_{n-r}) = (\varphi^1(x_{n-r}),\cdots,\varphi^r(x_{n-r})) \in \mathbb{R}^r$. Denoting the inverse of J_1 by T_1, one has

$$T_1[L] = \{ (0,x_{n-r}) \in \mathbb{R}^n \mid (\varphi(x_{n-r}),x_{n-r}) \in \mathbb{R}^n \}. \tag{3.55}$$

It follows that

$$\min_{x \in L} f(x) = \min_{PT_1x \in PT_1[L]} f(x) = \min_{x_{n-r} \in \mathbb{R}^{n-r}} f_2(x_{n-r}), \tag{3.56}$$

where

$$f_2(x_{n-r}) = f(\varphi^1(x_{n-r}),\cdots,\varphi^r(x_{n-r}),x^{r+1},\cdots,x^n). \tag{3.57}$$

Now, we can define the corresponding reduction measure for this method as

$$\mu_L(B) = \mu_{n-r}(PT_1[B]). \tag{3.58}$$

Applying Theorem 3.2, we have

Theorem 3.4: With respect to the problem (3.43) (under Assumptions A1 and A2), a point $\bar{x} \in L$ is a global minimum point and $\bar{c} = f(\bar{x})$ is the corresponding global minimum value of f over L if and only if one of the conditions (3.18) - (3.25) is satisfied for the reduction measure (3.53) or (3.58).

Reduction Method III

For $\delta > 0$, consider $L_\delta = \{x \in \mathbb{R}^n \mid \inf\|x-y\| \le \delta,\ y \in L\}$.

Definition 3.6: Suppose $c \ge \bar{c} = \min_{x \in L} f(x)$. The limits

$$M(f,c;L) = \lim_{c_k \downarrow c} \lim_{\delta \downarrow 0} \frac{1}{\mu(H_{c_k} \cap L_\delta)} \int_{H_{c_k} \cap L_\delta} f(x)d\mu, \tag{3.59}$$

$$V(f,c;L) = \lim_{c_k \downarrow c} \lim_{\delta \downarrow 0} \frac{1}{\mu(H_{c_k} \cap L_\delta)} \int_{H_{c_k} \cap L_\delta} [f(x)-M(f,c;L)]^2 d\mu, \qquad (3.60)$$

$$V_1(f,c;L) = \lim_{c_k \downarrow c} \lim_{\delta \downarrow 0} \frac{1}{\mu(H_{c_k} \cap L_\delta)} \int_{H_{c_k} \cap L_\delta} [f(x)-c]^2 d\mu, \qquad (3.61)$$

$$M_m(f,c;a;L) = \lim_{c_k \downarrow c} \lim_{\delta \downarrow 0} \frac{1}{\mu(H_{c_k} \cap L_\delta)} \int_{H_{c_k} \cap L_\delta} [f(x)-a]^m d\mu, \quad m \in I^+, \qquad (3.62)$$

are called, respectively, the <u>reduction</u> mean value, variance, modified variance and <u>mth</u> moment centered at a of f over level set H_c with linearly constrained set L.

The following lemma tells us that these definitions are well defined since they coincide with those of Reduction Method I.

<u>Lemma 3.5</u>: For $c > \bar{c}$,

$$\lim_{\delta \downarrow 0} \frac{1}{\mu(H_c \cap L_\delta)} \int_{H_c \cap L_\delta} f(x) d\mu = \frac{1}{\mu_L(H_c^1)} \int_{H_c^1} f_1(y) d\mu_L, \qquad (3.63)$$

where

$$H_c^1 = \{ y \in \mathbb{R}_1^{n-r} \mid f_1(y) \le c \}.$$

<u>Proof</u>: By (3.50), we have

$$\|Tx-Tu\|_{\mathbb{R}_1^n} = \|x-u\|_{\mathbb{R}^n}.$$

Hence,

$$\begin{aligned} T[L_\delta] &= \{ Tx \in \mathbb{R}_1^n \mid \inf \|Tx-Tu\|_{\mathbb{R}_1^n} \le \delta,\ u \in L \} \\ &= \{ (y,z) \in \mathbb{R}_1^n \mid \|(y,z)-(y,0)\|_{\mathbb{R}_1^n} \le \delta,\ y \in \mathbb{R}^{n-r} \} \\ &= \{ (y,z) \in \mathbb{R}_1^n \mid y \in \mathbb{R}_1^{n-r},\ \|z\|_{\mathbb{R}_1^r} \le \delta,\ z \in \mathbb{R}_1^r \} = \mathbb{R}_1^{n-r} \times B_\delta^r, \end{aligned}$$

where

$$B_\delta^r = \{ z \in \mathbb{R}_1^r \mid \|z\|_{\mathbb{R}_1^r} \le \delta \}.$$

Consequently,

$$T[H_c \cap L_\delta] = T[H_c] \cap T[L_\delta] = \bar{H}_c \cap (\mathbb{R}_1^{n-r} \times B_\delta^r), \qquad (3.64)$$

where

$$T[H_c] = \bar{H}_c = \{ (y,z) \in \mathbb{R}_1^n \mid f(\chi(y,z)) \le c \}.$$

Since the mapping $J = \mathbb{R}_1^n \to \mathbb{R}^n$ defined by $(y,z) \to \chi(y,z)$ is measure-preserving, we have

$$\mu(H_c \cap L_\delta) = \mu_1(\bar{H}_c \cap (\mathbb{R}_1^{n-r} \times B_\delta^r)),$$

where μ_1 is the Lebesque measure on $\mathbb{R}_1^n$. Hence,

$$\frac{1}{\mu(H_c \cap L_\delta)} \int_{H_c \cap L_\delta} f(x) d\mu = \frac{1}{\mu_1(\bar{H}_c \cap (\mathbb{R}_1^{n-r} \times B_\delta^r))} \int_{\bar{H}_c \cap (\mathbb{R}_1^{n-r} \times B_\delta^r)} f(\chi(y,z)) d\mu_1. \tag{3.65}$$

On the other hand, let $\mu_1 = \mu_L \times \mu_L^\perp$, where μ_L and $\mu_L^\perp$ are Lebesque measures on $\mathbb{R}_1^{n-r}$ and $\mathbb{R}_1^r$, respectively. Then

$$\frac{1}{\mu_1(H_c^1 \times B_\delta^r)} \int_{H_c^1 \times B_\delta^r} f(\chi(y,0)) d\mu_1$$

$$= \frac{1}{\mu_L(H_c^1)\mu_L^\perp(B_\delta^r)} \int_{B_\delta^r} d\mu_L^\perp \int_{H_c^1} f(\chi(y,0)) d\mu_L = \frac{1}{\mu_L(H_c^1)} \int_{H_c^1} f_1(y) d\mu_L. \tag{3.66}$$

Furthermore, we have

$$\lim_{d \downarrow 0} \bar{H}_c \cap (\mathbb{R}_1^{n-r} \times B_\delta^r) = \bigcap_{\delta > 0} (\bar{H}_c \cap (\mathbb{R}_1^{n-r} \times B_\delta^r)) = \lim_{\delta \downarrow 0} (H_c^1 \times B_\delta^r) = \bigcap_{\delta > 0} (H_c^1 \times B_\delta^r)$$

$$= \{ (y,0) \in \mathbb{R}_1^n \mid f_1(y) \le c \}, \tag{3.67}$$

and

$$\left| \frac{1}{\mu(H_c \cap L_\delta)} \int_{H_c \cap L_\delta} f(x) d\mu - \frac{1}{\mu_L(H_c^1)} \int_{H_c^1} f_1(y) d\mu_L \right|$$

$$= \left| \frac{1}{\mu_1(\bar{H}_c \cap (\mathbb{R}_1^{n-r} \times B_\delta^r))} \int_{\bar{H}_c \cap (\mathbb{R}_1^{n-r} \times B_\delta^r)} f(\chi(y,z)) d\mu_1 - \frac{1}{\mu_1(H_c^1 \times B_\delta^r)} \int_{H_c^1 \times B_\delta^r} f(\chi(y,0)) d\mu_1 \right|$$

$$\le \left| \frac{1}{\mu_1(\bar{H}_c \cap (\mathbb{R}_1^{n-r} \times B_\delta^r))} \int_{\bar{H}_c \cap (\mathbb{R}_1^{n-r} \times B_\delta^r)} f(\chi(y,z)) d\mu_1 - \frac{1}{\mu_1(H_c^1 \times B_\delta^r)} \int_{H_c^1 \times B_\delta^r} f(\chi(y,z)) d\mu_1 \right|$$

$$+ \left| \frac{1}{\mu_1(H_c^1 \times B_\delta^r)} \int_{H_c^1 \times B_\delta^r} [f(\chi(y,z)) - f(\chi(y,0))] d\mu_1 \right|$$

$$= a_1 + a_2.$$

Since (3.67) holds, a_1 will be smaller than any given $\epsilon > 0$ when δ is small enough. From the uniform continuity of $f(\chi(y,z))$ on a compact set, it follows that $a_2 < \epsilon$ whenever δ is sufficiently small. The proof is complete. ∎

Related results for variance and higher moments can be obtained in a similar way. For linear constraints, therefore, we can apply the reduction moments of f over the linear-equality-constrained level set $H_c \cap L$, using Theorem 3.2 instead of the decomposition approach (i.e., Reduction Methods I and II).

Theorem 3.6: With respect to the problem (3.43) (under Assumptions A1 and A2), a point $\bar{x} \in L$ is a global minimum point and $\bar{c} = f(\bar{x})$ is the corresponding global minimum value of f over L if and only if one of the conditions (3.18) - (3.25) is satisfied, where the mean value, variance, modified variance and mth moment are defined using Definition 3.6.

Reduction Method IV

Finally, we discuss another extension for L. Let

$$L^{\delta} = \{ x \in \mathbb{R}^n : |\ell_i(x)| \leq \delta,\ i = 1,2,\cdots,r \}. \tag{3.68}$$

For linear constraints, the connection between L^{δ} and L_{δ} is quite simple. The following lemma says that there is a smaller as well as a larger cylinder between which we can fit L^{δ}. In addition, their relative sizes need not change as δ changes.

Lemma 3.7: There exist $\beta \geq \alpha > 0$ independent of δ such that

$$L_{\alpha\delta} \subset L^{\delta} \subset L_{\beta\delta}. \tag{3.69}$$

Proof: Take $a = (\sqrt{n})\max_{i,j}|a_{ij}|$. From the Schwarz inequality, it follows that

$$|\Sigma_{j=1}^{n} a_{ij}(x^j-y^j)| \leq a\|x-y\|_{\mathbb{R}^n} \qquad \text{for } x,\ y \in \mathbb{R}^n.$$

Since $y \in L$ implies $\ell_i(x) = 0$, we have

$$|\ell_i(x)| = |\ell_i(x)-\ell_i(y)| = |\Sigma_{j=1}^{n} a_{ij}(x^j-y^j)| \leq a\|x-y\|_{\mathbb{R}^n}$$
$$\text{for } y \in L,\ i = 1,2,\cdots,r.$$

Hence, $L_{\alpha\delta} \subset L^{\delta}$, where $\alpha = 1/a$.

On the other hand, suppose that

$$\ell_i(x) = \langle \xi_i, x\rangle + \eta_i, \qquad i = 1,2,\cdots,r.$$

Since $\ell_i(x)$, $i = 1,2,\cdots,r$, are linearly independent, there exist u_1, u_2, $\cdots$, $u_r \in \mathbb{R}^n$ such that

$$\langle \xi_i, u_j\rangle = \delta_{ij},\ i,\ j = 1,2,\cdots,r.$$

For any $x \in L^\delta$, i.e., $|\ell_i(x)| \leq \delta$, let $\lambda_i = \ell_i(x)$ and $u = \Sigma_{j=1}^r \lambda_j u_j$. Then

$$\ell_i(x-u) = \langle \xi_i, x-u\rangle + \eta_i = \langle \xi_i, x\rangle + \eta_i - \langle \xi_i, u\rangle$$

$$= \ell_i(x) - \Sigma_{j=1}^r \lambda_j \langle \xi_i, u_j\rangle = \ell_i(x) - \lambda_i = 0.$$

That is, $x-u \in L$. Hence,

$$\|x-(x-u)\|_{\mathbb{R}^n} = \|u\|_{\mathbb{R}^n} \leq \delta \Sigma_{j=1}^r \|u_j\|_{\mathbb{R}^n} = \beta\delta,$$

where $\beta = \Sigma_{j=1}^r \|u_j\|$ is independent of x. We conclude that $x \in L_{\beta\delta}$. This completes the proof. ∎

From Lemma 3.7, it follows that

$$H_c \cap L_{\alpha\delta} \subset H_c \cap L^\delta \subset H_c \cap L_{\beta\delta}.$$

Therefore,

$$\bigcap_{\delta>0} (H_c \cap L_{\alpha\delta}) \subset \bigcap_{\delta>0} (H_c \cap L^\delta) \subset \bigcap_{\delta>0} (H_c \cap L_{\beta\delta}).$$

Thus,

$$\lim_{\delta\downarrow 0} (H_c \cap L^\delta) = \lim_{\delta\downarrow 0} (H_c \cap L_\delta). \tag{3.70}$$

Consequently, the following definitions of reduction moments for the linear-equality-constrained set L by taking limit of L^δ as $\delta \downarrow 0$ are equivalent to those of Definition 3.6, where the limit is applied to L^δ instead.

$$M(f,c;\ell) = \lim_{c_k\downarrow c} \lim_{\delta\downarrow 0} \frac{1}{\mu(H_c \cap L^\delta)} \int_{H_c \cap L^\delta} f(x)d\mu = M(f,c;L);$$

$$V(f,c;\ell) = \lim_{c_k\downarrow c} \lim_{\delta\downarrow 0} \frac{1}{\mu(H_c \cap L^\delta)} \int_{H_c \cap L^\delta} [f(x)-M(f,c;\ell)]^2 d\mu = V(f,c;L);$$

$$V_1(f,c;\ell) = \lim_{c_k\downarrow c} \lim_{\delta\downarrow 0} \frac{1}{\mu(H_c \cap L^\delta)} \int_{H_c \cap L^\delta} [f(x)-c]^2 d\mu = V_1(f,c;L);$$

and

$$M_m(f,c;a;\ell) = \lim_{c_k\downarrow c} \lim_{\delta\downarrow 0} \frac{1}{\mu(H_c \cap L^\delta)} \int_{H_c \cap L^\delta} [f(x)-a]^m d\mu = M_m(f,c;a;L); \quad m \in I^+.$$

The following is a trivial consequence of the above.

<u>Theorem 3.8</u>: With respect to the problem (3.43) (under Assumptions A1 and A2), a point $\bar{x} \in L$ is a global minimum point and $\bar{c} = f(\bar{x})$ is the corresponding global minimum value if and only if one of the conditions (3.18) - (3.25) is

satisfied for the mean value, variance, modified variance and higher moments defined above.

§4 Penalty Global Optimality Conditions

In this section, the concepts of mean value, variance, modified variance and higher moments over level sets will be extended to the case of penalty functions. The corresponding global optimality conditions turn out to be particularly implementable in our theoretical algorithms discussed in Chapter III. We will assume that the topological space X is a metric space in addition to the maintained assumptions A1 and A2.

4.1 Penalty Mean Value

Let S be a closed subset of X. Consider the constrained minimization problem:

$$\bar{c} = \min_{x \in S} f(x). \tag{4.1}$$

Definition 4.1: A function p on X is a penalty function for the constrained set S if

(i) p is continuous;

(ii) $p(x) \geq 0 \quad \forall\, x \in X$; and

(iii) $p(x) = 0$ if and only if $x \in S$.

In this section we consider the case where S is a robust set in X. We first introduce a sequence of penalty level sets useful in our definitions of a penalty mean value. Suppose $\{c_k\}$ is a decreasing sequence which tends to $c \geq \bar{c}$ as $k \to \infty$ and $\{\alpha_k\}$ is a positive increasing sequence which tends to infinity as

$k \to \infty$. Let

$$H_k = \{ x \mid f(x) + \alpha_k p(x) \le c_k \}, \quad k = 1,2,\cdots. \tag{4.2}$$

Lemma 4.1: The sequence $\{H_k\}$ given by (4.2) is decreasing by inclusion. Moreover,

$$\lim_{k\to\infty} H_k = \bigcap_{k=1}^{\infty} H_k = H_c \cap S. \tag{4.3}$$

Proof: Suppose $x \in H_{k+1}$. Then

$$f(x) + \alpha_{k+1}p(x) \le c_{k+1}.$$

Since $\alpha_{k+1} \ge \alpha_k$ and $c_{k+1} \le c_k$, it follows that

$$f(x) + \alpha_k p(x) \le f(x) + \alpha_{k+1}p(x) \le c_{k+1} \le c_k.$$

Therefore, $x \in H_k$, i.e., $H_{k+1} \subset H_k$.

Suppose $x \in \bigcap_{k=1}^{\infty} H_k$. Then $x \in H_k$ and

$$f(x) + \alpha_k p(x) \le c_k \le c_1, \quad \forall k. \tag{4.4}$$

If $x \in S$, then $p(x) > 0$. Hence, $\alpha_k p(x) \to \infty$ as $k \to \infty$ which contradicts (4.4). Therefore, $x \in S$ and

$$f(x) + \alpha_k p(x) = f(x) \le c_k \quad \forall k.$$

This implies that $x \in H_c$. Thus, we have proved

$$\bigcap_{k=1}^{\infty} H_k \subset H_c \cap S.$$

On the other hand, if $x \in H_c \cap S$, then

$$f(x) + \alpha_k p(x) = f(x) \le c \le c_k, \quad \forall k.$$

Hence, $x \in H_k$ $\forall k$, i.e.,

$$H_c \cap S \subset \bigcap_{k=1}^{\infty} H_k. \qquad \blacksquare$$

By using Lemma 4.1, we now proceed to prove:

Lemma 4.2: Suppose $c > \bar{c}$, $\{c_k\}$ is a decreasing sequence which tends to c as $k \to \infty$, and $\{\alpha_k\}$ is a positive increasing sequence which tends to infinity as $k \to \infty$. Then

$$\lim_{k\to\infty} \frac{1}{\mu(H_k)}\int_{H_k} f(x)d\mu = \frac{1}{\mu(H_c \cap S)}\int_{H_c \cap S} f(x)d\mu. \tag{4.5}$$

Proof: Since $c > \bar{c}$, we have $\mu(H_c \cap S) > 0$ by Lemma I.2.2. Applying Lemma 4.1, we have

$$\left|\frac{1}{\mu(H_k)}\int_{H_k} f(x)d\mu - \frac{1}{\mu(H_c \cap S)}\int_{H_c \cap S} f(x)d\mu\right|$$

$$\le \left|\frac{1}{\mu(H_k)} - \frac{1}{\mu(H_c \cap S)}\right| \cdot \left|\int_{H_k} f(x)d\mu\right| + \frac{1}{\mu(H_c \cap S)}\left|\int_{H_k} f(x)d\mu - \int_{H_c \cap S} f(x)d\mu\right| \to 0$$

as $k \to \infty$. This follows from the absolute continuity of integration and the convergence of $\mu(H_k)$ to $\mu(H_c \cap S)$ and that

$$\left|\int_{H_k} f(x)d\mu\right| \le c_1\mu(H_{c_1})$$

is bounded. ∎

We have defined in Section 3 the rejection mean value of f over its level set with robust constrained set S to be

$$M(f,c;S) = \frac{1}{\mu(H_c \cap S)}\int_{H_c \cap S} f(x)d\mu$$

if $c > \bar{c}$. Therefore,

$$\lim_{k\to\infty} \frac{1}{\mu(H_k)}\int_{H_k} f(x)d\mu = M(f,c;S) \tag{4.6}$$

and the limit does not depend on the choices of sequence $\{c_k\}$ and $\{\alpha_k\}$.

Definition 4.2: Suppose $c > \bar{c}$. The limit

$$M(f,c;p) = \lim_{k\to\infty} \frac{1}{\mu(H_k)}\int_{H_k} f(x)d\mu \tag{4.7}$$

is called the penalty mean value of f over its level set with respect to the penalty function p defined on the feasible set S.

Note that the penalty mean value $M(f,c;p)$ does not depend on the choice of $\{c_k\}$ and $\{\alpha_k\}$ when $c > \bar{c}$. What about the case $c = \bar{c}$?

Lemma 4.3: Suppose $\bar{c} = f(\bar{x})$ is the global minimum value of f over S. Then

$$\bar{c} = M(f,\bar{c};S) = M(f,\bar{c};p). \tag{4.8}$$

Proof: If $\bar{c} = f(\bar{x})$ is the global minimum value of f over S, then $\bar{c} = M(f,\bar{c};S)$. Suppose $\{c_k\}$ is a decreasing sequence which tends to $\bar{c}$ as $k \to \infty$ and

$\{\alpha_k\}$ is a positive increasing sequence which tends to infinity. Then

$$\frac{1}{\mu(H_k)}\int_{H_k} f(x)d\mu \le \frac{1}{\mu(H_k)}\int_{H_k} [f(x) + \alpha_k p(x)]d\mu \le c_k \quad \text{for } k \in I^+.$$

Hence,

$$\limsup_{k\to\infty} \frac{1}{\mu(H_k)}\int_{H_k} f(x)d\mu \le \bar{c}. \tag{4.9}$$

We will prove that

$$\liminf_{k\to\infty} \frac{1}{\mu(H_k)}\int_{H_k} f(x)d\mu \ge \bar{c}. \tag{4.10}$$

Otherwise, there is a subsequence of $\{\frac{1}{\mu(H_k)}\int_{H_k} f(x)d\mu\}$ such that

$$\lim_{k_i\to\infty} \frac{1}{\mu(H_{k_i})}\int_{H_{k_i}} f(x)d\mu = \hat{c} < c.$$

Let $2\eta = \bar{c}-\hat{c} > 0$. Then there is an integer N such that

$$\frac{1}{\mu(H_{k_i})}\int_{H_{k_i}} f(x)d\mu \; < \; \bar{c} - \eta, \quad \forall\, k_i > N. \tag{4.11}$$

It follows that there is at least a point $x_{k_i} \in H_{k_i}$ such that

$$f(x_{k_i}) \; < \; \bar{c} - \eta, \quad k_i > N. \tag{4.12}$$

Thus, we have constructed a sequence $\{x_{k_i}\}_{k_i=N}^{\infty}$ which has a convergent subsequence because of the assumption of compactness (Assumption A2). Without loss of generality, suppose $\{x_{k_i}\}$ is a convergent sequence $x_{k_i} \to \hat{x}$ as $k_i \to \infty$. It is clear that $\hat{x}$ is contained in $\bigcap_{k=1}^{\infty} H_k$ which is closed. Hence,

$$f(\hat{x}) = \lim_{k_i\to\infty} f(x_{k_i}) \; \le \; \bar{c} - \eta. \tag{4.13}$$

According to Lemma 4.1, $\hat{x} \in H_{\bar{c}} \cap S$. This implies that $f(\hat{x}) \ge \bar{c}$, which contradicts (4.13).

The result follows from the observation that

$$\bar{c} \le \liminf_{k\to\infty} \frac{1}{\mu(H_k)}\int_{H_k} f(x)d\mu \le \limsup_{k\to\infty} \frac{1}{\mu(H_k)}\int_{H_k} f(x)d\mu \le \bar{c}. \tag{4.14}$$

∎

4.2 Penalty Mean Value Conditions

Since the penalty mean value coincides with the rejection one, by Theorem 3.1, we have:

Theorem 4.4: The following are equivalent:

a. A point $\bar{x} \in S$ is a global minimum with $\bar{c} = f(\bar{x})$ being the corresponding global minimum value of f over S;

b.
$$M(f,c;p) \geq \bar{c} \quad \text{for } c > \bar{c}; \tag{4.15}$$

c.
$$M(f,\bar{c};p) = \bar{c}. \tag{4.16}$$

It is natural to think that one can use

$$M'(f,c;p) = \lim_{k\to\infty} \frac{1}{\mu(H_k)}\int_{H_k} [f(x)+\alpha_k p(x)]d\mu \tag{4.17}$$

as an alternative definition of the penalty mean value. The following two lemmas tell us that they are indeed equivalent.

Lemma 4.5: Suppose $c > \bar{c}$, $\{c_k\}$ is a decreasing sequence which tends to c as $k \to \infty$ and $\{\alpha_k\}$ is a positive increasing sequence which tends to infinity. Then

$$\lim_{k\to\infty} \frac{1}{\mu(H_k)}\int_{H_k} [f(x)+\alpha_k p(x)]d\mu = \frac{1}{\mu(H_c\cap S)}\int_{H_c\cap S} f(x)d\mu. \tag{4.18}$$

Proof: Since $c > \bar{c}$, we have $\mu(H_c\cap S) > 0$. After applying Lemma I.2.2, we have

$$\left|\frac{1}{\mu(H_k)}\int_{H_k} [f(x)+\alpha_k p(x)]d\mu - \frac{1}{\mu(H_c\cap S)}\int_{H_c\cap S} f(x)d\mu\right|$$
$$\leq \left|\frac{1}{\mu(H_k)} - \frac{1}{\mu(H_c\cap S)}\right| \left|\int_{H_k} [f(x)+\alpha_k p(x)]d\mu\right|$$
$$+ \frac{1}{\mu(H_c\cap S)} \left|\int_{H_k} [f(x)+\alpha_k p(x)]d\mu - \int_{H_c\cap S} [f(x)+\alpha_k p(x)]d\mu\right|.$$

By Lemma 4.1,

$$\left|\frac{1}{\mu(H_k)} - \frac{1}{\mu(H_c\cap S)}\right| \left|\int_{H_k} [f(x)+\alpha_k p(x)]d\mu\right| \leq L\,\frac{|\mu(H_c\cap S)-\mu(H_k)|}{\mu(H_c\cap S)} \to 0 \quad \text{as } k \to \infty,$$

and

$$\frac{1}{\mu(H_c \cap S)} \left| \int_{H_k} [f(x)+\alpha_k p(x)]d\mu - \int_{H_c \cap S} [f(x)+\alpha_k p(x)]d\mu \right|$$

$$\leq \frac{2L\,|\mu(H_k)-\mu(H_c \cap S)|}{\mu(H_c \cap S)} \to 0 \quad \text{as } k \to \infty. \qquad \blacksquare$$

Lemma 4.6: Suppose $\bar{c}$ is the global minimum value of f over S. Then

$$\lim_{k\to\infty} \frac{1}{\mu(H_k)} \int_{H_k} [f(x)+\alpha_k p(x)]d\mu = M(f,\bar{c};S) = \bar{c}. \tag{4.19}$$

Proof: Let $\{c_k\}$ be a decreasing sequence which tends to $\bar{c}$ as $k \to \infty$ and $\alpha_k > 0$, $\alpha_k \uparrow \infty$. We have

$$\frac{1}{\mu(H_k)} \int_{H_k} f(x)d\mu \leq \frac{1}{\mu(H_k)} \int_{H_k} [f(x)+\alpha_k p(x)]d\mu \leq c_k.$$

As $k \to \infty$, we have

$$\bar{c} = M(f,\bar{c};p) \leq \liminf_{k\to\infty} \frac{1}{\mu(H_k)} \int_{H_k} [f(x)+\alpha_k p(x)]d\mu$$

$$\leq \limsup_{k\to\infty} \frac{1}{\mu(H_k)} \int_{H_k} [f(x)+\alpha_k p(x)]d\mu \leq \bar{c}. \qquad \blacksquare$$

Hence, we have the following theorem.

Theorem 4.7: The following are equivalent:

a. A point $\bar{x} \in S$ is a global minimum with $\bar{c} = f(\bar{x})$ as the corresponding global minimum value of f over S;

b. $$M'(f,c;p) \geq \bar{c} \quad \text{for } c > \bar{c}; \tag{4.20}$$

c. $$M'(f,\bar{c};p) = \bar{c}.$$

Remark: Although $M'(f,c;p) = M(f,c;p)$ for $c \geq \bar{c}$, we adopt the latter as the definition of penalty mean value for computational cases. In practice, it is more convenient to compute $f(x)$ rather than $f(x)+\alpha_k p(x)$; especially when α_k becomes very large.

4.3 Penalty Variance and Higher Moment Conditions

As in the case of the preceding subsection, the corresponding concepts of penalty variance, modified variance and higher moments are introduced.

Definition 4.3: Suppose $c \geq \bar{c}$, where $\bar{c}$ is the global minimum value of f over S, $\{c_k\}$ is a decreasing sequence which tends to c as $k \to \infty$ and $\{\alpha_k\}$ is a positive, increasing and unbounded sequence. The limits

$$V(f,c;p) = \lim_{k\to\infty} \frac{1}{\mu(H_k)}\int_{H_k} [f(x)-M(f,c;p)]^2 d\mu, \tag{4.21}$$

$$V_1(f,c;p) = \lim_{k\to\infty} \frac{1}{\mu(H_k)}\int_{H_k} [f(x)-c]^2 d\mu, \tag{4.22}$$

and

$$M_m(f,c;a;p) = \lim_{k\to\infty} \frac{1}{\mu(H_k)}\int_{H_k} [f(x)-a]^m d\mu, \quad m \in I^+, \tag{4.23}$$

are called, respectively, the penalty variance, the penalty modified variance and the penalty mth moment of f over its level set H_c with respect to the penalty function p(x) depending on the constrained set S, where

$$H_k = \{\, x \mid f(x) + \alpha_k p(x) \leq c_k \,\}, \quad k \in I^+.$$

Again, we should prove that (4.21), (4.22) and (4.23) are well defined, i.e., the limits exist and do not depend on the choices of sequences $\{c_k\}$ and $\{\alpha_k\}$. This is the content of the following lemma.

Lemma 4.8: Suppose $c \geq \bar{c}$. Then

$$V(f,c;p) = V(f,c;S), \tag{4.24}$$

$$V_1(f,c;p) = V_1(f,c;S), \tag{4.25}$$

and

$$M_m(f,c;a;p) = M_m(f,c;a;S), \quad m \in I^+. \tag{4.26}$$

Proof: The results of Lemma 4.8 for the case of $c > \bar{c}$ follows from the method of the proof of Lemma 4.2. For the case $c = \bar{c}$, we will only prove (4.26). Since

$$\frac{1}{\mu(H_k)}\int_{H_k} [f(x)-a]^m d\mu = \Sigma_{i=0}^m (-1)^{m-i}\binom{m}{i}\frac{1}{\mu(H_k)}\int_{H_k} [f(x)-\bar{c}]^i d\mu\cdot[a-\bar{c}]^{m-i} \tag{4.27}$$

and

$$M_m(f,c;a;S) = \Sigma_{i=0}^m (-1)^{m-i}\binom{m}{i} M_i(f,c;\bar{c};S)[a-\bar{c}]^{m-i} \tag{4.28}$$

for $c \geq \bar{c}$, it is sufficient to prove that

$$\lim_{k\to\infty} \frac{1}{\mu(H_k)}\int_{H_k} [f(x)]^i d\mu = M_i(f,\bar{c};\bar{c};S), \quad \text{for } i \in I^+. \tag{4.29}$$

The proof for the case of i being odd is similar to that of Lemma 4.3. Suppose $i = 2\ell$ is even. Then

$$0 \le \frac{1}{\mu(H_k)}\int_{H_k} [f(x)-\bar{c}]^{2\ell} d\mu.$$

It follows that

$$0 \le \liminf_{k\to\infty} \frac{1}{\mu(H_k)}\int_{H_k} [f(x)-\bar{c}]^{2\ell} d\mu. \tag{4.30}$$

Suppose

$$\limsup_{k\to\infty} \frac{1}{\mu(H_k)}\int_{H_k} [f(x)-\bar{c}]^{2\ell} d\mu > \eta > 0. \tag{4.31}$$

Then we can also find a subsequence $\{x_{k_i}\}$ such that $x_{k_i} \in H_{k_i}$, $x_{k_i} \to \hat{x}$ as $k_i \to \infty$ so that

$$[f(\hat{x})-\bar{c}]^{2\ell} \ge \eta.$$

Hence, we have either

$$f(\hat{x})-\bar{c} \ge \eta^{1/2\ell} \tag{4.32}$$

or

$$f(\hat{x})-\bar{c} \ge -\eta^{1/2\ell}. \tag{4.33}$$

Suppose (4.32) holds, i.e., $f(\hat{x}) \ge \bar{c} + \eta^{1/2\ell}$. Note that, $f(\hat{x}) \le c_k$, and $x_k \in H_k$, $k = 1,2,\cdots$, so $\hat{x} \in H_{\bar{c}} \cap S$. Therefore, $f(\hat{x}) \le \bar{c}$, which is a contradiction. Condition (4.33), i.e., $f(\hat{x}) \le \bar{c} - \eta^{1/2\ell}$, contradicts the assumption that $\bar{c}$ is the global minimum value of f over S since $\hat{x} \in S$. This completes our proof for the even case since $M_{2\ell}(f,\bar{c};\bar{c};S) = 0$. ∎

Hence, we have the following theorem.

Theorem 4.9: The following are equivalent:

a. A point $\bar{x} \in S$ is a global minimum with $\bar{c} = f(\bar{x})$ as the corresponding global minimum value of f over S;

b. $$V(f,\bar{c};p) = 0; \tag{4.34}$$

c. $$V_1(f,\bar{c};p) = 0; \tag{4.35}$$

d. $$M_{2m-1}(f,c;0;p) \ge (\bar{c})^{2m-1} \quad \text{for } c > \bar{c} \text{ and some } m \in I^+; \tag{4.36}$$

e. $$M_{2m-1}(f,\bar{c};0;p) = (\bar{c})^{2m-1} \quad \text{for some } m \in I^+; \tag{4.37}$$

f. $$M_{2m}(f,\bar{c};M(f,\bar{c};p);p) = 0 \quad \text{for some } m \in I^+; \tag{4.38}$$

g. $$M_m(f,\bar{c};\bar{c};p) = 0 \quad \text{for some } m \in I^+. \tag{4.39}$$

We can also define respectively the penalty variance, modified variance and mth moments of f over its level sets with respect to a penalty function p as follows:

$$V'(f,c;p) = \lim_{k\to\infty} \frac{1}{\mu(H_k)}\int_{H_k} [f(x)+\alpha_k p(x)-M'(f,c;p)]^2 d\mu, \tag{4.40}$$

$$V_1'(f,c;p) = \lim_{k\to\infty} \frac{1}{\mu(H_k)}\int_{H_k} [f(x)+\alpha_k p(x)-\bar{c}]^2 d\mu, \tag{4.41}$$

and

$$M_m'(f,c;p) = \lim_{k\to\infty} \frac{1}{\mu(H_k)}\int_{H_k} [f(x)+\alpha_k p(x)-a]^m d\mu, \quad m \in I^+, \tag{4.42}$$

and prove that

$$V'(f,c;p) = V(f,c;p) = V(f,c;S), \tag{4.43}$$

$$V_1'(f,c;p) = V_1(f,c;p) = V(f,c;S), \tag{4.44}$$

and

$$M_m'(f,c;a;p) = M_m(f,c;a;p) = M_m(f,c;a;S), \quad m \in I^+. \tag{4.45}$$

Theorem 4.9 will also be valid for these alternative penalty variance, modified variance and higher moments.

Since the penalty mean value, variance, modified variance and higher moments of f coincide with the constrained ones, they share the same properties. For instance, the penalty mean value M(f,c;p) is an increasing function of c ($\geq \bar{c}$). In our discussion of theoretical algorithms and implementations, the penalty optimality conditions (in approximate forms) turn out to be more useful than the constrained ones.

§5 Convex Programming

In this section, we will discuss the optimality conditions for a convex programming problem in terms of the global optimality conditions introduced in the preceding sections.

5.1 Optimality Conditions for Differentiable Convex Functions

A subset S of a linear space X is convex if

$$\alpha x_1 + (1-\alpha)x_2 \in S \tag{5.1}$$

$\forall\ \alpha \in (0,1)$ and $x_1, x_2 \in S$. A function on S is convex if

$$f(\alpha x_1+(1-\alpha)x_2) \leq \alpha f(x_1) + (1-\alpha)f(x_2) \tag{5.2}$$

$\forall\ \alpha \in [0,1]$ and $x_1, x_2 \in S$.

Suppose X is a locally convex topological vector space, X^* its topological dual, and $\langle \cdot,\cdot \rangle$ the bilinear canonical pairing over $X^* \times X$. Let f be a convex function on X and S be a convex subset of X. Suppose Assumptions A1 and A2 hold. Consider the convex programming problem:

$$\min_{x \in S} f(x). \tag{5.3}$$

The <u>derivative</u> of function f <u>at point</u> x_o <u>along direction</u> $p \in X$ is defined by

$$D_p f(x_o) = \lim_{\lambda \downarrow 0} \frac{1}{\lambda}[f(x_o+\lambda p)-f(x_o)] \tag{5.4}$$

if the limit exists.

If $\exists\ x^* \in X^*$ such that

$$D_p f(x_o) = (x^*, p) \quad \forall\ x \in X, \tag{5.5}$$

we say that f is Gâteaux-differentiable at x_o. Call x^* the Gâteaux-derivative of f at x_o and denote it by $f'(x_o)$ or $\nabla f(x_o)$.

For a differentiable convex function the following is well known:

Proposition 5.1: Suppose f is Gâteaux-differentiable. Then the following are equivalent:

(1) f is convex on X;

(2) $f(x_1)-f(x_2) \geq \langle \nabla f(x_1), x_2-x_1\rangle$ for $x_1, x_2 \in X$;

(3) $\langle \nabla f(x+\alpha p), p\rangle$ is nonincreasing in α $\forall$ x, p $\in$ X;

(4) $\langle \nabla f(x_1)-\nabla f(x_2), x_1-x_2\rangle \geq 0$.

For a differentiable convex function, we have the following optimality condition:

Proposition 5.2: A point $\bar{x} \in S$ is a global minimum point of a Gâteaux-differentiable convex function f over a convex set if and only if

$$\langle \nabla f(\bar{x}), x-\bar{x}\rangle \geq 0 \quad \forall\, x \in S. \tag{5.6}$$

By using the concept of directional derivative we can weaken (5.6).

Proposition 5.3: Suppose f is a continuous convex function. Then, $\forall$ p $\in$ X, the directional derivative $D_p f(x)$ exists. Moreover, a point $\bar{x} \in S$ is a global minimum point of f over a convex set S if and only if, $\forall$ x $\in$ S,

$$D_{x-\bar{x}} f(\bar{x}) \geq 0. \tag{5.7}$$

The concept of subgradient is also used to describe the optimality conditions for a convex programming problem. A vector $x^* \in X^*$ is a subgradient of a convex function f at a point x_0 if

$$f(x) - f(x_0) \geq \langle x^*, x-x_0\rangle \tag{5.8}$$

$\forall$ x $\in$ X. The set $\partial f(x_0)$ of subgradients of f at a point x_0 is known as the subdifferential

$$\partial f(x_0) = \{\, x^* \in X^* \mid f(x)-f(x_0) \geq \langle x^*, x_0\rangle \ \forall\, x \in X \,\}. \tag{5.9}$$

Proposition 5.4: A vector $x^* \in X^*$ is a subgradient of f at a point x_0 if and only if

$$D_p f(x_0) \geq \langle x^*, p\rangle \quad \forall\, p \in X. \tag{5.10}$$

Proof: If x^* is a subgradient of f at x_0, then, for $\lambda > 0$,

$$f(x_0+\lambda p) - f(x_0) \geq \langle x^*, \lambda p\rangle$$

or

$$\frac{1}{\lambda}[f(x_o+\lambda p)-f(x_o)] \geq \langle x^*,p\rangle.$$

Therefore, $D_p f(x_o) \geq \langle x^*,p\rangle$.

On the other hand, if (5.10) holds, then for $0 < \lambda < 1$,

$$\langle x^*,x-x_o\rangle \leq D_{x-x_o} f(x_o) \leq \frac{1}{\lambda}\left[f(x_o+\lambda[x-x_o])-f(x_o)\right] \leq f(x)-f(x_o),$$

by the convexity of f. Therefore, x^* is a subgradient. ∎

For a continuous convex function f, the subdifferential is a nonempty, convex closed set. Moreover, if f is differentiable at x_o, then

$$\partial f(x_o) = \{\nabla f(x_o)\}.$$

That is, $\partial f(x_o)$ consists of a single vector $\nabla f(x_o)$, the gradient of f at x_o.

In general, however, condition (5.6) cannot be extended to the subgradient case: $\langle \xi,x-\bar{x}\rangle \geq 0$ for $x \in S$ and $\xi \in \partial f(\bar{x})$. In the following subsections, we will discuss relative optimality conditions described by subgradients.

5.2 Optimality Lemmas

Suppose $x_o \in S$ and $\xi \in \partial f(x_o)$ is a subgradient of f at a point x_o. Let $c_o = f(x_o)$ and

$$f_\xi(x_o;x) = c_o + \langle \xi;x-x_o\rangle. \tag{5.11}$$

Lemma 5.5: A point $\bar{x} \in S$ is a global minimum of f over S with $\bar{c} = f(\bar{x})$ being the corresponding global minimum value if and only if there exists a subgradient $\xi \in \partial f(\bar{x})$ such that

$$M(f_\xi(\bar{x};\cdot),c;S) \geq \bar{c}, \quad \text{for } c > \bar{c}. \tag{5.12}$$

Proof: Suppose (5.12) holds. Then $\bar{x}$ is a global minimum of $f_\xi(\bar{x};\cdot)$ over S, i.e.,

$$f_\xi(\bar{x};x) = \bar{c} + \langle \xi,x-\bar{x}\rangle \geq \bar{c} \quad \forall\, x \in S \quad \text{or} \quad \langle \xi,x-\bar{x}\rangle \geq 0 \quad \forall\, x \in S. \tag{5.13}$$

Furthermore, since $\xi \in \partial f(\bar{x})$,

$$f(x) - f(\bar{x}) \geq \langle \xi,x-\bar{x}\rangle \quad \forall\, x \in S.$$

From (5.13), we have

$$f(x) - f(\bar{x}) \geq 0 \quad \forall\, x \in S.$$

Suppose $\bar{x}$ is a global minimum of f over S. If $\bar{x} \in \mathrm{int}S$, (5.12) becomes trivial with $\xi = 0$. We now suppose $\bar{x} \in S\backslash \mathrm{int}S$ and proceed to prove that there is a subgradient $\xi \in \partial f(\bar{x})$ such that (5.12) holds. Consider the two subsets in $\mathbb{R}\times X$ given below:

$$A = \{ (c,x) \mid c < \infty,\ x \in \mathrm{int}S \} \tag{5.14}$$

and

$$H = \{ (c,x) \mid f(x) \leq c,\ c \leq \bar{c},\ x \in S \}. \tag{5.15}$$

We may assume that there is $c_o \leq \bar{c}$ such that $(c_o,\theta) \in H$ without loss of generality.

It is obvious that A and H are convex and disjoint. The interior of A is nonempty. According to the separation theorem, there is a nonzero vector $(c^*,x^*) \in \mathbb{R}\times X^*$ such that

$$c_1c^* + \langle x^*,y\rangle \leq c_2c^* + \langle x^*,x\rangle \tag{5.16}$$

$\forall\ (c_1,y) \in A$ and $(c_2,x) \in H$. If $c^* < 0$, then $c_1c^* + \langle x^*,x\rangle$ can be arbitrarily positive since c_1 can be arbitrarily negative. Hence $c^* \geq 0$. If $c^* = 0$, then

$$\langle x^*,y\rangle \leq \langle x^*,x\rangle \text{ for } (c_1,y) \in A \text{ and } (c_2,x) \in H. \tag{5.17}$$

A point $(f(x),x)$ is in intA and $(c_1,x+\epsilon z)$ in A, where z belongs to a neighborhood of 0 because f is continuous. Therefore,

$$\langle x^*,x+\epsilon z\rangle \leq 0, \quad \text{for } z \in B_\delta(0)$$

since $(c_o,\theta) \in H$, i.e.,

$$\langle x^*,z\rangle \leq 0 \quad \text{for } z \in B_\delta(0).$$

This implies that $x^* = 0$, which is a contradiction because (c^*,x^*) is supposed to be a nonzero vector. Hence, $c^* > 0$.

Set $c^* = 1$. Otherwise, divide (5.16) by c^*. We have

$$c_1 + \langle x^*,y\rangle \leq c_2 + \langle x^*,x\rangle \quad \text{for } (c_1,y) \in A \text{ and } (c_2,x) \in H. \tag{5.18}$$

Now, let $y = \bar{x}$, $c_1 = c_2 + f(\bar{x}) - f(x)$. Thus, (5.18) becomes

$$c_2 + f(\bar{x}) - f(x) + \langle x^*,\bar{x}\rangle \leq c_2 + \langle x^*,x\rangle \quad \text{for } x \in X. \tag{5.19}$$

It implies that

$$f(\bar{x}) + \langle x^*,\bar{x}\rangle \le f(x) + \langle x^*,x\rangle \quad \forall\, x \in X \tag{5.20}$$

or

$$f(x) - f(\bar{x}) \ge \langle -x^*,x-\bar{x}\rangle \quad \forall\, x \in X. \tag{5.21}$$

Thus, we have proved that the vector $-x^*$ is a subgradient of f.

Let $c_1 = c_2 + f(\bar{x}) - f(y)$, $x = \bar{x}$ and $\xi = -x^*$. In (5.18), we have

$$f(\bar{x}) - \langle \xi,x\rangle \le f(y) - \langle \xi,\bar{x}\rangle \quad \forall\, y \in \text{int}S.$$

Thus

$$f(\bar{x}) \le f(x) + \langle \xi,x-\bar{x}\rangle = f_\xi(\bar{x};x) \quad \forall\, x \in S. \tag{5.22}$$

This implies that

$$f_\xi(\bar{x};x) \ge f(\bar{x}) \quad \forall\, x \in S \tag{5.23}$$

so that $\bar{x}$ is a global minimum of $f_\xi(\bar{x},\cdot)$ over convex constrained set S. Applying the mean value condition to $f_\xi(\bar{x};\cdot)$, we have

$$M(f_\xi(\bar{x};\cdot),c;S) \ge \bar{c} \quad \text{for } c > \bar{c}.$$

This completes the proof of the lemma. ∎

In Lemma 5.5, the convex minimization problem (5.3) has been reduced to a related one for the affine function (5.11). Let $\bar{x} \in S$ and

$$\ell_\xi(x-\bar{x}) = \langle \xi,x-\bar{x}\rangle. \tag{5.24}$$

<u>Lemma 5.6</u>: The linear functional $\ell_\xi(x-\bar{x})$ is a supporting linear functional of S at $\bar{x}$, i.e.,

$$\langle \xi,x\rangle \ge \langle \xi,\bar{x}\rangle \quad \text{for } x \in S \tag{5.25}$$

if and only if (5.12) is satisfied.

<u>Proof</u>: Condition (5.12) is necessary and sufficient for $\bar{x} \in S$ to be a global minimum of f_ξ over S. It is equivalent to

$$f_\xi(\bar{x};x) = f(\bar{x}) + \langle \xi,x-\bar{x}\rangle \ge f(\bar{x}) \quad \forall\, x \in S$$

which is in turn equivalent to

$$\langle \xi,x-\bar{x}\rangle \ge 0 \quad \text{for } x \in S.$$ ∎

From Lemma 5.5, we obtain

<u>Lemma 5.7</u>: A point $\bar{x} \in S$ is a global minimum of f over S if and only if

$$\partial f(\bar{x}) \cap P \ne \emptyset, \tag{5.26}$$

where P denotes the set of supporting linear functionals of S at $\bar{x}$.

It is well known (Girsanov, 1972) that the set P of supporting linear functionals coincides with the dual cone of tangent directions, denoted by $T(\bar{x},S)^*$. (A set S^* of $x^* \in X$ is a dual of S if $\langle x^*,x\rangle \geq 0 \ \forall\ x \in S$, i.e., $S^* = \{x^* \in X \mid \langle x^*,x\rangle \geq 0,\ x \in S\}$.) If S is nonempty and robust, then P also coincides with the dual cone of feasible directions, $F(\bar{x},S)^*$. Therefore, (5.26) is equivalent to

$$\partial f(\bar{x}) \cap T(\bar{x},S)^* \neq \emptyset \tag{5.27}$$

which is in turn equivalent to

$$\partial f(\bar{x}) \cap F(\bar{x},S)^* \neq \emptyset \tag{5.28}$$

if S is nonempty and robust.

From the above discussion we see that, for a convex problem, the mean value condition plays the role of the theorem of support or the separation theorem. The former concerns the behavior of points on the boundary of a convex set S. In contrast, the constrained mean value condition (5.12) provides a less direct description of the boundary behavior near optimality. For the nonconvex case, where there may not exist supporting hyperplanes, the mean value condition still applies. This suggests an approach to generalize the theorem of support, which is still an open question.

5.3 Optimality Conditions for Convex Minimization

We provide, in this subsection, a brief summary of standard results using the preceding preliminary ones obtained by the mean value global optimality condition. We consider a problem where the constrained set S is an intersection of a finite number of subsets of X:

$$S = S_1 \cap S_2 \cap \cdots \cap S_n. \tag{5.29}$$

First, we prove some lemmas about properties of a cone generated by a set S:

$$\text{con}S = \{ x \mid x = \lambda y,\ y \in S \text{ and } \lambda > 0 \}. \tag{5.30}$$

Lemma 5.8: If S is convex, then conS is a convex cone. If $y \in \text{int}S$, $\lambda > 0$, and $x = \lambda y$, then $x \in \text{int}(\text{con}S)$.

Proof: Take $x_1, x_2 \in \text{con}S$ such that $x_1 = \lambda_1 y_1$, $x_2 = \lambda_2 y_2$, where $y_1, y_2 \in S$ and $\lambda_1, \lambda_2 > 0$. Let $\gamma_1, \gamma_2 > 0$ be arbitrary. Then

$$\begin{aligned}\gamma_1 x_1 + \gamma_2 x_2 &= \gamma_1\lambda_1 y_1 + \gamma_2\lambda_2 y_2 \\ &= (\gamma_1\lambda_1+\gamma_2\lambda_2)\left[\frac{\gamma_1\lambda_1}{\gamma_1\lambda_1+\gamma_2\lambda_2} y_1 + \frac{\gamma_2\lambda_2}{\gamma_1\lambda_1+\gamma_2\lambda_2} y_2\right] \in \text{con}S\end{aligned}$$

because the point within the brackets is in S.

If $x = \lambda y$, $y \in \text{int}S$ and $\lambda > 0$, then $y+\epsilon U \subset S$, where U is a neighborhood of 0 and $\epsilon > 0$ is sufficiently small. Hence,

$$x + \lambda\epsilon U = \lambda(y+\epsilon U) \subset \text{con}S,$$

i.e., $x \in \text{int}(\text{con}S)$. ∎

Lemma 5.9: Suppose $S_1,\cdots,S_n$ are convex sets and $0 \in S_i$, $i = 1,\cdots,n$. Then

$$\text{con}\left(\bigcap_{i=1}^{n} S_i\right) = \bigcap_{i=1}^{n} (\text{con}S_i). \tag{5.31}$$

Proof: If $x = \lambda y$, where $y \in \bigcap_{i=1}^{n} S_i$, then $x \in \text{con}S_i$, $i = 1,\cdots,n$. On the other hand, let $x \in \text{con}S_i$, $i = 1,\cdots,n$, i.e., $x = \lambda_i y_i$, $\lambda_i > 0$ and $y_i \in S_i$, $i = 1,\cdots,n$. It implies $\lambda_i^{-1}x \in S_i$ and

$$\lambda(\lambda_i^{-1}x) = (1-\lambda)0 + \lambda(\lambda_i^{-1}x) \in S_i \quad \text{for } 0 \le \lambda < 1.$$

Taking τ such that $0 < \tau \le \min \lambda_i^{-1}$, we obtain

$$\tau x = (\tau\lambda_i)(\lambda_i^{-1}x) \in S_i, \quad i = 1,\cdots,n,$$

i.e., $\tau x \in \bigcap_{i=1}^{n} S_i$ and $x = (\frac{1}{\tau})(\tau x) \in \text{con}(\bigcap_{i=1}^{n} S_i)$. ∎

Adopt the definition of dual C^* of C here. From Lemma 5.8, we have

Lemma 5.10: Suppose C is a convex cone. If $\langle x^*,x\rangle$ is bounded from below for $x \in C$, then $x^* \in C^*$. If $x \in \text{int}C$, then $\langle x^*,x\rangle > 0$ $\forall\, x^* \in C^*$ and $x^* \neq 0$.

Lemma 5.11: Let $C_1,\cdots,C_n$ be convex cones. If $C_1\cap\cdots\cap C_n = \emptyset$, then $\exists\, x_i^* \in C_i^*$ $(i = 1,\cdots,n)$ not all zero such that

$$x_1^* + \cdots + x_n^* = 0.$$

Proof: Consider a product space X^n. Construct two cones in X^n:

$$C = \prod_{i=1}^{n} C_i = \{ (x_1,\cdots,x_n) \mid x_1 \in C_1, \cdots, x_n \in C_n \}$$

and

$$P = \{ (x,\cdots,x) \in X^n \mid x \in X \}.$$

Since $C_1\cap\cdots\cap C_n = \emptyset$ and $C\cap P = \emptyset$, there exists a vector $(x_1^*,\cdots,x_n^*) \in (X^n)^*$ such that

$$\langle x_1^*,x\rangle + \cdots + \langle x_n^*,x\rangle \le \langle x_1^*,x_1\rangle + \cdots + \langle x_n^*,x_n\rangle \qquad (5.32)$$

$$\text{for } x \in X,\ x_1 \in C_1, \cdots, x_n \in C_n.$$

It follows from (5.31) that $\langle x_i^*,x_i\rangle$ is bounded from below for $x_i \in C_i$, $i = 1, \cdots,n$, i.e., $x_i^* \in C_i^*$, $i = 1,\cdots,n$. From (5.32), the left-hand side can be arbitrarily close to 0. Therefore $x_1^* + \cdots + x_n^* = 0$. ∎

Lemma 5.12: Suppose $C_1,\cdots,C_n$ are convex cones and $C = C_1\cap\cdots\cap C_n$. If

$$C_1\cap(\text{int}C_2)\cap\cdots\cap(\text{int}C_n) \neq \emptyset, \qquad (5.33)$$

then

$$C^* = C_1^* + \cdots + C_n^*.$$

Proof: By the definition of dual cones, $C_1^* + \cdots + C_n^* \subset C^*$. We now proceed to prove the opposite claim. Take a fixed $x_o^* \in C^*$, $x_o^* \neq 0$. Let $C_o = \{x \mid \langle x_o^*,x\rangle < 0\}$. Hence, we have $C_o\cap C = \emptyset$ and $C_o^* = \{y^* \mid y^* = \lambda x_o^*,\ \lambda \le 0\}$. Applying Lemma 5.11 we know that $\exists\ y^* \in C_o^*$, $x_i^* \in C_i^*$ $(i = 1,\cdots,n)$ such that

$$y^* + x_1^* + \cdots + x_n^* = 0 \qquad (5.34)$$

and y^*, x_i^* are not all equal to zero. From (5.34) we have

$$-\lambda x_o^* = x_1^* + \cdots + x_n^*, \quad \lambda \le 0. \qquad (5.35)$$

If $\lambda < 0$, then

$$x_o^* = (-\frac{1}{\lambda})x_1^* + \cdots + (-\frac{1}{\lambda})x_n^* \in C_1^* + \cdots + C_n^*.$$

We now prove that $\lambda \neq 0$. Otherwise $x_1^* + \cdots + x_n^* = 0$. Here, at least two vectors, for instance x_1^* and x_n^*, are nonzero. From (5.33), $\exists\ \hat{x} \in C_1\cap(\text{int}C_2)\cap \cdots\cap(\text{int}C_n)$ such that $\langle x_2^*,\hat{x}\rangle > 0$ and $\langle x_i^*,\hat{x}\rangle \ge 0$ for $i \neq 2$ since $\hat{x} \in \text{int}C_2$. This implies, however, that

$$0 = \langle x_1^* + \cdots + x_n^*, \hat{x}\rangle = \langle x_1^*, \hat{x}\rangle + \cdots + \langle x_n^*, \hat{x}\rangle > 0.$$

Hence, the proof is complete. ∎

From the proof of Lemma 5.12, we also have

Lemma 5.13: Suppose $C_1, \cdots, C_n$ are convex cones and $C = C_1 \cap \cdots \cap C_n$. Then either

$$C^* = C_1^* + \cdots + C_n^*,$$

or there exist vectors $x_i^* \in C_i^*$ $(i = 1, \cdots, n)$ not all zero such that

$$x_1^* + \cdots + x_n^* = 0$$

or both.

We are now ready to develop the optimality condition of convex minimization for intersecting constrained sets. Denoting

$$C_{\bar{x}}(S) = \mathrm{con}(S-\bar{x}) = \{ x \mid \bar{x}+\lambda x \in S \text{ for some } \lambda > 0 \}, \tag{5.36}$$

we have, by Lemma 5.6, the following:

Lemma 5.14: A point $\bar{x}$ is a global minimum of f over S if and only if

$$\partial f(\bar{x}) \cap C_{\bar{x}}(S)^* \neq \emptyset. \tag{5.37}$$

Theorem 5.15: Suppose $S_1, \cdots, S_n$ are convex sets, $C = S_1 \cap \cdots \cap S_n$, and $(\mathrm{int}S_1) \cap \cdots \cap (\mathrm{int}S_{n-1}) \cap S_n \neq \emptyset$. A point $\bar{x} \in S$ is a global minimum of f over S if and only if $\exists\ x_i^* \in C_{\bar{x}}(S_i)^*$ $(i = 1, \cdots, n)$ and $x^* \in \partial f(\bar{x})$ such that

$$x^* = x_1^* + \cdots + x_n^*. \tag{5.38}$$

Proof: Applying Lemma 5.9 and noting that $\bar{x}$ plays the role of a translated origin, we have

$$C_{\bar{x}}(S) = \bigcap_{i=1}^{n} C_{\bar{x}}(S_i). \tag{5.39}$$

If $\hat{x} \in \mathrm{int}S_i$ $(i = 1, \cdots, n-1)$ and $\hat{x} \in S_n$, then

$$\hat{x}-\bar{x} \in \mathrm{int}\Big[C_{\bar{x}}(S_i)\Big], \quad i = 1, \cdots, n-1 \text{ and } \hat{x}-\bar{x} \in C_{\bar{x}}(S),$$

according to Lemma 5.8. Therefore,

$$\mathrm{int}\Big[C_{\bar{x}}(S_1)\Big] \cap \cdots \cap \Big[\mathrm{int}C_{\bar{x}}(S_{n-1})\Big] \cap \Big[C_{\bar{x}}(S)\Big] \neq \emptyset. \tag{5.40}$$

If follows from Lemma 5.12 that

$$C_{\bar{x}}(S)^* = C_{\bar{x}}(S_1)^* + \cdots + C_{\bar{x}}(S_n)^*. \tag{5.41}$$

Now, a vector $x^* \in (\partial f(\bar{x})) \cap (C_{\bar{x}}(S)^*)$ exists by Lemma 5.14. This means that

$$x^* = x_1^* + \cdots + x_n^* \quad \text{for some } x_i^* \in C_{\bar{x}}(S_i)^*, \ i = 1,\cdots,n. \ \blacksquare$$

Theorem 5.16: Suppose $\bigcap_{i=1}^{n} S_i$, where S_i $(i = 1,\cdots,n)$ is a convex set. If $\bar{x} \in S$ is a global minimum of f over S, then $\exists$ vectors $x^* \in \partial f(\bar{x})$, $x_i^* \in C_{\bar{x}}(S_i)$ $(i = 1,\cdots,n)$ and a real number λ which equals either zero or unity such that

$$\lambda x^* = x_1^* + \cdots + x_n^*. \tag{5.42}$$

Moreover, if $\lambda = 0$, then $x_1^*,\cdots,x_n^*$ are not all zero. Otherwise, (5.42) is also sufficient.

Proof: According to Lemma 5.14, $\exists$ a vector $x^* \in \partial f(\bar{x})$ and $C_{\bar{x}}(S)^*$. Lemma 5.13 tells us that there are two possible cases. If (5.41) is valid, then $\lambda = 1$ and (5.42) is a necessary and sufficient condition. Otherwise, $\exists$ $x_i^* \in C_{\bar{x}}(S)^*$ $(i = 1,\cdots,n)$ such that they are not all zero and $x_1^* + \cdots + x_n^* = 0$. $\blacksquare$

5.4 Generalized Gradient

In this subsection, we will establish the link betweeen our integral characterization of global optimality and Clarke's (1975; 1976) generalized derivative approach to obtain necessary conditions for nonconvex programming.

Let X be a Banach space and f a real-valued function on X. The function f is said to be locally Lipschitz if, $\forall$ $x \in X$, there is a neighborhood $\mathcal{O}(x)$ such that for some K and any y, z in $\mathcal{O}(x)$, we have

$$|f(y)-f(z)| \le K\|y-z\|.$$

For each $v \in X$, the generalized directional derivative $f^o(x;v)$ in the direction v is defined by

$$f^o(x;v) = \limsup_{\substack{h\to 0\\ \lambda\downarrow 0}} \frac{1}{\lambda}[f(x+h+\lambda v)-f(x+h)]. \tag{5.43}$$

The generalized directional derivative $f^o(x;v)$ can be taken to be convex in direction v.

Definition 5.1: The generalized gradient of f at x, denoted $\partial_c f(x)$, is defined to be the subdifferential of the convex generalized directional derivative $f^o(x;\cdot)$ at 0.

Note that this definition requires neither convexity nor differentiability assumptions on f. If f is convex, then $\partial_c f(x)$ coincides with the subdifferential $\partial f(x)$ of f discussed in subsection 5.1. If for each point y in a neighborhood of x, f admits a Gâteaux derivative $\nabla f(y)$, then $\partial_c f(x) = \{\nabla f(x)\}$.

Lemma 5.17: If $\bar{x}$ is a local minimum for f, then 0 is a global minimum of $f^o(\bar{x};\cdot)$.

Proof: For any $v \in X$, by Definition 5.1, we have

$$f^o(\bar{x};v) = \limsup_{h\to 0,\lambda\downarrow 0} \frac{1}{\lambda}[f(\bar{x}+h+\lambda v)-f(\bar{x}+h)] \geq \limsup_{\lambda\downarrow 0} \frac{1}{\lambda}[f(\bar{x}+\lambda v)-f(\bar{x})] \geq 0$$

since $[f(\bar{x}+\lambda v)-f(\bar{x})]/\lambda \geq 0$ for $\lambda > 0$ sufficiently small. On the other hand, we have $f^o(\bar{x};0) = 0$ and $f^o(\bar{x};v)$ is convex in v. Hence 0 is a global minimum of $f(\bar{x};\cdot)$. ∎

Applying the global optimality conditions of Theorems 1.1, 2.1 and 2.2, on the generalized directional derivative $f^o(\bar{x};v)$ at a local minimum $\bar{x}$ in the above lemma, we obtain the following conditions:

Corollary 5.18: If $\bar{x}$ is a local minimum of f, then

$$M(f^o(\bar{x};\cdot),c) \geq 0 \quad \text{for } c > 0; \tag{5.44}$$

$$M(f^o(\bar{x};\cdot),0) = 0; \tag{5.45}$$

$$V(f^o(\bar{x};\cdot),0) = 0; \tag{5.46}$$

$$V_1(f^o(\bar{x};\cdot),0) = 0; \tag{5.47}$$

where M, V and V_1 are defined with respect to any Q-measure μ on a Borel field of X.

By Lemma 5.5, we have

Corollary 5.19: If $\bar{x}$ is a local minimum for f, then $\exists\ \xi \in \partial_c f(\bar{x})$ such that

$$M(\langle\xi,\cdot\rangle,c) \geq 0, \qquad \text{for } c > 0. \tag{5.48}$$

We will now consider the constrained case:

$$\min_{x \in S} f(x). \tag{5.49}$$

Recall that the cone of tangents of S at $\hat{x}$, denoted by $T = T(\hat{x},S)$, consists of all directions d such that $d = \lim_{k\to 0} \lambda_k(x_k-\hat{x})$, where $\lambda_k > 0$, $x_k \in S$ for each k and some $\{x_k\}$ which converges to $\hat{x}$. Note that T is a closed cone.

<u>Theorem 5.20</u>: If the point $\bar{x} \in S$ is a local minimum of f over S, then 0 is a global minimum of $f^o(\bar{x};\cdot)$ over $T(\bar{x},S)$.

<u>Proof</u>: Let $d \in T(\bar{x},S)$ and $\{x_k\} \subset S$ such that $x_k \to \bar{x}$, $\lambda_k(x_k-\bar{x}) \to d$ with $\lambda_k \to +\infty$. We have

$$\lambda_k[f(\bar{x} + \frac{1}{\lambda_k} d) - f(\bar{x})] = \lambda_k[f(\bar{x} + \frac{1}{\lambda_k} d) - f(x_k)] + \lambda_k[f(x_k) - f(\bar{x})],$$

where $x_k = \bar{x} + \frac{1}{\lambda_k}\lambda_k(x_k-\bar{x})$.

Since f is locally Lipschitz,

$$|\lambda_k[f(\bar{x} + \frac{1}{\lambda_k} d) - f(x_k)]| \le K \|d - \lambda_k(x_k-\bar{x})\|, \text{ for some } K > 0.$$

Moreover, $f(x_k) \ge f(\bar{x})$ for k sufficiently large. Therefore,

$$f^o(\bar{x};d) \ge \limsup_{k\to\infty} \lambda_k[f(\bar{x} + \frac{1}{\lambda_k} d) - f(\bar{x})] \ge 0.$$

But $f^o(\bar{x};0) = 0$. Hence,

$$f^o(\bar{x};d) \ge f(\bar{x};0) \quad \forall\, d \in T(\bar{x},S). \qquad \blacksquare$$

Suppose T_1 is a nonempty closed convex cone inclused in $T(\bar{x},S)$. Then $0 \in T_1$ and

$$\min_{d\in T_1} f^o(\bar{x};d) \ge \min_{d\in T} f^o(\bar{x};d) \ge f^o(\bar{x};0).$$

Then,

<u>Corollary 5.21</u>: If $\bar{x}$ is a local minimum of f over S, then 0 is a global minimum of $f^o(\bar{x};\cdot)$ over T_1.

We consider the reduced problem of minimizing the convex function $f^o(\bar{x};\cdot)$ over T_1. By Lemma 5.5 and Corollary 5.21, we have

<u>Theorem 5.22</u>: If $\bar{x}$ is a local minimum of f over S, then for any nonempty closed convex cone T_1 inclused in $T(\bar{x},S)$, $\exists\, \xi \in \partial_c f(\bar{x})$ such that

$$M(\langle\xi,\cdot\rangle,c;T_1) \geq 0, \quad \text{for } c > 0. \tag{5.50}$$

Lemma 5.6 tells us that if $\bar{x} \in S$ is a global minimum of f over S, then $\exists\ \xi \in \partial_c f(\bar{x})$ such that

$$\langle\xi,d\rangle \geq 0 \quad \forall\ d \in T_1.$$

That is, ξ is a vector in the dual of T_1. Hence,

Corollary 5.23: If $\bar{x}$ is a local minimum of f over S, then for any nonempty closed convex cone T_1 inclused in $T(\bar{x},S)$,

$$\partial_c f(\bar{x}) \cap (T_1)^* \neq \emptyset. \tag{5.51}$$

In his paper, Clarke introduced the concept of generalized normal cone to a set S at a point $x \in S$. Suppose S is a nonempty subset of X. Consider the distance function,

$$d_S(x) = \inf\ \{\ \|x-c\|\ \mid\ c \in S\ \}. \tag{5.52}$$

It is straightforward to show that $d_S(x)$ is a Lipschitz function. The normal cone N(x,S) of S at a point $x \in S$ is defined to be the conical hull of $\partial_c d_S(x)$, i.e.,

$$N(x,S) = \text{con}\ \{\ \lambda\xi\ \mid\ \lambda > 0 \text{ and } \xi \in \partial_c d_S(x)\ \}. \tag{5.53}$$

Corresponding to the concept of normal cone, we refer to the dual of $-\partial_c d_S(x)$, as the tangent cone of S at point x and denote it by J(x,S). Alternatively, J(x,S) can be defined by

$$J(x,S) = \{\ -d\ \mid\ d_S^o(x;d) = 0\ \}.$$

Note that the tangent cone J(x,S) is closed and convex. The following lemma shows that J(x,S) is included in the cone of tangents T(x,S).

Lemma 5.24: Suppose S is a closed subset of X and $\bar{x} \in S$. Then

$$J(\bar{x},S) \subset T(\bar{x},S).$$

Proof: Let $\{x_k\} \subset S$ be a sequence converging to $\bar{x}$ and $\{\lambda_k\}$ $(\lambda_k \geq 0)$ converging to 0. Let $d \in J(\bar{x},S)$. Then $d_S^o(\bar{x},d) = 0$, or

$$\limsup_{k\to\infty} \frac{1}{\lambda_k}\left[d_S(\bar{x}+[x_k-\bar{x}]+\lambda_k d) - d_S(\bar{x}+[x_k-\bar{x}])\right] = 0$$

so that

$$\lim_{k\to\infty} \frac{1}{\lambda_k}[d_S(x_k+\lambda_k d)] = 0. \tag{5.54}$$

Let $\tilde{x}_k \in S$ such that $\|\tilde{x}_k-(x_k+\lambda_k d)\| \le d_S(x_k+\lambda_k d)+(\lambda_k)^2$. We define $d_k = (\tilde{x}_k-x_k)/\lambda_k$ which is equal to $d + [\tilde{x}_k-(x_k+\lambda_k d)]/\lambda_k$. By (5.54), $d_S(x_k+\lambda_k d)/\lambda_k$ converges to 0. Hence $\|d_k-d\|$, which is bounded by $d_S(x_k+\lambda_k d)/\lambda_k$, converges to 0. That is, $d = \lim_{k\to\infty} (\tilde{x}_k-\bar{x})/\lambda_k$ belongs to $T(\bar{x},S)$. ∎

For completeness, the following results of Clarke (1976) and Hiriart-Urruty (1979) are stated without proof.

Theorem 5.25: If $\bar{x}$ is a local minimum of f over S, then

$$\partial_c f(\bar{x}) \cap \left[-N(\bar{x},S)\right] \neq \emptyset \tag{5.55}$$

and

$$\partial_c f(\bar{x}) \cap \left[-J(\bar{x},S)\right] \neq \emptyset. \tag{5.56}$$

§6 Optimality Conditions for Differentiable Functions

This section is, in a manner of speaking, an expository one. Applying the global optimality condition for continuous functions to obtain local optimality conditions for differentiable functions is somewhat contrived but serves to illustrate the connection as well as the gap between the two approaches.

We shall assume throughout this section that the space X is a normed linear space and that $f : X \to \mathbb{R}$ is Fréchet differentiable.

Definition 6.0: A function $f : X \to \mathbb{R}$, where X is a normed linear space, is Fréchet differentiable at $x_o \in X$ if $\exists\, y^* \in X^*$ such that

$$f(x) - f(x_o) = \langle y^*, x-x_o\rangle + o(\|x-x_o\|) \quad \text{for } x \in X.$$

The term $\langle y^*, x-x_o\rangle$ and the dual vector y^* in the above definition are referred to as the Fréchet differential of f at x_o with increment $x-x_o$ and the

Fréchet derivative of f at x_o, respectively.

6.1 General Discussion: the Unconstrained Case

Definition 6.1: Let $h \in X$ and $x \in S$. If there is a positive number $\epsilon_0 > 0$ such that $x+\epsilon h \in S \; \forall \; 0 < \epsilon \leq \epsilon_0$, then h is known as a feasible direction of S at point x.

Definition 6.2: A point $\bar{x} \in S$ is a local minimum of f over S if $\exists \; \delta > 0$ such that

$$f(\bar{x}) = \min_{B_\delta(\bar{x}) \cap S} f(x) \tag{6.1}$$

where $B_\delta(\bar{x})$ is a ball centered at $\bar{x}$ with radius δ; i.e.,

$$B_\delta(\bar{x}) = \{ x \mid \|x-\bar{x}\| \leq \delta \}. \tag{6.2}$$

Proposition 6.1: Suppose f(x) is differentiable at $\bar{x} \in S$ and h is a feasible direction of S at $\bar{x}$. If $\bar{x}$ is a local minimum, then

$$\langle \nabla f(\bar{x}), h \rangle \geq 0. \tag{6.3}$$

Proof: Construct a linear section,

$$L = \{ x \mid \bar{x}+th, \; 0 \leq t \leq \eta \},$$

where $\eta = \min\{\epsilon_0, \delta, \epsilon_1\}$. We will discuss how to select ϵ_1 later. Obviously, $L \subset B_\delta(\bar{x}) \cap S$ so that

$$f(\bar{x}) = \min_{x \in L} f(x).$$

We now define a Q-measure μ_L on L. Suppose $A \subset [0,\eta]$ and $A_L = \{x \mid \bar{x}+th, \; t \in A\}$. Then we define

$$\mu_L(A_L) = \mu(A) \cdot \|h\|, \tag{6.4}$$

where μ is the Lebesque measure on $\mathbb{R}^1$.

For $c > f(\bar{x}) = \bar{c}$, let $E_c = \{x \mid f(x) < c\}$. We have $\bar{x} \in E_c$ which is open. Thus, there is a ball $B_{\epsilon_1}(\bar{x}) \subset E_c$ and $L \subset H_c$.

By the mean value condition, we have

$$f(\bar{x}) \leq M(f,c;L) = \frac{1}{\mu_L(H_c \cap L)} \int_{H_c \cap L} f(x) d\mu_L$$

$$= \frac{1}{\mu_L(H_c \cap L)} \int_{H_c \cap L} \Big[f(\bar{x}) + \langle \nabla f(\bar{x}), x-\bar{x} \rangle + o(\|x-\bar{x}\|) \Big] d\mu_L$$

$$= f(\bar{x}) + \frac{\|h\|}{\eta \|h\|} \int_0^{\eta} \Big[\langle \nabla f(\bar{x}), th \rangle + o(\|th\|) \Big] dt.$$

This implies that

$$\frac{\eta}{2} \langle \nabla f(\bar{x}), h \rangle + o(\eta) \geq 0.$$

Hence,

$$\langle \nabla f(\bar{x}), h \rangle \geq 0. \qquad \blacksquare$$

If f is twice-differentiable at $\bar{x}$, then for $x = \bar{x}+th$,

$$f(x) = f(\bar{x}) + \langle \nabla f(\bar{x}), th \rangle + \langle th^*, A(\bar{x})th \rangle + o(t^2\|h\|^2),$$

where $A(\bar{x})$ is the Henssian operator of f at $\bar{x}$. By a similar argument, we can prove:

<u>Proposition 6.2</u>: Suppose f is twice-differentiable at $\bar{x}$ and h is a feasible direction of S at $\bar{x}$. If $\bar{x}$ is a local minimum of f over S and $\langle \nabla f(\bar{x}), h \rangle = 0$, then

$$\langle h^*, A(\bar{x})h \rangle \geq 0. \tag{6.5}$$

From Propositions 6.1 and 6.2, we can derive the optimality condition for an unconstrained local minimum immediately.

<u>Proposition 6.3</u>: Suppose f is differentiable at $\bar{x} \in \text{int}S$. If $\bar{x}$ is a local minimum, then

$$\nabla f(\bar{x}) = 0. \tag{6.6}$$

If, in addition, f is twice-differentiable at $\bar{x}$, then

$$\langle h^*, A(\bar{x})h \rangle \geq 0 \quad \forall\, h \in X,\ h^* \in X^*. \tag{6.7}$$

(The latter is referred to as the second order condition.)

The following sufficient global optimality condition for a differentiable convex function f is well known. Since

$$f(x) \geq f(\bar{x}) + \langle \nabla f(\bar{x}), x-\bar{x} \rangle \quad \forall\, x \in S,$$

where $S \subset X$ is convex, we have

Proposition 6.4: Suppose f is a convex function differentiable at $\bar{x} \in \text{int}S$. If

$$\langle \nabla f(\bar{x}), x-\bar{x} \rangle \geq 0 \quad \forall\, x \in S,$$

then $\bar{x}$ is a global minimum of f over S.

Proof: For the purpose of illustration, we provide a short mean-value-based proof. For each $c > f(\bar{x})$, we have

$$c \geq \frac{1}{\mu(H_c \cap S)} \int_{H_c \cap S} f(x) d\mu \geq f(\bar{x}) + \frac{1}{\mu(H_c \cap S)} \int_{H_c \cap S} \langle \nabla f(\bar{x}), x-\bar{x} \rangle d\mu \geq f(\bar{x}).$$

Letting $c \to \bar{c}$, we obtain

$$f(\bar{x}) \leq M(f,\bar{c};S) \leq f(\bar{x})$$

i.e.,

$$M(f,\bar{c};S) = \bar{c}.$$

Hence, $\bar{x}$ is a global minimum of f over S. ∎

6.2 The Inequality Constrained Case in $\mathbb{R}^n$

In this subsection, we will consider the nonlinear programming problem:

$$\min_{x \in G} f(x), \tag{6.8}$$

where G is a robust set defined by inequality constraints:

$$G = \{\, x \in \mathbb{R}^n \mid g_i(x) \leq 0,\ i = 1,\cdots,r \,\} \tag{6.9}$$

with continuous, real-valued functions f and g_i $(i = 1,\cdots,r)$ on $\mathbb{R}^n$. Let

$$I = \{\, i \mid g_i(\bar{x}) = 0 \,\}$$

denote the index of the set of active constraints at $\bar{x}$. Suppose $\forall\, i \in I$, $g_i(x)$ is differentiable at $\bar{x}$. Consider

$$G_I = \{\, h \in \mathbb{R}^n \mid \langle \nabla g_i(\bar{x}), h \rangle < 0,\ i \in I \,\}. \tag{6.10}$$

Lemma 6.5: If, for $i \in I$, $g_i(x)$ is differentiable at $\bar{x}$, and for $i \notin I$, $g_i(x)$ is continuous at $\bar{x}$, then each $h \in G_I$ is a feasible direction of G at $\bar{x}$.

Proof: Suppose $h \in G_I$. For $i \notin I$, since $g_i(\bar{x}) < 0$ and $g_i(x)$ is continuous,

$\exists\, \epsilon_1 > 0$ such that $g_i(\bar{x}+\epsilon h) \leq 0$ for $0 \leq \epsilon < \epsilon_1$. We have $g_i(\bar{x}+\epsilon h) = g_i(\bar{x}) + \langle \nabla g_i(\bar{x}), \epsilon h\rangle + o(\epsilon)$ for $i \in I$ since $g_i(x)$ is differentiable. Hence, $g_i(\bar{x}+\epsilon_2 h) \leq 0$ for $i \in I$ when ϵ_2 is small enough since $\langle \nabla g_i(\bar{x}), h\rangle < 0$ for $i \in I$. Let $\epsilon_0 = \min\{\epsilon_1, \epsilon_2\}$. It follows that $g_i(\bar{x}+\epsilon h) \leq 0$, $i = 1,\cdots,r$, for $0 < \epsilon < \epsilon_0$. This means that h is a feasible direction. ∎

From Proposition 6.1 and Lemma 6.5, we have proved that if $\bar{x}$ is a local minimum of f over G, then the system

$$\begin{cases} \langle \nabla f(\bar{x}), h\rangle < 0 \\ \langle \nabla g_i(\bar{x}), h\rangle < 0 \quad \text{for } i \in I \end{cases} \tag{6.11}$$

has no solutions. Applying the Alternative Theorem, we know that there exists a nonzero vector $u = (u_0, u_I) \geq 0$ such that

$$u_0 \nabla f(\bar{x}) + \sum_{i \in I} u_i \nabla g_i(\bar{x}) = 0. \tag{6.12}$$

Hence,

<u>Proposition 6.6</u>: Suppose f, g_i ($i \in I$) are differentiable at $\bar{x}$, and g_i ($i \notin I$) is continuous at $\bar{x}$. If $\bar{x}$ is a local minimum of f over G, then there exists a nonzero vector $u = (u_0, u_I) \geq 0$ such that (6.12) is satisfied.

Adding some kind of qualification, we can arrive at the standard Kuhn-Tucker conditions.

<u>Proposition 6.7</u>: Under the hypothesis of Proposition 6.6 as well as Slater's condition (or other alternative ones), if $\bar{x}$ is a local minimum of f over G, then there exists a nonzero vector $u = (u_1, \cdots, u_r)$ such that

(1) $$\nabla f(\bar{x}) + \sum_{i \in I} u_i \nabla g_i(\bar{x}) = 0,$$

(2) $$u_i g_i(\bar{x}) = 0, \quad i = 1,2,\cdots,r,$$

(3) $$u_i \geq 0, \quad i = 1,2,\cdots,r.$$

With enough convexity imposed on f and g_i, $i \in I$, these conditions are also sufficient.

<u>Proposition 6.8</u>: Suppose f is convex at $\bar{x}$ and g_i is quasi-convex at $\bar{x}$ for $i \in I$. Let $\bar{x} \in G$. If there are $u_i \geq 0$, $i \in I$, such that

$$\nabla f(\bar{x}) + \sum_{i \in I} u_i \nabla g_i(\bar{x}) = 0, \tag{6.13}$$

then $\bar{x}$ is a global minimum of f over G.

Proof: We provide a mean-value based proof. Since g_i is differentiable and quasi-convex at $\bar{x}$ and $u_i \geq 0$ for $i \in I$, we have

$$\langle \sum_{i \in I} u_i \nabla g_i(\bar{x}), x-\bar{x} \rangle \leq 0, \tag{6.14}$$

because $g_i(x) \leq g_i(\bar{x}) = 0$ for $i \in I$ and $x \in S$. Hence, for each $c > \bar{c} = f(\bar{x})$, we have

$$\begin{aligned} c &\geq \frac{1}{\mu(H_c \cap G)} \int_{H_c \cap G} f(x) d\mu \\ &\geq f(\bar{x}) + \frac{1}{\mu(H_c \cap G)} \int_{H_c \cap G} \langle \nabla f(\bar{x}), x-\bar{x} \rangle d\mu \\ &= f(\bar{x}) - \frac{1}{\mu(H_c \cap G)} \int_{H_c \cap G} \langle \sum_{i \in I} u_i \nabla g_i(\bar{x}), x-\bar{x} \rangle d\mu \geq f(\bar{x}) = \bar{c}. \end{aligned}$$

Letting $c \downarrow \bar{c}$, $M(f, \bar{c}; G) = \bar{c}$. Hence, $\bar{x}$ is a global minimum of f over G. ∎

6.3 Equality and Inequality Constrained Cases in $\mathbb{R}^n$

When we consider the optimality conditions for the equality and inequality constrained problems, we require the equality constrained set

$$L = \{ x \in \mathbb{R}^n \mid \ell_j(x) = 0, \ j = 1, \cdots, s \} \tag{6.15}$$

to be a manifold. For $\bar{x} \in G \cap L$, suppose the gradients $\nabla \ell_j(\bar{x})$, $j = 1, \cdots, s$, are continuous and linearly independent. Then the appropriate measure and integration can be defined on L. The global optimality conditions can then be applied. Let

$$L_0 = \{ h \mid \langle \nabla \ell_j(\bar{x}), h \rangle = 0, \ j = 1, \cdots, s \} \tag{6.16}$$

Lemma 6.9: Suppose for each $i \in I$, g_i is differentiable at $\bar{x} \in G \cap L$; for each $i \notin I$, g_i is continuous at $\bar{x}$; each ℓ_j, $j = 1, \cdots, s$, is continuously differentiable at $\bar{x}$; and $\nabla \ell_j(\bar{x})$, $j = 1, \cdots, s$, are linearly independent. Then, for each $h \in G_I \cap L_0$, there is a continuously differentiable arc $\lambda(t)$ over $[0,\epsilon_0]$ for some $\epsilon_0 > 0$ with $\lambda(0) = \bar{x}$ such that $\lambda(t)$ is contained in $G \cap L$.

<u>Proof</u>: We define an arc $\lambda(t)$ in $\mathbb{R}^n$ by the following differentiable equation:

$$\frac{d\lambda(t)}{dt} = P_t h, \qquad \lambda(0) = \bar{x}, \tag{6.17}$$

where P_t is a projection matrix which projects the vector h to the annihilator of the matrix $[\nabla \ell_1(\lambda(t)),\cdots,\nabla \ell_s(\lambda(t))]$, i.e., $\langle \nabla \ell_j(\lambda(t)), P_t h\rangle = 0$, $j = 1,\cdots,s$. Since $\nabla \ell_j(\bar{x})$, $j = 1,\cdots,s$, are continuous and independent, $\exists\ \epsilon_1 > 0$ such that (6.17) has a continuously differentiable solution $\lambda(t)$ for $0 \leq t \leq \epsilon_1$.

Moreover, we have $d\ell_j(\lambda(t))/dt = \langle \nabla \ell_j(\lambda(t)), P_t h\rangle = 0$ and $\ell_j(\lambda(0)) = 0$, $j = 1,\cdots,s$. Hence $\ell_j(\lambda(t)) = 0$, $j = 1,\cdots,s$, for $0 \leq t \leq \epsilon_1$. For $i \notin I$, since g_i is continuous at $\bar{x}$ and $g_i(\lambda(0)) < 0$, $\exists\ \epsilon_2 > 0$ such that $g_i(\lambda(t)) \leq 0$ for $0 \leq t \leq \epsilon_2$. Finally, for $i \in I$, we have $g_i(\lambda(0)) = g_i(\bar{x}) = 0$ and $\frac{d}{dt}g_i(\lambda(t))|_{t=0} = \langle \nabla g_i(\bar{x}), P_0 h\rangle = \langle \nabla g_i(\bar{x}), h\rangle < 0$. Therefore, there is $\epsilon_3 > 0$ such that $g_i(\lambda(t)) \leq 0$, $i \in I$, for $0 \leq t \leq \epsilon_3$. Letting $\epsilon_0 = \min\{\epsilon_1,\epsilon_2,\epsilon_3\}$, we conclude that the arc $\lambda(t)$, $t \in [0,\epsilon_0]$ is contained in $G \cap L$. ∎

Expanding $f(\lambda(t))$ along the arc $\lambda(t)$, we have

$$f(\lambda(t)) = f(\lambda(0)) + \langle \nabla f(\lambda(0)), P_0 h\rangle t + o(t) = f(\bar{x}) + \langle \nabla f(\bar{x}), h\rangle t + o(t).$$

Thus, similar to the proof of Proposition 6.1, we can prove using the global optimality condition that if $\bar{x}$ is a local minimum of f over $G \cap L$, then

$$\langle \nabla f(\bar{x}), h\rangle \geq 0, \quad \text{for } h \in G_I \cap L_0.$$

That is, the system

$$\begin{cases} \langle \nabla f(\bar{x}), h\rangle < 0 & \\ \langle \nabla g_i(\bar{x}), h\rangle < 0, & i \in I \\ \langle \nabla \ell_j(\bar{x}), h\rangle < 0, & j = 1,\cdots,s \end{cases}$$

has no solutions. Applying again the Alternative Theorem, we obtain:

<u>Proposition 6.10</u>: Under the hypotheses of Lemma 6.9, suppose f is differentiable at $\bar{x} \in G \cap L$. If $\bar{x}$ is a local minimum of f over $G \cap L$, then there is a nonzero vector (u_0,u_I,v) such that $(u_0,u_I) \geq 0$ and

$$u_0 \nabla f(\bar{x}) + \sum_{i \in I} u_i \nabla g_i(\bar{x}) + \sum_{j=1}^{s} v_j \nabla \ell_j(\bar{x}) = 0. \tag{6.18}$$

Similarly, we have

Proposition 6.11: Under the hypotheses of Proposition 6.10 as well as Slater's (or other alternative) qualification, there is a vector (u_I, v) such that

(1) $$\nabla f(\bar{x}) + \sum_{i \in I} u_i \nabla g_i(\bar{x}) + \sum_{j=1}^{s} v_j \nabla \ell_j(\bar{x}) = 0; \tag{6.19}$$

(2) $$u_i \nabla g_i(\bar{x}) = 0, \quad i = 1, \cdots, r;. \tag{6.20}$$

(3) $$u_i \geq 0, \quad i \in I. \tag{6.21}$$

Proposition 6.12: Suppose f is convex at $\bar{x} \in G \cap L$, $g_i(x)$, $i \in I$, is quasi-convex at $\bar{x}$, and $\ell_j(\bar{x})$, $j = 1, \cdots, s$, is linear. If the condition (6.19) holds for $u_i \geq 0$, $i \in I$, then $\bar{x}$ is a global minimum of f over $G \cap L$.

§7 Integer and Mixed Programming

This section concerns the global optimality conditions for integer and mixed minimization problems. After introducing a special topological structure and a corresponding Q-measure space, the problem becomes a special case of the general problem treated in Sections 1 - 4. Therefore, all relevant results apply here.

7.1 Integer Minimization Problems

Let $X = \{x_1, \cdots, x_n, \cdots\}$, and $\mathcal{P} = 2^X$ be the power set of X. Under the discrete topology, $(X, \mathcal{P})$ is a topological space.

Let S be a subset of X and $f : X \to \mathbb{R}$ be a real-valued function. We are interested in finding the minimum value $\bar{c}$ of f over the constrained set S:

$$\bar{c} = \lim_{x \in S} f(x). \tag{7.1}$$

and the set $\bar{H}$ of global minima

$$\bar{H} = \{ x \mid f(x) = \bar{c} \}, \tag{7.2}$$

if there are solutions to (7.1).

For each real c, the level set

$$H_c = \{ x \mid f(x) \leq c \}$$

and the set

$$H_c^o = \{ x \mid f(x) < c \}$$

are subsets of X. Since any subset of X is open as well as closed, each real-valued function on X is continuous.

We replace Assumption A2 in Chapter I by the following:

<u>Assumption A2'</u>: There is a real number α such that the level set

$$H_\alpha = \{ x \mid f(x) \leq \alpha \} \tag{7.3}$$

is finite and the intersection $H_\alpha \cap S$ is nonempty.

Suppose for each $x_i \in X$ we are given $a_i > 0$, $i \in I^+$. Define the measure μ on $\mathcal{P}$ by:

$$\mu(A) = \sum_{x_i \in A} a_i. \tag{7.4}$$

<u>Proposition 7.1</u>: (X, Ω, μ) is a Q-measure space.

<u>Proof</u>: This is true since each open set is in Ω, the measure of each non-empty (open) set is positive, and the measure of any finite set is finite. ∎

7.2 Optimality Conditions

We define mean value, variance, modified variance and higher moments of function f as follows:

<u>Definition 7.1</u>: Suppose $\alpha \geq c \geq \bar{c} = \min f(x)$.

$$M(f,c) = \frac{1}{\sum_{x_i \in H_c} a_i} \sum_{x_i \in H_c} a_i f(x_i), \tag{7.5}$$

$$V(f,c) = \frac{1}{\sum_{x_i \in H_c} a_i} \sum_{x_i \in H_c} a_i [f(x_i) - M(f,c)]^2, \tag{7.6}$$

$$V_1(f,c) = \frac{1}{\sum_{x_i \in H_c} a_i} \sum_{x_i \in H_c} a_i [f(x_i) - c]^2, \tag{7.7}$$

and

$$M_m(f,c;d) = \frac{1}{\sum_{x_i \in H_c} a_i} \sum_{x_i \in H_c} a_i [f(x_i) - d]^m, \quad m \in I^+, \tag{7.8}$$

are labeled respectively as the mean value, the variance, the modified variance and the m<u>th</u> moment centered at d of f over level set H_c.

Since $\mu(H_c) = \sum_{x_i \in H_c} a_i > 0$ and $|f(x_i)|$ is bounded on H_c, (7.5) - (7.8) are well defined so that there is no need for limit-based definitions as in the general case.

We can also define the constrained version of the above concepts as follows:

<u>Definition 7.2</u>: Suppose $\alpha \geq c \geq \bar{c} = \min_{x \in S} f(x)$. We label

$$M(f,c;S) = \frac{1}{\sum_{x_i \in H_c \cap S} a_i} \sum_{x_i \in H_c \cap S} a_i f(x_i), \tag{7.9}$$

$$V(f,c;S) = \frac{1}{\sum_{x_i \in H_c \cap S} a_i} \sum_{x_i \in H_c \cap S} a_i [f(x_i) - M(f,c)]^2, \tag{7.10}$$

$$V_1(f,c;S) = \frac{1}{\sum_{x_i \in H_c \cap S} a_i} \sum_{x_i \in H_c \cap S} a_i [f(x_i) - c]^2, \tag{7.11}$$

and

$$M_m(f,c;d;S) = \frac{1}{\sum_{x_i \in H_c \cap S} a_i} \sum_{x_i \in H_c \cap S} a_i [f(x_i) - d]^m, \quad m \in I^+, \tag{7.12}$$

respectively as the <u>constrained</u> mean value, variance, modified variance and m<u>th</u> moment centered at d of f over $H_c \cap S$.

All the properties obtained for various moments of a continuous function f are satisfied except for the differential properties since the concept of derivative is not properly defined. For example, $\lim_{\Delta c \uparrow 0} \mu(H_{c+\Delta c}) \neq \mu(H_c)$.

Now, the optimality conditions for the integer minimization problem can be stated as follows:

Theorem 7.2: The following are equivalent:

a. A point $\bar{x} \in S$ is a global minimum and $\bar{c} = f(\bar{x})$ is the corresponding global minimum value of f over S;

b. $$M(f,c;S) \geq \bar{c}, \quad \text{for } c > \bar{c}; \tag{7.13}$$

c. $$M(f,\bar{c};S) = \bar{c}; \tag{7.14}$$

d. $$V(f,\bar{c};S) = 0; \tag{7.15}$$

e. $$V_1(f,\bar{c};S) = 0; \tag{7.16}$$

f. $$M_{2m-1}(f,\bar{c};0;S) \geq (\bar{c})^{2m-1} \quad \text{for } c > \bar{c} \text{ and some } m \in I^+; \tag{7.17}$$

g. $$M_{2m-1}(f,\bar{c};0;S) = (\bar{c})^{2m-1} \quad \text{for some } m \in I^+; \tag{7.18}$$

h. $$M_{2m}(f,\bar{c};M(f,\bar{c};S);S) = 0 \quad \text{for some } m \in I^+; \tag{7.19}$$

i. $$M_m(f,\bar{c};\bar{c};S) = 0 \quad \text{for some } m \in I^+. \tag{7.20}$$

7.3 Mixed Minimization Problems

In this subsection, we will consider two kinds of mixed minimization problems: (i) $X = I \times Z$ and (ii) $X = I \cup Z$, where I is discrete and Z is a Hausdorff topological space.

Consider the case of product space. Define a product Borel field to be

$$\Omega = \{ A \times B \mid A \in \Omega_1 \text{ and } B \in \Omega_2 \}. \tag{7.21}$$

A product measure for an element $A \times B$ of Ω is a rectangle with measurable sides:

$$\mu(A \times B) = \mu_1(A) \cdot \mu_2(B), \tag{7.22}$$

where the two Q-measure spaces (I,Ω_1,μ_1) and (Z,Ω_2,μ_2) are given in advance. The measure space (I,Ω_1,μ_1) is of the integer-type defined in the previous subsection and (Z,Ω_2,μ_2) is a familiar Q-measure space. The new mixed measure space is also a Q-measure space since if a set $O = O_1 \times O_2$ is nonempty and open, then

$$\mu(O) = \mu_1(O_1)\cdot\mu_2(O_2) > 0.$$

For each nonempty open set A in I×Z, there is a neighborhood $O = O_1 \times O_2$ such that $O \subset A$. Hence, $\mu(A) \geq \mu(O) > 0$.

Now, let $f : I\times Z \to \mathbb{R}$ be a real-valued function, continuous with respect to the product topology. Let $c \geq \bar{c} = \min f(i,z)$ and

$$H_c(i) = \{ z \mid f(i,z) \leq c \}$$

for fixed i. Note that $H_c(i)$, which is the ith cross-section of level set H_c, might be empty for some i. The measure of level set $H_c = \{(i,z) \mid f(i,z) \leq c\}$ is given by:

$$\mu(H_c) = \int_I \mu_2(H_c(i))d\mu_1 = \Sigma_i a_i \mu_2(H_c(i)). \tag{7.23}$$

Definition 7.3: Suppose $c \geq \bar{c} = \min f(x)$. The limits

$$M(f,c) = \lim_{c_k \downarrow c} \frac{1}{\Sigma_i a_i \mu(H_{c_k}(i))} \Sigma_i a_i \int_{H_{c_k}(i)} f(i,z)d\mu_2, \tag{7.24}$$

$$V(f,c) = \lim_{c_k \downarrow c} \frac{1}{\Sigma_i a_i \mu(H_{c_k}(i))} \Sigma_i a_i \int_{H_{c_k}(i)} [f(i,z)-M(f,c)]^2 d\mu_2, \tag{7.25}$$

$$V_1(f,c) = \lim_{c_k \downarrow c} \frac{1}{\Sigma_i a_i \mu(H_{c_k}(i))} \Sigma_i a_i \int_{H_{c_k}(i)} [f(i,z)-c]^2 d\mu_2, \tag{7.26}$$

and

$$M_m(f,c;d) = \lim_{c_k \downarrow c} \frac{1}{\Sigma_i a_i \mu(H_{c_k}(i))} \Sigma_i a_i \int_{H_{c_k}(i)} [f(i,z)-d]^m d\mu_2, \quad m \in I^+, \tag{7.27}$$

are respectively called the product-mixed mean value, variance, modified variance, and mth moment centered at d of f over level set H_c.

If $X = I\cup Z$ and $I\cap Z = \emptyset$, then the structure of X is rather simple. An open set in X is just the union of an open set of I and that of Z. The union Borel field Ω is given by:

$$\Omega = \{ A\cup B \mid A \in \Omega_1 \text{ and } B \in \Omega_2 \}$$

and the union measure μ on Ω is given by

$$\mu(A\cup B) = \mu_1(A) + \mu_2(B),$$

where the two Q-measure spaces (I,Ω_1,μ_1) and (Z,Ω_2,μ_2) are given in advance.

Let $O = O_1 \cup O_2$ be a nonempty open set of X, i.e., $O_1 \cup O_2 \neq \emptyset$ and at least one of them is nonempty. Then

$$\mu(O) = \mu_1(O_1) + \mu_2(O_2) > 0$$

and (X,Ω,μ) is a Q-measure space.

Let $f : I \cup Z \to \mathbb{R}$ be a real-valued function which is continuous with respect to the union topology. Let $c \geq \bar{c} = \min f(x)$ and

$$H_c = \{ I_c \cup Z_c \mid f(x) \leq c \} = H_c(I) \cup H_c(Z),$$

where for some $i \in I$ and some $z \in Z$, $f(x) = f(i,z) \leq c$. The measure of the level set H_c is

$$\mu(H_c) = \mu_1(H_c(I)) + \mu_2(H_c(Z)) = \sum_{i \in H_c(I)} a_i + \mu_2(H_c(Z)). \tag{7.28}$$

Definition 7.4: Suppose $c \geq \bar{c} = \min f(x)$. The limits

$$M(f,c) = \lim_{c_k \downarrow c} \frac{1}{\sum_{i \in H_c(I)} a_i + \mu_2(H_c(Z))} \left[\sum_{i \in H_c(I)} a_i f(i) + \int_{H_c(Z)} f(z) d\mu_2 \right], \tag{7.29}$$

$$V(f,c) = \lim_{c_k \downarrow c} \frac{1}{\sum_{i \in H_c(I)} a_i + \mu_2(H_c(Z))} \left[\sum_{i \in H_c(I)} a_i [f(i) - M(f,c)]^2 + \int_{H_c(Z)} [f(z) - M(f,c)]^2 d\mu_2 \right], \tag{7.30}$$

$$V_1(f,c) = \lim_{c_k \downarrow c} \frac{1}{\sum_{i \in H_c(I)} a_i + \mu_2(H_c(Z))} \left[\sum_{i \in H_c(I)} a_i [f(i) - c]^2 + \int_{H_c(Z)} [f(z) - c]^2 d\mu_2 \right], \tag{7.31}$$

and

$$M_m(f,c;d) = \lim_{c_k \downarrow c} \frac{1}{\sum_{i \in H_c(I)} a_i + \mu_2(H_c(Z))} \left[\sum_{i \in H_c(I)} a_i [f(i) - d]^m + \int_{H_c(Z)} [f(z) - d]^m d\mu_2 \right], \quad m \in I^+, \tag{7.32}$$

are called, respectively, the <u>union-mixed</u> mean value, variance, modified variance, and m<u>th</u> moment centered at d of f over level set H_c.

Again, Theorem 7.2 is also valid for mixed programming which we will not state here.

§8 Optimality Conditions for a Class of Discontinuous Functions

In this section, we weaken the requirement of continuity of the objective function in order to treat a considerably larger domain of problems than hitherto possible. Examples include the likelihood function and the expected utility function when the probability distributions possess discontinuities. The class of functions developed here, called robust functions, is in a sense the largest class consistent with an objective function having accessible global minima. We begin by proving additional properties of robust sets.

8.1 Robust Sets

Let X be a topological space. Recall that a subset $G \subset X$ is said to be robust if

$$cl(intG) = clG. \tag{8.1}$$

Clearly, any open set is robust. This is not necessarily the case for a closed set. Consider the example of a single point in $\mathbb{R}^2$.

If G is a nonempty robust set, then $intG \neq \emptyset$. Otherwise $cl(intG) = \emptyset \neq clG$.

We will now prove more properties of a robust set.

Proposition 8.1: A set G is robust if and only if for any open neighborhood $\mathcal{O}(x)$ around a point $x \in clG$,

$$\mathcal{O}(x) \cap intG \neq \emptyset. \tag{8.2}$$

Proof: (Necessity) Since $x \in cl(intG)$ $\forall$ $x \in clG$, we have, for any neighborhood $\mathcal{O}(x)$ of x, $\mathcal{O}(x) \cap intG \neq \emptyset$.

(Sufficiency) If condition (8.2) is satisfied but G is not robust, then $\exists$ a point x such that $x \in (clG)\backslash cl(intG)$. But (8.2) implies that $x \in cl(intG)$, which is a contradiction. ∎

Definition 8.1: A point $x \in S \subset X$ is said to be robust with respect to S if

$$\mathcal{O}(x) \cap \text{int}S \neq \emptyset$$

for any open neighborhood $\mathcal{O}(x)$ of x.

Hence, each point in a robust set is robust with respect to this set.

Proposition 8.2: A set G is robust if and only if

$$\partial G = \partial(\text{int}G), \tag{8.3}$$

where $\partial G = (\text{cl}G)\backslash(\text{int}G)$ denotes the boundary of G.

Proof: Suppose G is a robust set. Then

$$\partial(\text{int}G) = \text{cl}(\text{int}G)\backslash\text{int}(\text{int}G) = (\text{cl}G)\backslash(\text{int}G) = \partial G.$$

If (8.3) is valid, then

$$\partial(\text{int}G) = \text{cl}(\text{int}G)\backslash\text{int}(\text{int}G) = \text{cl}(\text{int}G)\backslash\text{int}G.$$

Hence,

$$\partial G = \text{cl}G\backslash\text{int}G = \text{cl}(\text{int}G)\backslash\text{int}G.$$

Thus,

$$\text{cl}G = \text{cl}(\text{int}G). \qquad \blacksquare$$

Proposition 8.3: If G_k, $k \in I^+$, are robust sets, then $\bigcup_{k=1}^{\infty} G_k$ is also robust.

Proof: Since G_k, $k \in I^+$, are robust, we have

$$\text{cl}\left(\bigcup_{k=1}^{\infty} G_k\right) = \bigcup_{k=1}^{\infty} \text{cl}G_k = \bigcup_{k=1}^{\infty} \text{cl}(\text{int}G_k) = \text{cl}\left(\bigcup_{k=1}^{\infty} \text{int}G_k\right) \subset \text{cl}\left(\bigcup_{k=1}^{\infty} G_k\right).$$

Suppose $x \in \text{cl}(\bigcup_{k=1}^{\infty} G_k)$. This implies that for any neighborhood $\mathcal{O}(x)$ of x

$$\mathcal{O}(x) \cap \bigcup_{k=1}^{\infty} G_k \neq \emptyset,$$

say, $y \in \mathcal{O}(x) \cap \bigcup_{k=1}^{\infty} G_k$, i.e., $y \in \bigcup_{k=1}^{N} G_k$ for some N. It follows that

$$y \in \text{cl}\left(\bigcup_{k=1}^{N} G_k\right) = \text{cl}\left(\bigcup_{k=1}^{N} \text{int}G_k\right) \subset \text{cl}\left(\text{int}\left(\bigcup_{k=1}^{\infty} G_k\right)\right).$$

Therefore,

$$\mathcal{O}(x) \cap cl(int(\bigcup_{k=1}^{\infty} G_k)) \neq \emptyset.$$

This implies that

$$x \in cl(cl(int(\bigcup_{k=1}^{\infty} G_k))) = cl(int(\bigcup_{k=1}^{\infty} G_k)).$$

Thus

$$cl(\bigcup_{k=1}^{\infty} G_k) \subset cl(int(\bigcup_{k=1}^{\infty} G_k)).$$

On the other hand, we always have

$$cl(int(\bigcup_{k=1}^{\infty} G_k)) \subset cl(\bigcup_{k=1}^{\infty} G_k).$$

Therefore,

$$cl(\bigcup_{k=1}^{\infty} G_k) = cl(int(\bigcup_{k=1}^{\infty} G_k)).$$ ∎

<u>Proposition 8.4</u>: Suppose G is robust and D is open, then $G \cap D$ is robust.

<u>Proof</u>: Suppose $G \cap D \neq \emptyset$. Otherwise the proposition is trivial. If $G \cap D$ is not robust, i.e.,

$$cl\left[int(G \cap D)\right] \subsetneq cl(G \cap D),$$

then there exists a point $x \in cl(G \cap D)$ but $x \notin cl(int(G \cap D))$. Therefore, there exists a neighborhood $\mathcal{O}(x)$ of x such that

$$\mathcal{O}(x) \cap int(G \cap D) = \emptyset$$

or

$$\mathcal{O}(x) \cap intG \cap D = (\mathcal{O}(x) \cap D) \cap intG = \emptyset. \tag{8.4}$$

But $\mathcal{O}(x) \cap D = \mathcal{O}_1(x)$ is also a neighborhood of x and G is robust. According to Proposition 8.1,

$$\mathcal{O}_1(x) \cap intG \neq \emptyset.$$

This contradicts (8.4). ∎

<u>Remark</u>: The intersection of two robust sets need not be robust.

<u>Corollary 8.5</u>: Suppose G is robust and D is closed, then $G \setminus D$ is robust.

<u>Proof</u>: The result follows from the observation that $G \setminus D = G \cap D^c$ and that D^c is open. ∎

8.2 The Structure of a Robust Set on the Real Line $\mathbb{R}$

It is obvious that either an open interval or a nondegenerate closed interval is robust on the real line. Half open intervals which are unions of open and closed intervals are also robust. What is surprising is that a robust set can also include certain points which are not in any interval within it.

Definition 8.2: A robust point x of a robust set G on the real line is said to be singular if it is not in any interval within G.

Example 8.1: Let $G = (\bigcup_{n=1}^{\infty} (\frac{1}{2^{n-1}}, \frac{1}{2^{n+1}})) \cup \{0\}$. Then G is a robust set and 0 is a singular robust point of G.

Lemma 8.6: Every singualr point x of a robust set G is associated with a sequence of disjoint intervals $\{J_n\}$ such that x is the common limit of the endpoints of J_n, $n \in I^+$. Moreover, the set of singular robust points, if nonempty, is at most countable.

Proof: Suppose $x \in G$ is singular robust. Take $\delta_1 > 0$. Then $B_{\delta_1}(x) \cap \text{int}G \neq \emptyset$. Let $y_1 \in B_{\delta_1}(x) \cap \text{int}G$ and look for the largest interval $J_1 \subset G$ containing y_1. Choose $\delta_1 > \delta_2 > 0$ such that $(B_{\delta_2}(x)) \cap J_1 = \emptyset$. We have $(B_{\delta_2}(x)) \cap (\text{int}G) \neq \emptyset$. Let $y_2 \in (B_{\delta_2}(x)) \cap (\text{int}G)$ and again find the largest interval J_2 containing y_2. Repeating this process with $0 < \delta_3 < \delta_2$ such that $(B_{\delta_3}(x)) \cap J_2 = \emptyset$, and so on, we have constructed an infinite sequence $\{J_n\}$ of disjoint intervals whose endpoints tend to the point x. Let $y \neq x$ be another singular robust point of G and $G_1 = G \setminus (\bigcup_{n=1}^{\infty} J_n) \neq \emptyset$. Then $B_\delta(y) \cap \text{int}G_1 \neq \emptyset \ \forall \ \delta > 0$. Otherwise, we have $B_\delta(y) \cap (\bigcup_{n=1}^{\infty} J_n) \neq \emptyset \ \forall \ \delta > 0$. Now y is a singular robust point of $\bigcup_{n=1}^{\infty} J_n$ and $\exists \ y_n \in J_n$, $n = 1, 2, \cdots$, such that $y_n \to y$. This implies a contradiction, i.e. $y = x$. Applying the same procedure to G_1, we can construct another infinite sequence of disjoint intervals. ∎

Proposition 8.7: A robust set G on the real line is the countable union of disjoint intervals and a possibly nonempty set of singular robust points.

Proof: If G is such a set, then for each $x \in \text{cl}G$, $\exists$ a sequence $\{x_n\} \subset G$

such that $x_n \to x$ and each x_n is in some interval J_n or it is a singular robust point. For each open neighborhood $B_\delta(x)$ of x there is a positive integer N such that $x_n \in B_\delta(x)$ for $n > N$. Pick an $n > N$. Then there is an open neighborhood $B_{\delta_1}(x_n)$ of x_n such that $B_{\delta_1}(x_n) \subset B_\delta(x)$. Now, $B_{\delta_1}(x_n) \cap \mathrm{int}G \neq \emptyset$ since x_n is a robust point. This implies that $B_\delta(x) \cap \mathrm{int}G \neq \emptyset$. We conclude from Proposition 8.1 that G is robust.

Suppose G is robust on the real line. Take a point $x \in \mathrm{int}G$. Find a largest interval J contained in G which contains x. Take another point $y \in \mathrm{int}(G\backslash J)$ (if it is nonempty) and find another largest interval J_1 contained in $G\backslash J$ which contains y_1 and so on. The number of such disjoint intervals is at most countable since each interval has at least one rational number.

By definition, all remaining points, if any, are singular robust. ∎

8.3 Robust Continuity

Let $f : X \to \mathbb{R}$ be a real-valued function on the topological space X. In this subsection, we will consider a class of possibly discontinuous functions which stems from the properties of robust sets discussed previously.

Definition 8.3: A function f is said to be robust if

$$H_c^o = \{ x \mid f(x) < c \} \tag{8.5}$$

is robust for any real c.

Proposition 8.8: Suppose f is robust and g is continuous. Then the following functions are also robust:

(i) αf ($\alpha \geq 0$ and is real);

(ii) $f + g$;

(iii) $f \cdot g$ (g is strictly positive on X);

(iv) f/g (g is strictly positive on X).

Proof: (i) If $\alpha = 0$, then αf is continuous. Suppose $\alpha > 0$. $\forall\, c \in \mathbb{R}$,

$$\{ x \mid \alpha f(x) < c \} = \{ x \mid f(x) < c/\alpha \} \tag{8.6}$$

is robust if f is robust.

(ii) We enumerate all rational numbers $\gamma_1, \gamma_2, \gamma_3, \cdots$, and then prove that, for real c,

$$\{ x \mid f(x)+g(x) < c \} = \bigcup_{k=1}^{\infty} \Big[\{ x \mid f(x) < \gamma_k \} \cap \{ x \mid g(x) < c-\gamma_k \} \Big]. \quad (8.7)$$

Let $x \in \bigcup_{k=1}^{\infty} \Big[\{x \mid f(x) < \gamma_k\} \cap \{x \mid g(x) < c-\gamma_k\} \Big]$. Then there is at least an index k such that $x \in \Big[\{x \mid f(x) < \gamma_k\} \cap \{x \mid g(x) < c-\gamma_k\} \Big]$. Then $f(x)+g(x) < \gamma_k+c-\gamma_k = c$. If $f(x)+g(x) < c$, let $f(x) = a$, $g(x) = b$ and $c-(a+b) = 2\eta > 0$. Since the rational numbers are dense in $\mathbb{R}$, we can find a γ_k such that $0 < \gamma_k-a < \eta$. This implies that $f(x) = a < \gamma_k$ and $g(x) = b = c-a-2\eta < c-\gamma_k$. In other words, $x \in \Big[\{x \mid f(x) < \gamma_k\} \cap \{x \mid g(x) < c-\gamma_k\} \Big]$. We have proved (8.7). For $k = 1,2,3,\cdots$, $\{x \mid f(x) < \gamma_k\}$ is robust and $\{x \mid g(x) < c-\gamma_k\}$ is open. Therefore, $\{x \mid f(x) < \gamma_k\} \cap \{x \mid g(x) < c-\gamma_k\}$ is robust. As $\{x \mid f(x)+g(x) < c\}$ is the countable union of robust sets, we conclude that it is also robust.

(iii) For any real c, we can prove similarly that

$$\{ x \mid f(x)\cdot g(x) < c \} = \bigcup_{k=1}^{\infty} \Big[\{ x \mid f(x) < \gamma_k \} \cap \{ x \mid g(x) < c/\gamma_k \} \Big] \quad (8.8)$$

so that $\{x \mid f(x)\cdot g(x) < c\}$ is robust.

(iv) Since $f(x)/g(x) = f(x)\cdot\frac{1}{g(x)}$, where $\frac{1}{g(x)}$ is strictly positive and continuous, the result follows from (iii). ∎

<u>Example 8.2</u>: A monotone function f is robust since for each real c the less-than level set $\{x \mid f(x) < c\}$ is an interval which is unbounded from the left or the right.

<u>Example 8.3</u>: The function

$$f(x) = \begin{cases} \sin(1/x), & x \neq 0 \\ \alpha \quad , & x = 0 \end{cases} \quad (8.9)$$

is lower semi-continuous if $\alpha \leq -1$, and is robust if $\alpha \geq -1$.

<u>Example 8.4</u>: Let

$$f_1(x) = \begin{cases} 1, & x < 0 \\ 0, & x \geq 0 \end{cases} \quad \text{and} \quad f_2(x) = \begin{cases} 0, & x \leq 0 \\ 1, & x > 0. \end{cases} \quad (8.10)$$

Then f_1 and f_2 are both robust. But

$$f_1(x) + f_2(x) = \begin{cases} 1, & x \neq 0 \\ 0, & x = 0 \end{cases} \tag{8.11}$$

is not robust.

8.4 Optimality Conditions

We now proceed to consider the global optimality conditions of robust functions. We need to weaken the continuity assumption (i.e. Assumption A1) to the following:

Assumption A1': f is lower semi-continuous and robust.

The previous framework for global optimization can then be adopted for robust objective functions. We will only state results corresponding to those in Sections 1 and 2. The extensions with the constrained cases and penalty methods are straightforward and will not be presented here.

Lemma 8.9: Suppose f is robust and the level set $H_c = \{x \mid f(x) \leq c\}$ is nonempty. If $\mu(H_c) = 0$ for a Q_1-measure μ, then c is the global minimum of f and H_c is the corresponding set of global minima.

Proof: Suppose c is not the global minimum value while $\hat{c} < c$ is. Let $2\eta = c-\hat{c} > 0$. Then $H^o_{c-\eta} = \{x \mid f(x) < c-\eta\}$ is nonempty and robust so that $\text{int}H^o_{c-\eta} \neq \emptyset$ and

$$\emptyset \neq \text{int}H^o_{c-\eta} \subset \text{int}H_c.$$

But

$$\mu(H_c) \geq \mu(\text{int}H_c) > 0.$$

This is a contradiction. ∎

Note that, if $c > \bar{c} = \min f(x)$, then Lemma 8.9 implies that $\mu(H_c) > 0$.

Definition 8.4: Suppose $c \geq \bar{c} = \min f(x)$. The limits

$$M(f,c) = \lim_{c_k \downarrow c} \frac{1}{\mu(H_{c_k})} \int_{H_{c_k}} f(x) d\mu, \tag{8.12}$$

$$V(f,c) = \lim_{c_k \downarrow c} \frac{1}{\mu(H_{c_k})} \int_{H_{c_k}} [f(x)-M(f,c)]^2 d\mu, \tag{8.13}$$

$$V_1(f,c) = \lim_{c_k \downarrow c} \frac{1}{\mu(H_{c_k})} \int_{H_{c_k}} [f(x)-c]^2 d\mu, \tag{8.14}$$

and

$$M_m(f,c;a) = \lim_{c_k \downarrow c} \frac{1}{\mu(H_{c_k})} \int_{H_{c_k}} [f(x)-a]^m d\mu, \quad m \in I^+, \tag{8.15}$$

are respectively called the mean value, the variance, the modified variance and the m<u>th</u> moment centered at a of f over its level set H_c, where $\{c_k\}$ is a decreasing sequence which tends to c.

By Lemma 8.9, we can prove that the above limits exist and do not depend on the choice of $\{c_k\}$.

It is straightforward to verify that all properties of mean value and higher moments in Sections 1 and 2 are valid for robust functions. In particular, we have the following global optimality conditions:

<u>Theorem 8.10</u>: For Problem (P) under Assumptions A1' and A2, the following are equivalent:

a. A point $\bar{x}$ is a global minimum and $\bar{c} = f(\bar{x})$ is the corresponding global minimum value of f;

b. $$M(f,c) \geq \bar{c}, \quad \text{for } c > \bar{c};$$

c. $$M(f,\bar{c}) = \bar{c};$$

d. $$V(f,\bar{c}) = 0;$$

e. $$V_1(f,\bar{c}) = 0;$$

f. $$M_{2m-1}(f,c;0) \geq (\bar{c})^{2m-1} \quad \text{for } c > \bar{c} \text{ and some } m \in I^+;$$

g. $$M_{2m-1}(f,\bar{c};0) = (\bar{c})^{2m-1} \quad \text{for some } m \in I^+;$$

h. $$M_{2m}(f,\bar{c};M(f,\bar{c})) = 0 \quad \text{for some } m \in I^+;$$

i. $$M_m(f,\bar{c};\bar{c}) = 0 \quad \text{for some } m \in I^+.$$

CHAPTER III

THEORETICAL ALGORITHMS AND TECHNIQUES

In this chapter, we will deal with the theoretical algorithms for finding global minima of a function over a constrained set. The mean value-level set method will be introduced in Section 1. Two simple techniques for finding constrained global minima based on the rejection and the reduction methods will be treated in Section 2 where we discuss the special case of finding the global minima of a function with linear equality constraints. The "global" version of the penalty method is the subject of Section 3. We first consider the sequential unconstrained minimization technique (SUMT). After pointing out some of its shortcomings, we introduce an improved SUMT. For robust constrained sets, we develop in Section 4 a nonsequential penalty technique which seems to be more effective. In Section 5, the technique of adaptive change of search domains is presented. This technique is useful when the initial search domain is difficult to determine. Section 6 considers the problem of stability of the mean value and the global minimization method when the objective function and the constrained set have perturbations in their specifications. Finally, in Section 7, we will briefly consider the problem of lower approximation.

The Monte Carlo implementation of the above mentioned theoretical algorithms will be dealt with in the next chapter.

§1 The Mean Value-Level Set (M-L) Method

Let X be a Hausdorff topological space, (X,Ω,μ) a Q-measure space and f :

$X \to \mathbb{R}$ a real-valued function. In this section we will introduce the mean value-level set (M-L) method for finding global minima; and assume that Assumptions A1 (or A1') and A2 (or A2') are satisfied.

1.1 Algorithm

Take a real number c_o such that the level set

$$H_{c_o} = \{ x \mid f(x) \le c_o \} \tag{1.1}$$

is nonempty. For example, we can take $c_o \ge \bar{c} = \min f(x)$ or $x_o \in X$ and set $c_o = f(x_o)$. If the measure of H_{c_o} is equal to zero, then c_o is the global minimum value and H_{c_o} is the set of global minima of f due to Lemma I.2.1. Otherwise, compute the mean value $M(f,c_o)$ of f over its level set H_{c_o}; and set

$$c_1 = M(f,c_o) = \frac{1}{\mu(H_{c_o})}\int_{H_{c_o}} f(x)\, d\mu. \tag{1.2}$$

Obviously,

$$c_o \ge c_1 \ge \bar{c} = \min f(x). \tag{1.3}$$

Consider the level set at c_1,

$$H_{c_1} = \{ x \mid f(x) \le c_1 \}. \tag{1.4}$$

In general, let

$$c_{k+1} = M(f,c_k) \tag{1.5}$$

and

$$H_{c_{k+1}} = \{ x \mid f(x) \le c_{k+1} \}. \tag{1.6}$$

We have

$$c_k \ge c_{k+1} \ge \bar{c}. \tag{1.7}$$

In this way, we have constructed a decreasing sequence of mean value of f,

$$c_o \ge c_1 \ge \cdots \ge c_k \ge c_{k+1} \ge \cdots \ge \bar{c}$$

and a decreasing sequence of level sets

$$H_{c_0} \supset H_{c_1} \supset \cdots \supset H_{c_k} \supset H_{c_{k+1}} \supset \cdots \supset H_{\bar{c}} .$$

Summerizing this discussion and applying the global optimality condition, we have the following algorithm.

Mean Value-Level Set (M-L) Method

Step 0: Take a point $x_0 \in X$. Give a small positive ϵ. Let

$$c_0 = f(x_0), \quad H_{c_0} = \{ x \mid f(x) \le c_0 \}, \quad k = 0.$$

Step 1: Compute the mean value

$$c_{k+1} = M(f, c_k) = \frac{1}{\mu(H_{c_k})} \int_{H_{c_k}} f(x)\, d\mu.$$

Let
$$H_{c_{k+1}} = \{ x \mid f(x) \le c_{k+1} \}.$$

Step 2: Compute the modified variance

$$VF = V_1(f, c_k) = \frac{1}{\mu(H_{c_k})} \int_{H_{c_k}} [f(x) - c_k]^2\, d\mu.$$

Step 3: If $VF \ge \epsilon$, let $k = k+1$ and go to Step 1; otherwise, go to Step 4.

Step 4: Set $\hat{c} = c_{k+1}$ and $\hat{H} = H_{c_{k+1}}$. Stop.

The number $\hat{c}$ and the set $\hat{H}$ approximate the global minimum value and the set of global minima, respectively. Step 3 applies the global optimality condition $V_1(f, \bar{c}) = 0$ in an approximation form.

1.2 Convergence

If we set $\epsilon = 0$ in the M-L algorithm, the iterative process will not terminate. We will obtain two decreasing sequences $\{c_k\}$ and $\{H_{c_k}\}$ which are both bounded from below. Therefore, they are convergent. Let

$$\bar{c} = \lim_{k \to \infty} c_k \tag{1.8}$$

and

$$\bar{H} = \lim_{k\to\infty} H_{c_k} = \bigcap_{k=1}^{\infty} H_{c_k} . \tag{1.9}$$

Furthermore, we have the following convergence theorem:

Theorem 1.1: The limit $\bar{c} = \lim_{k\to\infty} c_k$ is the global minimum value and the limit $\bar{H} = \lim_{k\to\infty} H_{c_k}$ is the set of global minima of f.

Proof: From the construction of the algorithm, we have

$$c_{k+1} = M(f,c_k), \quad k = 1,2,\cdots \tag{1.10}$$

since $\{c_{k+1}\}$ and $\{c_k\}$ are decreasing sequences and have the same limit $\bar{c}$. According to Proposition II.1.3,

$$\lim_{k\to\infty} M(f,c_k) = M(f,\bar{c}), \tag{1.11}$$

so that

$$\bar{c} = M(f,\bar{c}). \tag{1.12}$$

Applying Theorem II.1.8, we conclude that $\bar{c}$ is the global minimum value of f. Moreover, we also have

$$\lim_{k\to\infty} H_{c_k} = H_{\bar{c}} = \bar{H} = \{ x \mid f(x) = \bar{c} \}. \tag{1.13}$$

∎

1.3 The Actual Descent Property

The iterative process of the M-L algorithm has an actual descent property which we state below.

Theorem 1.2: Suppose X is a connected topological space. If the function f is not a constant on H_{c_o}, then the sequences $\{c_k\}$ and $\{H_{c_k}\}$ defined by (1.5) and (1.6) are both strictly decreasing.

Proof: If $c_k = c_{k+1}$, then clearly $\mu(H_{c_k}) = \mu(H_{c_{k+1}})$. We shall prove that $\mu(H_{c_k})$ also equals $\mu(H_{c_{k-1}})$. Let $\Delta H_k = H_{c_{k-1}} \backslash H_{c_k}$. Then

$$c_k\mu(H_{c_{k-1}}) - c_{k+1}\mu(H_{c_k})\int_{\Delta H_k} f(x)d\mu.$$

Since $c_k = c_{k+1}$, we have

$$c_{k+1}\mu(\Delta H_k) = \int_{\Delta H_k} f(x)d\mu$$

or

$$\int_{\Delta H_k} [f(x)-c_{k+1}]d\mu = 0. \tag{1.14}$$

But $f(x)-c_{k+1} \geq 0$ for $x \in \Delta H_k$. Therefore, either $\mu(\Delta H_k) = \mu(H_{c_{k-1}})-\mu(H_{c_k}) = 0$ or $f(x) = c_{k+1}$ on the set ΔH_k. The latter is ruled out since $\Delta H_k = \{x \mid c_k < f(x) \leq c_{k-1}\}$. Hence, we have proved that $\mu(H_{c_{k-1}}) = \mu(H_{c_k})$.

Next, we will prove that $c_k = c_{k+1}$ if $\mu(H_{c_k}) = \mu(H_{c_{k+1}})$. Suppose $c_k > c_{k+1}$. Since the function is continuous, there is an open set B such that

$$B \subset E = \{ x \mid c_{k+1} < f(x) < c_k \} \subset \Delta H_k.$$

It follows that

$$\mu(\Delta H_k) \geq \mu(B) > 0. \tag{1.15}$$

This contradicts $\mu(H_{c_k}) = \mu(H_{c_{k+1}})$. Therefore, if $c_k = c_{k+1}$ for a fixed k, then $\mu(H_{c_k}) = \mu(H_{c_{k-1}}) = \mu(H_{c_{k+1}})$. This in turn means that $c_{k-1} = c_k$ and $c_{k+1} = c_{k+2}$, and so on. Finally, we have $c_0 = c_1 = \cdots = c_k = c_{k+1} = \cdots = \bar{c}$ and $H_{c_0} = H_{c_1} = \cdots = H_{c_k} = H_{c_{k+1}} = \cdots = \bar{H}$. That is, $f(x) = \bar{c}\ \forall\ x \in H_{c_0}$.

If $\mu(H_{c_k}) = \mu(H_{c_{k+1}})$ for a fixed k, then $c_k = c_{k+1}$. And the same argument follows. ∎

Let

$$\frac{c_{k+1}-\bar{c}}{c_k-\bar{c}} = c(f,k) \tag{1.16}$$

and

$$\frac{\mu(H_{c_{k+1}})-\mu(\bar{H})}{\mu(H_{c_k})-\mu(\bar{H})} = h(f,k). \tag{1.17}$$

The above measures tell us something about the rate of convergence of mean values and the measures of level sets, respectively. We have

$$0 < c(f,k) < 1, \quad k = 0,1,2,\cdots \tag{1.18}$$

and

$$0 < h(f,k) < 1, \quad k = 0,1,2,\cdots \tag{1.19}$$

as long as the function f is not a constant.

Remark: If the function f is not constant and $c > \bar{c}$, then

$$c - M(f,c) > 0.$$

Therefore,

$$\partial_\mu M(f,c) = \frac{c-M(f,c)}{\mu(H_c)} > 0.$$

Also, $\partial_\mu M(f,c) = 0$ for $c > \bar{c}$ if and only if $f(x) = c \ \forall\ x \in H_c$.

1.4 The Influence of Errors

The M-L algorithm has the desirable property of stability. The convergence of this algorithm does not depend on the choice of initial data. We shall show that it is also robust with respect to certain changes in the sequence of intermediate mean value induced by possible computational errors at every stage. The limited influence of any single error in accessing the global minimum value follows from the nondependence of convergence on initial data. The following theorem provides a necessary and sufficient condition for convergence even if computational errors arise at every stage.

Suppose at stage k there is a computational error Δ_k such that the computed mean value equals $d_k = M(f,d_{k-1})+\Delta_k$, given the computed mean value d_{k-1} at stage k-1 (with possible errors). Interestingly, the M-L algorithm has a useful forgiving property -- the error in computing the former mean value does not directly affect the error arising from the current computation of the mean value. This is made more precise in the following theorem.

Theorem 1.3: Suppose $\{d_k\}$ is a decreasing sequence such that $\lim_{k\to\infty} d_k = \bar{d}$ and $\mu(H_{d_k}) > 0$. Let

$$c_k = \frac{1}{\mu(H_{d_{k-1}})}\int_{H_{d_{k-1}}} f(x)d\mu, \quad k = 1,2,\cdots. \tag{1.20}$$

Then $\bar{d}$ is the global minimum value of f if and only if

$$\Delta_k = d_k - c_k \to 0 \quad \text{as } k \to \infty. \tag{1.21}$$

Proof: (Necessity) Suppose $\bar{d}$ is the global minimum value of f. From (1.20), we have

$$\bar{d} \le c_k \le d_{k-1}, \quad k = 1,2,\cdots. \tag{1.22}$$

As k tends to infinity,

$$0 \le d_{k-1} - c_k \le d_{k-1} - \bar{d} \to 0. \tag{1.23}$$

This implies (1.21).

(Sufficiency) We have

$$c_k = M(f, d_{k-1}), \quad k = 1,2,\cdots. \tag{1.24}$$

But condition (1.21) implies that

$$\lim_{k\to\infty} c_k = \lim_{k\to\infty} d_k = \bar{d}. \tag{1.25}$$

Let $k \to \infty$ in (1.24), we have

$$\bar{d} = M(f, \bar{d}).$$

Hence, $\bar{d}$ is the global minimum value of f. ∎

Example 1.1: Let $f(x) = |x|^\alpha$, $\alpha > 0$. Find its global minimum value and the set of global minima.

Let $c_o = 1$. Then $H_{c_o} = [-1,1]$. Set

$$c_1 = \frac{1}{2}\int_{-1}^{1} |x|^\alpha dx = \frac{1}{1+\alpha}.$$

We find that

$$H_{c_1} = [-(\tfrac{1}{1+\alpha})^{1/\alpha}, (\tfrac{1}{1+\alpha})^{1/\alpha}] \quad \text{and} \quad \mu(H_{c_1}) = 2(\tfrac{1}{1+\alpha})^{1/\alpha}.$$

In general, we have

$$c_k = (\tfrac{1}{1+\alpha})c_{k-1} = (\tfrac{1}{1+\alpha})^k, \quad k = 1,2,\cdots,$$

$$H_{c_k} = [-(\frac{1}{1+\alpha})^{k/\alpha}, (\frac{1}{1+\alpha})^{k/\alpha}], \quad k = 1,2,\cdots,$$

and

$$\mu(H_{c_k}) = 2(\frac{1}{1+\alpha})^{k/\alpha}, \quad k = 1,2,\cdots.$$

Therefore,

$$\bar{c} = \lim_{k\to\infty} c_k = 0$$

and

$$\bar{H} = \bigcap_{k=1}^{\infty} [-(\frac{1}{1+\alpha})^{k/\alpha}, (\frac{1}{1+\alpha})^{k/\alpha}] = \{0\}.$$

§2 The Rejection and Reduction Methods

For constrained problems, a simple way of finding global minima is using rejection measure and reduction measure. In this section we will consider problems of this kind. Subsections 2.1 and 2.2 deal with rejection and reduction methods, respectively. As an example, we will discuss in subsection 2.3 the linear equality constrained problem in more detail.

2.1 <u>The Rejection Method</u>

Consider the following constrained minimization problem:

$$\min_{x\in S} f(x), \tag{2.1}$$

where S is a closed robust set. We assume that Assumptions A1 and A2 are satisfied.

As in subsection II.3.1, we introduce a rejection measure μ_S from the original Q-measure. So, we have a rejection Q-measure space $(X\cap S, \Omega_S, \mu_S)$, where $\Omega_S = \{S\cap B \mid B \in \Omega\}$ and

$$\mu_S(A) = \mu(A \cap S), \quad \text{for } A \in \Omega. \tag{2.2}$$

A rejection algorithm for finding the global minimum value and the set of global minima of f over the constrained set S is described below.

Rejection Algorithm

Step 0: Take a point $x_o \in S$. Pick a small positive ϵ. Let

$$c_o = f(x_o), \quad H_{c_o} = \{ x \mid f(x) \le c_o \}, \quad k = 0.$$

Step 1: Compute the rejection mean value of f over $H_{c_k} \cap S$:

$$c_{k+1} = M(f, c_k; S) = \frac{1}{\mu(H_{c_k} \cap S)} \int_{H_{c_k} \cap S} f(x) d\mu.$$

Let $$H_{c_{k+1}} = \{ x \mid f(x) \le c_{k+1} \}.$$

Step 2: Compute the rejection modified variance:

$$VF = V_1(f, c_k; S) = \frac{1}{\mu(H_{c_k} \cap S)} \int_{H_{c_k} \cap S} [f(x) - c_k]^2 d\mu.$$

Step 3: If $VF \ge \epsilon$, let $k = k+1$ and go to Step 1; otherwise, go to Step 4.

Step 4: Set $\hat{c} = c_{k+1}$ and $\hat{H} = H_{c_{k+1}}$. Stop.

The number $\hat{c}$ is an approximation of the global minimum value and the set $\hat{H}$ is the corresponding approximation of the set of global minima of f over the constrained set S. Again, in Step 3, the global optimality condition $V_1(f, \bar{c}; S) = 0$ is applied in an approximation form.

If we set $\epsilon = 0$ in this algorithm, then the iterative procedure will not terminate and we obtain two decreasing sequences, $\{c_k\}$ and $\{H_{c_k}\}$, which are bounded from below. Therefore, they are convergent. Let

$$\bar{c} = \lim_{k \to \infty} c_k \tag{2.3}$$

and

$$\bar{H} = \lim_{k \to \infty} (H_{c_k} \cap S) = \bigcap_{k=1}^{\infty} (H_{c_k} \cap S). \tag{2.4}$$

Using the rejection mean value condition, we can easily prove the following convergence theorem.

Theorem 2.1: The limit $\bar{c} = \lim_{k\to\infty} c_k$ is the global minimum value and $\bar{H} = \lim_{k\to\infty}(H_{c_k} \cap S)$ is the set of global minima of f over the constrained set S.

Note here that Theorems 1.2 and 1.3 also apply to the rejection method with minor modifications.

2.2 The Reduction Method

The reduction method is usually applied to solving a minimization problem over a manifold L:

$$\min_{x\in L} f(x). \tag{2.5}$$

Again, we assume that Assumptions A1 and A2 are satisfied.

As we have seen in subsection II.3.1, a reduction measure μ_L can be introduced to treat problem (2.5) in a derived reduction Q-measure space (L,Ω_L,μ_L).

The reduction algorithm for approximating the global minimum value and the corresponding set of global minima of f over manifold L is described below.

Reduction Algorithm

Step 0: Take a point $x_o \in L$. Pick a small positive ϵ. Let

$$c_o = f(x_o), \quad H_{c_o} = \{ x \mid f(x) \le c_o \}, \quad k = 0.$$

Step 1: Compute the reduction mean value of f over $H_{c_k} \cap L$:

$$c_{k+1} = M(f,c_k;L) = \frac{1}{\mu_L(H_{c_k} \cap L)} \int_{H_{c_k} \cap L} f(x)d\mu_L .$$

Let $$H_{c_{k+1}} = \{ x \mid f(x) \le c_{k+1} \}.$$

Step 2: Compute the reduction modified variance:

$$VF = V_1(f,c_k;L) = \frac{1}{\mu_L(H_{c_k} \cap L)} \int_{H_{c_k} \cap L} [f(x)-c_k]^2 d\mu_L.$$

Step 3: If VF $\geq \epsilon$, let $k = k+1$ and go to Step 1; otherwise, go to Step 4.

Step 4: Set $\hat{c} = c_{k+1}$ and $\hat{H} = H_{c_{k+1}}$. Stop.

The number $\hat{c}$ and the set $\hat{H}$ approximate respectively the global minimum value and the corresponding set of global minima of f over the constrained set L. As before, we apply in Step 3 the global optimality condition $V_1(f,\bar{c};L) = 0$ in an approximation form.

If we take $\epsilon = 0$ in this reduction algorithm, then the iterative process will not terminate, resulting in two decreasing and convergent sequences, $\{c_k\}$ and $\{H_{c_k}\}$. They are convergent since they are bounded from below. Let

$$\bar{c} = \lim_{k\to\infty} c_k \tag{2.6}$$

and

$$\bar{H} = \lim_{k\to\infty}(H_{c_k} \cap L) = \bigcap_{k=1}^{\infty} (H_{c_k} \cap L). \tag{2.7}$$

Using the reduction mean value condition, we can easily prove the following convergence theorem.

<u>Theorem 2.2</u>: The limit $\bar{c} = \lim_{k\to\infty} c_k$ is the global minimum value and $\bar{H} = \lim_{k\to\infty}(H_{c_k} \cap L)$ is the set of global minima of f over the constrained set L.

Again with minor modifications, Theorems 1.2 and 1.3 apply to the reduction mean value. The reduction measure can also be extended to the case with a constrained set $S = L \cap G$, where L is a manifold and G is a robust set. We refrain from further details here.

The key point of the reduction method is the introduction of the reduction measure. For nonlinear programming in $\mathbb{R}^n$ with a differentiable m-manifold as the constrained set, we can introduce a Lebesque measure on the manifold. The next subsection will consider in detail the example of a linear equality constrained problem.

2.3 The Ruduction Method for Linear Equality Constrained Cases in $\mathbb{R}^n$

Consider a linear constrained minimization problem of f in $\mathbb{R}^n$. Suppose the constrained set is given by:

$$L = \{ x \mid \ell_i(x) = 0,\ i = 1,\cdots,r,\ x \in \mathbb{R}^n \}, \tag{2.8}$$

where

$$\ell_i(x) = \Sigma_{j=1}^{n} a_{ij} x^j + b_i, \quad i = 1,\cdots,r. \tag{2.9}$$

We assume that

$$\operatorname{rank}(A) = \operatorname{rank}(\bar{A}) = r, \tag{2.10}$$

where $A = (a_{ij})$ and $\bar{A} = (A,b)$, and $b = (b_1,\cdots,b_r)^T$.

In this subsection, we present two reduction methods for finding global minima with linear equality constraints constructed in subsection II.3.3, and reduce the problem to unconstrained ones in an n-r dimensional subspace.

Method I

As in subsection II.3.3, we introduce a projection P of $\mathbb{R}_1^n$ into $\mathbb{R}_1^{n-r}$ and a linear transformation $T : \mathbb{R}_1^n \to \mathbb{R}_1^n$ so that PT is a one-to-one mapping from L onto $\mathbb{R}_1^{n-r}$ and

$$L = \{ x \mid Tx \in T[L] \} = \{ x \mid PTx \in PT[L] \}. \tag{2.11}$$

It follows from (II.3.51) that

$$\min_{x \in L} f(x) = \min_{PTx \in PT[L]} f(x) = \min_{y \in \mathbb{R}_1^{n-r}} f_1(y), \tag{2.12}$$

where

$$f_1(y) = f(\chi(y,0)) \tag{2.13}$$

since $x = \chi(y,z)$. (See (II.3.46) and (II.3.47).)

Note that the problem has been transformed into an unconstrained one. The level set

$$H_{c_o} = \{ y \in \mathbb{R}_1^{n-r} \mid f_1(y) \le c_o \} \tag{2.14}$$

is by assumption compact in $\mathbb{R}_1^{n-r}$ for some c_o. We construct a convergent decreasing sequence of mean values and a convergent decreasing sequence of level sets as follows:

$$c_k = \frac{1}{\mu(H_{c_{k-1}})}\int_{H_{c_{k-1}}} f_1(y)d\mu, \quad k = 1,2,\cdots \tag{2.15}$$

and

$$H_{c_k} = \{ y \in \mathbb{R}_1^{n-r} \mid f_1(y) \le c_k \}, \quad k = 0,1,2,\cdots, \tag{2.16}$$

where μ is the Lebesque measure on $\mathbb{R}_1^{n-r}$.

An analogous theorem on convergence is stated below.

Theorem 2.3: The limit $\bar{c} = \lim_{k\to\infty} c_k$ is the global minimum value of f subject to the linear equality constraints (2.8) and (2.9), and

$$\bar{H} = \{ x \in \mathbb{R}^n \mid x = \chi(y,0),\ y \in \bigcap_{k=1}^{\infty} H_{c_k} \} \tag{2.17}$$

is the corresponding set of global minima.

Method II

We have known from (II.3.54) that $x^1, \cdots, x^r$ can be expressed as linear combinations of $x^{r+1}, \cdots, x^n$:

$$x^i = \varphi^i(x^{r+1},\cdots,x^n), \quad i = 1,2,\cdots,r. \tag{2.18}$$

Consider the function

$$f_2(x_{n-r}) = f(\varphi^1(x^{r+1},\cdots,x^n),\cdots,\varphi^r(x^{r+1},\cdots,x^n),x^{r+1},\cdots,x^n), \tag{2.19}$$

where $x_{n-r} \in \mathbb{R}^{n-r}$ and $\mathbb{R}^n = \mathbb{R}^r \times \mathbb{R}^{n-r}$. Note that f_2 is continuous on $\mathbb{R}^{n-r}$.

Since L can be written as

$$L = \{ (x_r,x_{n-r}) \mid x_r = (\varphi^1(x^{r+1},\cdots,x^n),\cdots,\varphi^r(x^{r+1},\cdots,x^n)) \}, \tag{2.20}$$

we have, from (II.3.56),

$$\min_{x\in L} f(x) = \min_{PT_1x \in PT_1[L]} f(x) = \min_{x_{n-r} \in \mathbb{R}^{n-r}} f_2(x_{n-r}). \tag{2.21}$$

Once again the problem is transformed into an unconstrained one of n-r dimensions. The level set

$$H_{c_o} = \{ x_{n-r} \in \mathbb{R}^{n-r} \mid f_2(x_{n-r}) \le c_o \} \tag{2.22}$$

is by assumption bounded in $\mathbb{R}^{n-r}$ for some c_o.

Again, we construct a convergent decreasing sequence of mean values and a convergent decreasing sequence of level sets in the following way:

$$c_k = \frac{1}{\mu_{n-r}(H_{c_{k-1}})} \int_{H_{c_{k-1}}} f_2(x_{n-r}) d\mu_{n-r}, \quad k = 1,2,\cdots \tag{2.23}$$

and

$$H_{c_k} = \{ x_{n-r} \in \mathbb{R}^{n-r} \mid f_2(x_{n-r}) \le c_k \}, \quad k = 0,1,2,\cdots, \tag{2.24}$$

where μ_{n-r} is the Lebesque measure on $\mathbb{R}^{n-r}$. Our corresponding theorem on convergence is stated below.

Theorem 2.4: The limit $\bar{c} = \lim_{k\to\infty} c_k$ is the global minimum value of f subject to the linear equality constraints (2.8) and (2.9), and

$$\bar{H} = \{ x \in \mathbb{R}^n \mid x = (\varphi^1(x_{n-r}),\cdots,\varphi^r(x_{n-r}),x_r), \ x_r \in \bigcap_{k=1}^{\infty} H_{c_k} \} \tag{2.25}$$

is the corresponding set of global minima.

§3 Global SUMT and Discontinuous Penalty Functions

This section considers the penalty method for constrained minimization problems. We begin by combining the M-L Algorithm with the traditional SUMT (Sequential Unconstrained Minimization Technique). While we are able to find global minima, often, only a subset can be identified. This problem is addressed via an improved SUMT in the following subsection. We assume throughout this sectioin that (X,ρ) is a metric space, where ρ is the metric on X.

3.1 SUMT and the Set of Global Minima

Recall that a nonnegative continuous function $p(x)$ on X is called a penalty function with respect to the feasible set S if $p(x) = 0$ if and only if $x \in S$.

Suppose $\{\alpha_k\}$ is a positive, strictly increasing and unbounded sequence. Let

$$F(x,\alpha_k) = f(x) + \alpha_k p(x), \quad k = 1,2,\cdots. \tag{3.1}$$

Find the unconstrained global minimum value of the penalized function $F(x,\alpha_k)$,

$$d_k = \min F(x,\alpha_k). \tag{3.2}$$

Let

$$A_k = \{ x \mid F(x,\alpha_k) = d_k \} \tag{3.3}$$

and

$$\bar{H} = \{ x \in S \mid f(x) = \bar{c}, \ \bar{c} = \min_{x \in S} f(x) \}. \tag{3.4}$$

The global minimum values and the sets of global minima of the penalized functions $F(x,\alpha_k)$, $k = 1,2,\cdots$, have the following properties:

(i) $$d_k \le d_{k+1} \le \bar{c}; \tag{3.5}$$

(ii) $$p(x_k) \ge p(x_{k+1}) \text{ for } x_k \in A_k \text{ and } x_{k+1} \in A_{k+1},\ k = 1,2,\cdots; \tag{3.6}$$

(iii) $$f(x_k) \le f(x_{k+1}) \le \bar{c} \text{ for } x_k \in A_k \text{ and } x_{k+1} \in A_{k+1},\ k = 1,2,\cdots; \tag{3.7}$$

Since $\alpha_k < \alpha_{k+1}$, we have $F(x,\alpha_k) \le F(x,\alpha_{k+1})$ for all x and $k = 1,2,\cdots$. It is obvious that $d_k \le d_{k+1} \le \bar{c}$. The points x_k and x_{k+1} are global minima of $F(x,\alpha_k)$ and $F(x,\alpha_{k+1})$, respectively. For $x_k \in A_k$ and $x_{k+1} \in A_{k+1}$, we have

$$f(x_k) + \alpha_k p(x_k) \le f(x_{k+1}) + \alpha_k p(x_{k+1}) \tag{3.8}$$

and

$$f(x_{k+1}) + \alpha_{k+1} p(x_{k+1}) \le f(x_k) + \alpha_{k+1} p(x_k). \tag{3.9}$$

Combine (3.8) and (3.9) to obtain

$$(\alpha_{k+1}-\alpha_k)p(x_{k+1}) \le (\alpha_{k+1}-\alpha_k)p(x_k).$$

Hence $p(x_k) \geq p(x_{k+1})$ since $\alpha_{k+1} > \alpha_k$. Also, from (3.8), $f(x_{k+1}) \geq f(x_k) + \alpha_k[p(x_k)-p(x_{k+1})] \geq f(x_k)$. Moreover, if $\bar{x} \in \bar{H}$, then $p(\bar{x}) = 0$. Consequently, $f(\bar{x}) = f(\bar{x}) + \alpha_k p(\bar{x}) \geq f(x_k) + \alpha_k p(x_k) \geq f(x_k)$ for $x_k \in A_k$ and $k = 1,2,\cdots$. Therefore, (3.7) holds.

We now proceed to consider a set B which consists of all points x such that there is a subsequence $\{x_{k_i}\}$ with $x_{k_i} \in A_{k_i}$ and $\lim_{k_i\to\infty} x_{k_i} = x$. It is known in previous studies of SUMT that we can only find those global minima in the set B. The following lemma gives the structure of B.

<u>Lemma 3.1</u>:

$$B = \bigcap_{m=1}^{\infty} \mathrm{cl}\Big(\bigcup_{k=m}^{\infty} A_k\Big). \tag{3.10}$$

<u>Proof</u>: Suppose $x \in B$, i.e., $\exists$ a subsequence $\{x_{k_i}\}$ such that $x_{k_i} \to x$ as $k_i \to \infty$. Given m, $x_{k_i} \in \bigcup_{k=m}^{\infty} A_k$ for $k_i \geq m$. It follows that $x \in \mathrm{cl}(\bigcup_{k=m}^{\infty} A_k)$ $\forall$ m. Hence, $x \in \bigcap_{m=1}^{\infty} \mathrm{cl}(\bigcup_{k=m}^{\infty} A_k)$.

If $x \in \bigcap_{m=1}^{\infty} \mathrm{cl}(\bigcup_{k=m}^{\infty} A_k)$, i.e., $x \in \mathrm{cl}(\bigcup_{k=m}^{\infty} A_k)$ $\forall$ m, then $\exists$ a sequence $\{x_j^m\} \subset \bigcup_{k=m}^{\infty} A_k$ such that $\lim_{j\to\infty} x_j^m = x$, $m = 1,2,\cdots$. Since $\lim_{j\to\infty} x_j^1 = x$, $\exists$ j_1 such that $\rho(x_j^1,x) < 1/2$ and $x_{j_1}^1 \in \bigcup_{k=1}^{\infty} A_k$. Therefore, $x_{j_1}^1 \in A_{m_1}$ for some m_1. Let $\bar{x}_{m_1} = x_{j_1}^1$. Now, $\lim_{j\to\infty} x_j^{m_1+1} = x \in \bigcup_{k=m_1+1}^{\infty} A_k$. Hence, $\exists$ $x_{j_2}^{m_1+1} \in \bigcup_{k=m_1+1}^{\infty} A_k$ such that $\rho(x_{j_2}^{m_1+1},x) < 1/2^2$ and $x_{j_2}^{m_1+1} \in A_{m_2}$ for some $m_2 > m_1$. Letting $x_{m_2} = x_{j_2}^{m_1+1}$ and repeating the above process, we have constructed a sequence $\{x_{m_k}\}$, where $x_{m_k} \in A_{m_k}$, $m_1 < m_2 < \cdots < m_k < \cdots$, and $\rho(x_{m_k},x) < 1/2^k$. Therefore, $x \in B$. ∎

<u>Theorem 3.2</u>:

$$\bar{H} \supset B \neq \emptyset.$$

<u>Proof</u>: The sets $B_m = \mathrm{cl}(\bigcup_{k=m}^{\infty} A_k)$, $m = 1,2,\cdots$, are nonempty, closed, and contained in a compact set H_{c_o} for some c_o (Assumption A2). Since it is decreasing, $\bigcap_{m=1}^{\infty} B_m = B \neq \emptyset$.

If $\hat{x} \in B$, then $\exists$ a subsequence $\{x_{k_i}\}$ such that $x_{k_i} \in A_{k_i}$ and $x_{k_i} \to \hat{x}$.

According to (3.7), $\{f(x_k)\}$ is an increasing sequence bounded by $\bar{c}$. From (3.5), we have

$$\lim_{k_i\to\infty} [f(x_{k_i}) + \alpha_{k_i} p(x_{k_i})] \le \bar{c}. \tag{3.11}$$

It follows that

$$\lim_{k_i\to\infty} p(x_{k_i}) = p(\hat{x}) = 0$$

since $\alpha_k \uparrow +\infty$ and both $\lim_{k_i\to\infty} \alpha_{k_i} p(x_{k_i})$ and $\lim_{k_i\to\infty} p(x_{k_i})$ exist. This means that $\hat{x} \in S$. But $f(x) \ge \bar{c}$ for $x \in S$. Hence $f(\hat{x}) = \bar{c}$ and $\hat{x} \in \bar{H}$. ∎

In general, however, the set B does not coincide with the set of global minima $\bar{H}$.

Counter Example: Suppose

$$f(x) = \begin{cases} x & \text{for } 0 \le x \le 4/3, \\ 2 - (1/2)x & \text{for } 4/3 \le x \le 3. \end{cases} \tag{3.12}$$

Find the global minimum value of f over $S = \{x \mid 1 \le x \le 2\}$ and the set of global minima.

Obviously the global minimum value is $\bar{c} = 1$ and the set of global minima is given by $\bar{H} = \{1,2\}$.

Suppose the penalty function $p(x)$ is taken as

$$p(x) = \begin{cases} (1-x)^2 & \text{for } 0 \le x \le 1, \\ 0 & \text{for } 1 \le x \le 2, \\ (x-2)^2 & \text{for } 2 \le x \le 3. \end{cases} \tag{3.13}$$

Then,

$$F(x,\alpha) = \begin{cases} x + \alpha(1-x)^2 & \text{for } 0 \le x \le 1, \\ x & \text{for } 1 \le x \le \frac{4}{3}, \\ 2 - \frac{1}{2}x, & \text{for } \frac{4}{3} \le x \le 2, \\ 2 - \frac{1}{2}x + \alpha(x-2)^2 & \text{for } 2 \le x \le 3. \end{cases} \tag{3.14}$$

The minimum point of the penalized function $F(x,\alpha)$ over [0,1] is $x_1 = 1-(1/2\alpha)$ where $F(x_1,\alpha) = 1-(1/4\alpha)$. The corresponding minimum point over [2,3] is $x_2 = 2+(1/4\alpha)$ with $F(x_2,\alpha) = 1-(1/16\alpha)$. There is not a minimum point in (1,2) and $F(1,\alpha) = F(2,\alpha) = 1$. Hence, the global minimum of $F(x,\alpha)$ over [0,3] is $x_1 =$

1-(1/2α) for any $\alpha > 0$. This implies that

$$B = \{1\} \neq \bar{H} = \{1,2\}. \quad \blacksquare$$

We now proceed to consider the condition under which the set B is equal to the set of global minima $\bar{H}$.

The closed ball $B_\delta(x)$ with radius δ around $x \in X$ is defined by:

$$B_\delta(x) = \{ y \in X \mid \rho(x,y) \leq \delta \}.$$

<u>Proposition 3.3</u>: $B = \bar{H}$ if and only if, $\forall \bar{x} \in \bar{H}$ and $\delta > 0$, $\exists$ an integer k_δ such that

$$B_\delta(\bar{x}) \cap A_{k_\delta} \neq \emptyset. \tag{3.15}$$

<u>Proof</u>: (Sufficiency) It suffices to prove that $\bar{H} \subset B$ given (3.15) since we already know from Theorem 3.2 that $B \subset \bar{H}$. Consider a strictly positive sequence $\{\delta_i\}$ such that $\delta_i \to 0$ as $i \to \infty$. By condition (3.15), for each i, $\exists\, k_i$ such that

$$B_{\delta_i}(\bar{x}) \cap A_{k_i} \neq \emptyset.$$

Take $x_{k_i} \in B_{\delta_i}(\bar{x}) \cap A_{k_i}$, $i = 1,2,\cdots$. Since $x_{k_i} \in B_{\delta_i}(\bar{x})$, the distance $\rho(x_{k_i},\bar{x})$ between $\bar{x}$ and x_{k_i} tends to zero as $k_i \to \infty$, i.e., $x_{k_i} \to \bar{x}$ as $k_i \to \infty$. Furthermore, $x_{k_i} \in A_{k_i}$ so that $\bar{x} \in B$ and $\bar{H} \subset B$.

(Necessity) Suppose $\bar{H} = B$. For each $\bar{x} \in \bar{H} = B$, $\exists\, x_{k_i} \in A_{k_i}$, $i = 1,2,\cdots$ such that $x_{k_i} \to \bar{x}$ as $k_i \to \infty$. In addition, for any $\delta > 0$, we have $x_{k_i} \in B_\delta(\bar{x})$ for k_i sufficiently large. Letting $k_\delta = k_i$, we have $x_{k_i} \in B_\delta(\bar{x}) \cap A_{k_\delta} \neq \emptyset$. $\blacksquare$

<u>Corollary 3.4</u>: Suppose, $\forall \bar{x} \in \bar{H}$, $\exists$ a positive integer k_o and $x_{k_o} \in A_{k_o}$ such that

$$F(x_{k_o},\alpha_{k_o}) = f(\bar{x}).$$

Then, $\bar{H} = B$.

<u>Proof</u>: For $k \geq k_o$, we have

$$F(x_{k_o},\alpha_{k_o}) \leq F(x_k,\alpha_k) = f(\bar{x}).$$

Hence $F(x_k,\alpha_k) = f(\bar{x})$ so that $\bar{x} \in A_k\ \forall \bar{x} \in \bar{H}$, i.e., $\bar{H} \subset A_k$. This implies, $\forall \bar{x} \in$

$\bar{H}$ and $\delta > 0$, that $B_\delta(\bar{x}) \cap A_k \neq \emptyset$. Hence $B = \bar{H}$ by Proposition 3.3. ■

Corollary 3.5: If $\exists\ \bar{x} \in \bar{H}$ and $\delta > 0$ such that

$$F(x_k,\alpha_k) < f(x), \qquad x_k \in A_k$$

$\forall\ x \in B_\delta(\bar{x})$ and $k = 1,2,\cdots$, then $B \neq \bar{H}$.

Proof: $\forall\ x \in B_\delta(\bar{x})$, we have

$$F(x,\alpha_k) = f(x) + \alpha_k p(x) \geq f(x) > F(x_k,\alpha_k).$$

Hence, for $k = 1,2,\cdots$, $x \notin A_k$ or $B_\delta(\bar{x}) \cap A_k = \emptyset$. It follows from Proposition 3.3 that $\bar{H} \neq B$. ■

Corollary 3.6: If the set of global minima $\bar{H}$ intersects the interior of the feasible set S and

$$F(x_k,\alpha_k) < f(\bar{x}), \qquad \text{for } x_k \in A_k,\ \bar{x} \in \bar{H},\ k = 1,2,\cdots,$$

then $\bar{H} \neq B$.

Proof: This follows from Corollary 3.5 immediately. ■

Note that the counter-example given previously in this subsection is just the case described by Corollary 3.6.

3.2 Discontinuous Penalty Functions

In this subsection, we will utilize the concept of robustness (cf. Chapter II, Section 8) by introducing a class of discontinuous penalty functions which can be applied to transform a constrained minimization problem into an unconstrained one.

Consider the following minimization problem over a constrained set S:

$$\min_{x \in S} f(x) \tag{3.16}$$

with

$$S = \{\ x \mid g_i(x) \leq 0,\ i = 1,\cdots,r\ \}, \tag{3.17}$$

where each $g_i(x)$, $i = 1,\cdots,r$, is continuous. Define

$$p(x) = \begin{cases} 0 & x \in S \\ \delta + d(x) & x \notin S \end{cases} \tag{3.18}$$

where d(x) is a continuous function related to $g_i(x)$, $i = 1,\cdots,r$, and $\delta > 0$. For example:

$$d(x) = \Sigma_{i=1}^{r}(\max\{g_i(x),0\})^{\rho}, \tag{3.19}$$

or

$$d(x) = \max_i \left[(\max\{g_i(x),0\})^{\rho}\right], \tag{3.20}$$

where $\rho > 0$.

<u>Proposition 3.7</u>: The function p(x) given by (3.18) is robust.

<u>Proof</u>: For each c, we have

$$H_c^o = \{ x \mid p(x) < c \} = \begin{cases} \emptyset & \text{if } c < 0 \\ S & \text{if } 0 \leq c \leq \delta \\ \{ x \mid \delta + d(x) < c \} & \text{if } c > \delta. \end{cases} \tag{3.21}$$

We know that $\emptyset$ is robust and S is supposed to be robust. The set

$$\{ x \mid \delta + d(x) < c \} \tag{3.22}$$

is open since $\delta+d(x)$ is continuous. It follows that H_c^o is robust for every real number c. This implies that p(x) is robust. ∎

From Proposition II.8.8, $\alpha p(x)$ is robust if $\alpha > 0$; $f(x)+\alpha p(x)$ is robust if f(x) is continuous. Hence, we have

<u>Proposition 3.8</u>: Suppose the objective function f is continuous and the penalty parameter α is positive. Then the penalized function

$$F(x,\alpha) = f(x) + \alpha p(x) \tag{3.23}$$

is robust.

The following proposition states that a constrained minimization problem can be reduced to an unconstrained one by utilizing a robust penalty function.

<u>Proposition 3.9</u>: Suppose the constrained set S is robust and compact, and the objective function f is bounded from below. Then, there is a constraint α_o such that

$$\bar{c} = \min_{x \in S} f(x) = \inf_{x \in X} F(x,\alpha_o) = \min_{x \in X} F(x,\alpha_o) \tag{3.24}$$

and

$$\bar{H} = \{ x \mid f(x) = \bar{c},\ x \in S \} = \{ x \mid F(x,\alpha_o) = \bar{c} \}. \tag{3.25}$$

Proof: Since $f(x)$ is bounded from below, $\exists\ M < \infty$ such that $-f(x) < M\ \forall\ x \in X$. Suppose $\max_{x \in S} |f(x)| = M_1$. Take $\alpha_o = (M+M_1)/\delta$. It is clear that

$$\inf_{x \in X} F(x,\alpha_o) \le \min_{x \in S} F(x,\alpha_o). \tag{3.26}$$

Suppose

$$\inf_{x \in X} F(x,\alpha_o) < \min_{x \in S} F(x,\alpha_o).$$

Then there is a point $\hat{x} \in X$ such that

$$F(\hat{x},\alpha_o) < \bar{c}. \tag{3.27}$$

If $\hat{x} \in S$, then, given (3.18), we have

$$F(\hat{x},\alpha_o) = f(\hat{x}) + \alpha_o p(\hat{x}) = f(\hat{x}) \ge \bar{c}, \tag{3.28}$$

contradicting (3.27). If $\hat{x} \notin S$, then

$$F(\hat{x},\alpha_o) = f(\hat{x}) + \alpha_o p(\hat{x}) > f(\hat{x}) + M + M_1 \ge M_1 \ge \bar{c}. \tag{3.29}$$

This also contradicts (3.27). Therefore, we conclude that

$$\inf_{x \in X} F(x,\alpha_o) = \min_{x \in S} F(x,\alpha_o). \tag{3.30}$$

But $p(x) = 0$ on S. Hence,

$$\min_{x \in S} F(x,\alpha_o) = \min_{x \in S} f(x). \tag{3.31}$$

These prove (3.24). Since $F(x,\alpha_o) > \bar{c}\ \forall\ x \notin S$ (see (3.29)), and $F(x,\alpha_o) = f(x)\ \forall\ x \in S$, (3.25) obtains. ∎

§4 The Nonsequential Penalty Method

In Section 3 we dealt with sequential unconstrained minimization techniques for finding global minima under constraints. One shortcoming of SUMT is that it requires excessive computing time. In this section, a new nonsequential penalty technique will be introduced to treat global minimization problems with a robust feasible set.

4.1 Construction

Suppose X is a metric space, S is a closed robust set and Assumptions A1 and A2 are satisfied. The nonsequential minimization algorithm is given below.

Take a real number $c_o > \bar{c} = \min_{x\in S} f(x)$ and $\alpha_o > 0$. Let

$$H_o^{(o)} = \{ x \mid f(x) + \alpha_o p(x) \leq c_o \}, \tag{4.1}$$

where $p(x)$ is a penalty function with respect to the constrained set S. The measure of $H_o^{(o)}$ is positive, i.e. $\mu(H_o^{(o)}) > 0$. Otherwise, $H_o^{(o)}$ would be the set of global minima with c_o as the corresponding global minimum value of function $f(x)+\alpha_o p(x)$ due to Lemma I.2.1. Let $\bar{x} \in S$ be a global minimum of f over S. We have

$$c_o > f(\bar{x}) = f(\bar{x}) + \alpha_o p(\bar{x}) \geq f(x) + \alpha_o p(x) = c_o, \quad \forall\, x \in H_o^{(o)}, \tag{4.2}$$

which is a contradiction.

We know that the measure of the intersection of H_{c_o} and S is also positive because $c_o > f(\bar{x})$. We can therefore compute the following mean values:

$$a_1^{(o)} = \frac{1}{\mu(H_o^{(o)})}\int_{H_o^{(o)}} f(x)d\mu, \tag{4.3}$$

$$b_1^{(o)} = \frac{1}{\mu(H_o^{(o)})}\int_{H_o^{(o)}} p(x)d\mu, \tag{4.4}$$

and

$$d_1^{(o)} = \frac{1}{\mu(H_{c_o} \cap S)}\int_{H_{c_o} \cap S} f(x)d\mu. \tag{4.5}$$

There are two possibilities: (i) $f(x) + \alpha_o p(x) \geq c_o \; \forall\, x \in X\backslash S$, or (ii) $\exists\, x_o \in S$ such that $f(x_o) + \alpha_o p(x_o) < c_o$. In case (i), $f(x) + 2\alpha_o p(x) > c_o$ because $p(x) >$

$0 \ \forall\, x \notin S$. Hence $x \notin H_o^{(1)} = \{ x \mid f(x) + 2\alpha_o p(x) \le c_o \}$ if $x \notin S$, i.e., $H_o^{(1)} \subset S$ and $\{ x \mid f(x) + 2\alpha_o p(x) \le c \} \subset S$ for all $\bar{c} \le c \le c_o$. In this case, we have an unconstrained problem of minimizing the function $f(x) + 2\alpha_o p(x)$. This has been discussed before.

Consider case (ii). The continuity of the function $f(x) + \alpha_o p(x)$ implies that there is a ball $B_\delta(x_o) \subset X\backslash S$ with radius δ and centered at x_o such that $f(x) + \alpha_o p(x) < c_o$ for $x \in B_\delta(x_o)$. Hence, $B_\delta(x_o) \subset H_o^{(o)}$ and $p(x) > 0$ for $x \in B_\delta(x_o)$. Thus $b_1^{(o)} > 0$.

Suppose

$$a_1^{(o)} + \alpha_o b_1^{(o)} \le d_1^{(o)}. \tag{4.6}$$

Let

$$a_1^{(1)} = \frac{1}{\mu(H_o^{(1)})}\int_{H_o^{(1)}} f(x)d\mu, \tag{4.7}$$

$$b_1^{(1)} = \frac{1}{\mu(H_o^{(1)})}\int_{H_o^{(1)}} p(x)d\mu, \tag{4.8}$$

and

$$d_1^{(1)} = \frac{1}{\mu(S\cap H_{d_1^{(o)}})}\int_{S\cap H_{d_1^{(o)}}} f(x)d\mu. \tag{4.9}$$

Clearly, $\mu(H_o^{(1)}) > 0$. Moreover, since $c_o > \min_{x\in S} f(x)$, $f(x)$ is not constant on S, hence $d_1^{(o)}$ is not the global minimum value of f over S and the measure of $S\cap H_{d_1^{(o)}}$ is positive.

There are again two cases. In the first case, $f(x) + 2\alpha_o p(x) \ge c_o \ \forall\, x \in X\backslash S$, giving rise to an unconstrained problem of minimizing the function $f(x) + 2^2\alpha_o p(x)$. In the second case, we have $b_1^{(1)} > 0$.

If, again,

$$a_1^{(1)} + 2\alpha_o b_1^{(1)} \le d_1^{(1)}, \tag{4.10}$$

then we continue the procedure. After a certain number of steps, we either have

$$f(x) + 2^k\alpha_o p(x) \ge c_o$$

$\forall\, x \in X\backslash S$, in which case the problem reduces to an unconstrained minimization of $f(x) + 2^{k+1}\alpha_o p(x)$, or $\exists\, x \in X\backslash S$ such that $f(x) + 2^k\alpha_o p(x) < c_o$ so that $b_1^{(k)} > 0$. Consider the latter case. Let

$$H_o^{(k)} = \{ x \mid f(x) + 2^k\alpha_o p(x) \le c_o \}. \tag{4.11}$$

We can similarly prove that the measures of $H_o^{(k)}$ and $S\cap H_{d_1^{(k-1)}}$ are positive.

Let

$$a_1^{(k)} = \frac{1}{\mu(H_o^{(k)})}\int_{H_o^{(k)}} f(x)d\mu, \tag{4.12}$$

$$b_1^{(k)} = \frac{1}{\mu(H_o^{(k)})}\int_{H_o^{(k)}} p(x)d\mu, \tag{4.13}$$

and

$$d_1^{(k)} = \frac{1}{\mu(S\cap H_{d_o^{(k-1)}})}\int_{S\cap H_{d_o^{(k-1)}}} f(x)d\mu. \tag{4.14}$$

Obviously, we have

$$H_o^{(o)} \supset H_o^{(1)} \supset \cdots \supset H_o^{(k-1)} \supset H_o^{(k)} \supset \cdots, \tag{4.15}$$

$$c_o \ge d_1^{(o)} \ge d_1^{(1)} \ge \cdots \ge d_1^{(k-1)} \ge d_1^{(k)} \ge \cdots \ge \bar{c} \tag{4.16}$$

and

$$b_1^{(k)} > 0, \quad k = 1,2,\cdots. \tag{4.17}$$

Lemma 4.1: Repeating the above procedure, we have

$$a_1^{(k)} + 2^k\alpha_o b_1^{(k)} > d_1^{(k)}, \tag{4.18}$$

for some finite integer k.

Proof: To prove by contradiction, suppose the contrary. Then, we have sequences $\{H_o^{(k)}\}$, $\{a_1^{(k)}\}$, $\{b_1^{(k)}\}$ and $\{d_1^{(k)}\}$. The conclusion that

$$\bigcap_{k=0}^{\infty} H_o^{(k)} \subset S \tag{4.19}$$

follows from the observation that

$$f(x) + 2^k\alpha_o p(x) \to \infty \quad \text{as } k \to \infty \quad \text{for } x \notin S,$$

so that $x \notin \bigcap_{k=0}^{\infty} H_o^{(k)}$ for $x \notin S$. From Lemma II.4.1 with $\alpha_k = 2^k\alpha_o$, we have

$$H_o^{(k)} \to H_{c_o} \cap S. \tag{4.20}$$

Consequently, as $k \to \infty$,

$$a_1^{(k)} = \frac{1}{\mu(H_o^{(k)})}\int_{H_o^{(k)}} f(x)d\mu \to \frac{1}{\mu(S\cap H_{c_o})}\int_{S\cap H_{c_o}} f(x)d\mu = d_1^{(o)} > d_1^{(k)} \tag{4.21}$$

so that, for k sufficiently large,

$$a_1^{(k)} + 2^k\alpha_o b_1^{(k)} \geq d_1^{(k)}. \qquad \blacksquare$$

Thus, with no loss of generality, we can assume that α_o is chosen sufficiently large at the beginning so that

$$c_1^1 = a_1 + \alpha_o b_1 > d_1, \tag{4.22}$$

where

$$a_1 = \frac{1}{\mu(H_o)}\int_{H_o} f(x)d\mu, \tag{4.23}$$

$$b_1 = \frac{1}{\mu(H_o)}\int_{H_o} p(x)d\mu, \tag{4.24}$$

and

$$d_1 = \frac{1}{\mu(S\cap\hat{H}_o)}\int_{S\cap\hat{H}_o} f(x)d\mu \tag{4.25}$$

with $H_o = \{x \mid f(x) + \alpha_o p(x) \leq c_o\}$ and $\hat{H}_o = \{x \mid f(x) \leq c_1'\}$, $\bar{c} < c_1' = d_1^{(k)} \leq c_o$, for some k such that (4.22) holds.

Let $c_1 = \min\{c_1', c_1^1\}$, $\alpha_1 = \alpha_o \cdot \beta$ $(\beta > 1)$ and

$$H_1 = \{\, x \mid f(x) + \alpha_1 p(x) \leq c_1 \,\}. \tag{4.26}$$

We have $\mu(H_1) > 0$. If $c_1 = c_1' \leq c_1^1$, then $\mu(H_1) > 0$ because $\hat{H}_o \cap S \subset H_1$. Otherwise $c_1' > c_1^1 = c_1 > d_1$, $H_{c_1}\cap S \subset H_1$. If $H_{c_1}\cap S$ is empty, then $f(x) > c_1$ for $x \in S$ so that

$$d_1 \cdot \mu(\hat{H}_o\cap S) = \int_{\hat{H}_o\cap S} f(x)d\mu \geq c_1\mu(\hat{H}_o\cap S) > d_1\mu(\hat{H}_o\cap S),$$

which is a contradiction since $\mu(\hat{H}_o\cap S) > 0$. Therefore $H_{c_1}\cap S \neq \emptyset$. Also, $\mu(H_{c_1}\cap S) > 0$, or else c_1 would be the global minimum value of f over S, contradicting the fact that $\bar{c} < d_1 < c_1$. Hence, $\mu(H_1) \geq \mu(H_{c_1}\cap S) > 0$. Thus, we can compute

$$a_2 = \frac{1}{\mu(H_1)}\int_{H_1} f(x)d\mu, \tag{4.27}$$

$$b_2 = \frac{1}{\mu(H_1)}\int_{H_1} p(x)d\mu, \tag{4.28}$$

and

$$d_2 = \frac{1}{\mu(S\cap\hat{H}_1)}\int_{S\cap\hat{H}_1} f(x)d\mu, \tag{4.29}$$

where $\hat{H}_1 = \{x \mid f(x) \leq c_2'\}$, $\bar{c} < c_2' = d_2^{(k)} \leq c_1$ for some integer k such that

$$c_2' = a_2 + \alpha_1 b_2 > d_2. \tag{4.30}$$

And so on, we have constructed the sequences $\{H_j\}$, $\{a_j\}$, $\{b_j\}$, $\{d_j\}$ and $\{c_j\}$. The following relations apply:

$$H_o \supset H_1 \supset \cdots \supset H_j \supset H_{j+1} \supset \cdots, \tag{4.31}$$

$$c_o \geq c_1 \geq \cdots \geq c_j \geq c_{j+1} \geq \cdots, \tag{4.32}$$

and

$$c_j > d_j, \quad j = 1,2,\cdots. \tag{4.33}$$

Note that (4.32) follows from the fact that $f(x) + \alpha_j p(x) \leq c_j$ for $x \in H_j$ so that

$$\begin{aligned} c_{j+1} \leq a_{j+1} + \alpha_j b_{j+1} &= \frac{1}{\mu(H_j)}\int_{H_j} f(x)d\mu + \alpha_j \frac{1}{\mu(H_j)}\int_{H_j} p(x)d\mu \\ &= \frac{1}{\mu(H_j)}\int_{H_j} [f(x) + \alpha_j p(x)]d\mu \leq c_j, \quad j = 1,2,\cdots. \end{aligned} \tag{4.34}$$

4.2 Convergence

Let

$$\bar{H} = \bigcap_{j=1}^{\infty} H_j = \lim_{j\to\infty} H_j \tag{4.35}$$

and

$$\bar{c} = \lim_{j\to\infty} c_j. \tag{4.36}$$

<u>Theorem 4.2</u>: The limit $\bar{c}$ is the global minimum value and $\bar{H}$ is the corres-

ponding set of global minima of f over the constrained set S.

Proof: Letting $j \to \infty$ in (4.34), we have

$$\bar{c} \le \lim_{j\to\infty} \frac{1}{\mu(H_j)}\int_{H_j} [f(x) + \alpha_j p(x)]d\mu \le \bar{c},$$

i.e.,

$$M'(f,\bar{c};p) = \bar{c}. \tag{4.37}$$

Hence $\bar{c}$ is the global minimum value of f over S due to Theorem II.4.7.

Correspondingly, we have from Lemma 4.1 that

$$\lim_{k\to\infty} H_k = H_{\bar{c}} \cap S.$$

Hence, $\bar{H} = H_{\bar{c}} \cap S$ is the set of global minima. ∎

§5 The Technique of Adaptive Change of Search Domain

In order to reduce the possibly excessive amount of computation associated with too large an initial level set corresponding to a particular choice of a starting objective function value, we will develop, in this section, two models of adaptive change of search domains. The change-of-domain techniques allow an initial choice of a computationally manageable domain G_0 and then move on to better performing domains while still holding down their "sizes". This, in some sense, achieves a more judicial use of computationally generated information than in the case with the methods discussed earlier. This section provides the convergence and optimality conditions. Details concerning implementation will be discussed in the next chapter in the appropriate section.

5.1 A Simple Model

Let c_o be a real number and G_0 be an initial search domain such that $\mu(H_{c_o} \cap G_0) > 0$. Let

$$c_1 = M(f,c_o;G_0) = \frac{1}{\mu(H_{c_o} \cap G_0)} \int_{H_{c_o} \cap G_0} f(x) d\mu. \tag{5.1}$$

Then,

$$c_o \geq c_1 \geq \bar{c}_o = \min_{x \in G_0} f(x). \tag{5.2}$$

Take a search domain G_1 such that

$$G_0 \cap H_{c_1} \subset G_1. \tag{5.3}$$

Note that (5.3) does not require $G_0 \subset G_1$, but rather $H_{c_1} \cap G_0 \subset H_{c_1} \cap G_1$ and

$$\mu(H_{c_1} \cap G_1) \geq \mu(H_{c_1} \cap G_0) > 0.$$

Let

$$c_2 = M(f,c_1;G_1). \tag{5.4}$$

In general, we require that

$$G_k \cap H_{c_{k+1}} \subset G_{k+1}, \quad k = 0,1,2,\cdots \tag{5.5}$$

and set

$$c_{k+1} = M(f,c_k;G_k), \quad k = 0,1,2,\cdots. \tag{5.6}$$

In this manner, we have constructed the following two sequences:

$$c_o \geq c_1 \geq \cdots \geq c_k \geq c_{k+1} \geq \cdots \tag{5.7}$$

and

$$H_{c_o} \supset H_{c_1} \supset \cdots \supset H_{c_k} \supset H_{c_{k+1}} \supset \cdots. \tag{5.8}$$

5.2 Convergence

Let

$$\bar{c} = \lim_{k\to\infty} c_k \tag{5.9}$$

and

$$\bar{H} = \lim_{k\to\infty} H_{c_k} = \bigcap_{k=1}^{\infty} H_{c_k}. \tag{5.10}$$

Theorem 5.1: The limit $\bar{c}$ is the global minimum value and $\bar{H}\cap G_L$ is the corresponding global minima of f over set

$$G_L = cl(\bigcup_{k=1}^{\infty} G_k). \tag{5.11}$$

Proof: From (5.6) and the mean value property,

$$\min_{x\in G_k} f(x) \le c_{k+1}, \quad k = 1,2,\cdots \tag{5.12}$$

so that

$$\min_{x\in G_L} f(x) \le c_{k+1}, \quad k = 1,2,\cdots. \tag{5.13}$$

Hence,

$$\min_{x\in G_L} f(x) \le \bar{c}. \tag{5.14}$$

We proceed to prove that $\min_{x\in G_L} f(x) = \bar{c}$. If $\min_{x\in G_L} f(x) < \bar{c}$, then there exists at least a point $\hat{x} \in G_L$ such that

$$\hat{c} = f(\hat{x}) = \bar{c} - 2\eta, \tag{5.15}$$

where

$$\eta = (\bar{c}-\hat{c})/2 > 0. \tag{5.16}$$

We can find a sequence $\{x_j\} \subset \bigcup_{k=1}^{\infty} G_k$ which tends to $\hat{x}$, and an integer N sufficiently large such that

$$f(x_j) < \bar{c} - \eta, \quad \text{for } j > N,$$

and $x_j \in G_{k_j}$, i.e., $E_{\bar{c}-\eta} \cap G_{k_j} \neq \emptyset$, where

$$E_{\bar{c}-\eta} = \{ x \mid f(x) < \bar{c}-\eta \}. \tag{5.17}$$

Since $H_{\bar{c}-\eta}$ is open and G_{k_j} is robust, $\mu(E_{\bar{c}-\eta} \cap G_{k_j}) > 0$ or $\mu(H_{\bar{c}-\eta} \cap G_{k_{j_0}}) > 0$ for some fixed j_0.

We have

$$c_{m+1}\mu(H_{c_m} \cap G_m) = \int_{H_{c_m} \cap G_m} f(x)d\mu$$

$$= \int_{(H_{c_m} \cap G_m)\setminus(H_{\bar{c}-\eta} \cap G_m)} f(x)d\mu + \int_{H_{\bar{c}-\eta} \cap G_m} f(x)d\mu$$

$$\leq c_m[\mu(H_{c_m} \cap G_m) - \mu(H_{\bar{c}-\eta} \cap G_m)] + (\bar{c}-\eta)\mu(H_{\bar{c}-\eta} \cap G_m).$$

Rearranging terms, we have

$$c_m - c_{m+1} \geq \eta\left[\mu(H_{\bar{c}-\eta} \cap G_m)/\mu(H_{c_m} \cap G_L)\right] \geq \eta\left[\mu(H_{\bar{c}-\eta} \cap G_m)/\mu(H_{c_0} \cap G_L)\right]. \tag{5.18}$$

From (5.5), we have

$$G_k \cap H_{c_{k+1}} \subset G_{k+1} \cap H_{c_{k+1}}$$

and

$$G_k \cap H_{c_{k+1}} \cap H_{\bar{c}-\eta} \subset G_{k+1} \cap H_{c_{k+1}} \cap H_{\bar{c}-\eta},$$

i.e.,

$$H_{\bar{c}-\eta} \cap G_k \subset H_{\bar{c}-\eta} \cap G_{k+1}, \quad k = 1,2,\cdots$$

since $H_{\bar{c}-\eta} \subset H_{c_{k+1}}$. Hence,

$$\mu(H_{\bar{c}-\eta} \cap G_m) \geq \mu(H_{\bar{c}-\eta} \cap G_{k_{j_0}}) > 0 \tag{5.19}$$

if $m > k_{j_0}$. Taking the limit of (5.18) as $m \to \infty$, we have

$$\bar{c} - \bar{c} \geq \eta\left[\mu(H_{\bar{c}-\eta} \cap G_{j_0})/\mu(H_{c_0} \cap G_L)\right] > 0, \tag{5.20}$$

which is a contradiction. Therefore, $\bar{c}$ is the global minimum value of f over G_L. It is obvious that $\bar{H} \cap G_L$ is the corresponding set of global minima of f over G_L. ∎

5.3 Optimality Conditions of the Simple Model

Suppose $\{c_k\}$ is a decreasing sequence which tends to $\bar{c}$ and $\{G_k\}$ is a sequence of domains such that

$$H_{c_{k+1}} \cap G_k \subset G_{k+1}, \quad \text{for } k = 0,1,2,\cdots. \tag{5.21}$$

It is clear that

$$H_{\bar{c}} \cap G_L \neq \emptyset, \tag{5.22}$$

where

$$G_L = \mathrm{cl}\left(\bigcup_{k=1}^{\infty} G_k\right). \tag{5.23}$$

Theorem 5.2: The following are equivalent:

(a) $\bar{c}$ is the global minimum value of f over G_L;

(b)
$$\lim_{k\to\infty} \frac{1}{\mu(H_{c_k} \cap G_k)} \int_{H_{c_k} \cap G_k} f(x)d\mu = \bar{c}; \tag{5.24}$$

(c)
$$\lim_{k\to\infty} \frac{1}{\mu(H_{c_k} \cap G_k)} \int_{H_{c_k} \cap G_k} [f(x)-\bar{c}]^2 d\mu = 0; \tag{5.25}$$

(d)
$$\lim_{k\to\infty} \frac{1}{\mu(H_{c_k} \cap G_k)} \int_{H_{c_k} \cap G_k} [f(x)-c_k]^m d\mu = 0, \quad \text{for some } m \in I^+. \tag{5.26}$$

Proof (a) ⇒ (b): Suppose $\bar{c}$ is the global minimum value of f over G_L. Then

$$M(f,c_k;G_k) = \min_{x\in G_k} f(x) \geq \min_{x\in G_L} f(x) = \bar{c}, \quad k = 0,1,2,\cdots. \tag{5.27}$$

On the other hand,

$$M(f,c_k;G_k) = \frac{1}{\mu(H_{c_k} \cap G_k)} \int_{H_{c_k} \cap G_k} f(x)d\mu \leq c_k, \quad k = 0,1,2,\cdots. \tag{5.28}$$

Letting $k \to \infty$ in (5.27) and (5.28), we have

$$\bar{c} \leq \liminf_{k\to\infty} M(f,c_k;G_k) \leq \limsup_{k\to\infty} M(f,c_k;G_k) \leq \bar{c}.$$

Thus, the limit exists and (5.24) holds.

(b) ⇒ (a): The proof is omitted since it is the same as that of Theorem 5.1.

(a) ⇒ (d): Suppose $\bar{c}$ is the global minimum value of f over G_L. Then, $\bar{c} \leq$

$f(x)$ for $x \in G_k$, $k = 1,2,\cdots$. Noting that $f(x) \le c_k$ for $x \in G_k \cap H_{c_k}$ and that $c_k \downarrow \bar{c}$, we have

$$0 \le \left|\frac{1}{\mu(H_{c_k} \cap G_k)}\int_{H_{c_k} \cap G_k} [f(x)-c_k]^m d\mu\right| \le (c_k-\bar{c})^m \to 0 \text{ as } k \to \infty.$$

Hence,

$$\lim_{k\to\infty} \frac{1}{\mu(H_{c_k} \cap G_k)}\int_{H_{c_k} \cap G_k} [f(x)-c_k]^m d\mu = 0.$$

(d) ⇒ (a): According to (5.21), we have

$$\min_{x\in G_L} f(x) \le \min_{x\in G_k} f(x) = \min_{x\in H_{c_k}\cap G_k} f(x) \le c_k,$$

so that $\min_{x\in G_L} f(x) \le \bar{c}$. Suppose $\min_{x\in G_L} f(x) = \hat{c} < \bar{c}$. As in the proof of Theorem 5.1, we can find a j_0 such that $\mu(H_{\bar{c}-\eta} \cap G_{j_0}) > 0$, where $\eta = (\bar{c}-\hat{c})/2$.

If m is even, then

$$\frac{1}{\mu(H_{c_k} \cap G_k)}\int_{H_{c_k} \cap G_k} [f(x)-c_k]^m d\mu \ge \frac{1}{\mu(H_{c_k} \cap G_k)}\int_{H_{\bar{c}-\eta} \cap G_{j_0}} [f(x)-c_k]^m d\mu$$

$$\ge [\bar{c}-\eta-c_k]^m \left[\mu(H_{\bar{c}-\eta} \cap G_{j_0})/\mu(H_{c_0} \cap G_L)\right], \quad \text{for } k \ge j_0,\ k = 1,2,\cdots.$$

Taking limit, we have

$$\lim_{k\to\infty} \frac{1}{\mu(H_{c_k} \cap G_k)}\int_{H_{c_k} \cap G_k} [f(x)-c_k]^m d\mu \ge \eta^m \left[\mu(H_{\bar{c}-\eta} \cap G_{j_0})/\mu(H_{c_0} \cap G_L)\right] > 0,$$

which contradicts (5.26).

If m is odd so that $[f(x)-c_k]^m \le 0$ for $x \in H_{c_k} \cap G_k$, then

$$\frac{1}{\mu(H_{c_k} \cap G_k)}\int_{H_{c_k} \cap G_k} [f(x)-c_k]^m d\mu \le \frac{1}{\mu(H_{c_k} \cap G_k)}\int_{H_{\bar{c}-\eta} \cap G_{j_0}} [f(x)-c_k]^m d\mu$$

$$\le [\bar{c}-\eta-c_k]^m \left[\mu(H_{\bar{c}-\eta} \cap G_{j_0})/\mu(H_{c_0} \cap G_L)\right],$$

and

$$\lim_{k\to\infty} \frac{1}{\mu(H_{c_k} \cap G_k)}\int_{H_{c_k} \cap G_k} [f(x)-c_k]^m d\mu \le -\eta^m \left[\mu(H_{\bar{c}-\eta} \cap G_{j_0})/\mu(H_{c_0} \cap G_L)\right] < 0,$$

which also contradicts (5.26). ∎

5.4 The General Model

In the simple model of Section 5.1, we require that the sequence of search domains $\{G_k\}$ satisfy

$$G_k \cap H_{c_{k+1}} \subset G_{k+1}.$$

We remove the above restriction in this subsection.

Let c_o be a real number and G_0 be an initial search domain such that $\mu(H_{c_o} \cap G_0) > 0$. Let

$$c_1 = M(f,c_o;G_0) = \frac{1}{\mu(H_{c_o} \cap G_0)}\int_{H_{c_o} \cap G_0} f(x)d\mu. \tag{5.29}$$

Then,

$$\min_{x \in G_0} f(x) \leq c_1 = M(f,c_o;G_0) \leq c_o.$$

Note that $H_{c_1} \neq \emptyset$ and $\mu(H_{c_1}) > 0$. Take a domain G_1 such that $\mu(H_{c_1} \cap G_1) > 0$ and let $c_2 = M(f,c_1;G_1)$. In general, at the k<u>th</u> step, we choose a domain G_k such that $\mu(H_{c_k} \cap G_k) > 0$ and set

$$\begin{aligned} \min_{G_k} f(x) \leq c_{k+1} &= M(f,c_k;G_k) \\ &= \frac{1}{\mu(H_{c_k} \cap G_k)}\int_{H_{c_k} \cap G_k} f(x)d\mu \leq c_k, \quad k = 1,2,\cdots. \end{aligned} \tag{5.30}$$

We have consequently constructed the following two sequences:

$$c_o \geq c_1 \geq \cdots \geq c_k \geq c_{k+1} \geq \cdots$$

and

$$H_{c_o} \supset H_{c_1} \supset \cdots \supset H_{c_k} \supset H_{c_{k+1}} \supset \cdots,$$

both of which are bounded from below. Let

$$\bar{c} = \lim_{k\to\infty} c_k \tag{5.31}$$

and

$$\bar{H} = \lim_{k\to\infty} H_{c_k} = \bigcap_{k=1}^{\infty} H_{c_k}. \tag{5.32}$$

Theorem 5.3: If the limit $\bar{G} = \lim_{k\to\infty} G_k$ exists and is robust and $\bar{H}\cap\bar{G}$ is non-empty, then the limit $\bar{c}$ is the global minimum value of f over $\bar{G}$ and $\bar{H}\cap\bar{G}$ is the corresponding set of global minima.

Proof: Since $\bar{H}\cap\bar{G} \neq \emptyset$,

$$\min_{x\in\bar{G}} f(x) \leq \min_{x\in\bar{G}\cap\bar{H}} f(x) \leq \bar{c}.$$

We proceed to prove that $\min_{x\in\bar{G}} f(x) = \bar{c}$. Suppose $\exists\ \hat{x} \in \bar{G}$ such that $f(\hat{x}) = \hat{c} < \bar{c}$. Then, there is an integer N such that $\hat{x} \in \bigcap_{k=N}^{\infty} G_k$. Let $\bar{c}-\hat{c} = 2\eta > 0$.

$$c_{m+1}\mu(H_{c_m}\cap G_m) = \int_{(H_{c_m}\cap G_m)\setminus(H_{\bar{c}-\eta}\cap G_m)} f(x)d\mu + \int_{H_{\bar{c}-\eta}\cap G_m} f(x)d\mu$$

$$\leq c_m[\mu(H_{c_m}\cap G_m)-\mu(H_{\bar{c}-\eta}\cap G_m)] + (\bar{c}-\eta)\mu(H_{\bar{c}-\eta}\cap G_m)$$

$$\leq c_m\mu(H_{c_m}\cap G_m) - \eta\mu(H_{\bar{c}-\eta}\cap G_m).$$

This implies that

$$c_m - c_{m+1} \geq \eta\,\frac{\mu(H_{\bar{c}-\eta}\cap G_m)}{\mu(H_{c_m}\cap G_m)} \geq \eta\,\frac{\mu(H_{\bar{c}-\eta}\cap G_m)}{\mu(H_{c_o})}.$$

We have $\lim_{m\to\infty} (c_m-c_{m+1}) = 0$ and $\lim_{m\to\infty} \mu(H_{\bar{c}-\eta}\cap G_m) = \mu(H_{\bar{c}-\eta}\cap\bar{G})$. Since $\hat{x} \in E_{\bar{c}-\eta} = \{ x \mid f(x) < \bar{c}-\eta \}$, it follows that $\hat{x} \in \bar{G}$ and $\bar{G}$ is robust. Hence, $\mu(H_{\bar{c}-\eta}\cap\bar{G}) > 0$, which gives a contradiction. ■

It is reasonable to require $\bar{G}$ be given by $\lim_{k\to\infty} G_k$. The requirement $\bar{H}\cap\bar{G} \neq \emptyset$ is more subtle, the necessity of which is demonstrated in the following counter-example.

Example 5.1: Let $G = \{(x,y)\mid 0\leq x\leq 1; 0\leq y\leq 2\}$ and $G_k = G\setminus\Delta_k$, where Δ_k is a triangle with apexes $A_1(0,2)$, $A_2(0,2-1/k)$ and $A_3(1/k,2)$. Then $\lim_{k\to\infty} G_k = G\setminus\{(0,2)\}$. Let f(x) be an affine function with $f(0,0) = 2$, $f(1,0) = 3$, $f(1,1) = 1$ and $f(0,1) = 0$. Then $\min_{x\in G_L} f(x) = -2$ ($G_L = cl(\bigcup_{k=1}^{\infty} G_k)$), $H_{\bar{c}} = \{(0,2)\}$. But

$$H_{\bar{c}}\cap\bar{G} = \emptyset.$$

For this general model, we can also prove a similar optimality conditions theorem. Suppose $\{c_k\}$ is a decreasing sequence which tends to $\bar{c}$ and $\{G_k\}$ is a sequence of search domains such that $\mu(H_{c_k} \cap G_k) > 0$ $(k = 1,2,\cdots)$, $\bar{G} = \lim_{k\to\infty} G_k$ is robust and $H_{\bar{c}} \cap \bar{G} \neq \emptyset$.

Theorem 5.4: The following are equivalent:

(a) a real number $\bar{c}$ is the global minimum value of f over set $\bar{G}$;

(b)
$$\lim_{k\to\infty} \frac{1}{\mu(H_{c_k} \cap G_k)} \int_{H_{c_k} \cap G_k} f(x) d\mu = \bar{c}; \tag{5.33}$$

(c)
$$\lim_{k\to\infty} \frac{1}{\mu(H_{c_k} \cap G_k)} \int_{H_{c_k} \cap G_k} [f(x)-\bar{c}]^2 d\mu = 0; \tag{5.34}$$

(d)
$$\lim_{k\to\infty} \frac{1}{\mu(H_{c_k} \cap G_k)} \int_{H_{c_k} \cap G_k} [f(x)-c_k]^m d\mu = 0, \quad \text{for some } m \in I^+. \tag{5.35}$$

§6 Stability of Global Minimization

The question of sensitivity and stability for certain nonlinear programming problems has been considered for local minima by several researches. Nevertheless, there has not been any such treatment of a global nature by measure-integration approach. This section considers the stability in $X = \mathbb{R}$ of continuous objective function f and constraint function g. The related global sensitivity analysis will be treated in subsequent papers.

In this section, we assume that Assumptions A1 and A2 are satisfied.

6.1 Continuity of Mean Value

In this subsection, we consider the continuity of mean value and higher moments with respect to perturbations in the objective function f, level set parameter c and the constraints. We begin by proving two lemmas.

The relevant conditions and definitions for the statements of the lemmas are given below:

(1) $$\lim_{\epsilon \to 0} f_\epsilon(x) = f(x) \quad \text{and} \quad \lim_{\delta \to 0} g_\delta(x) = g(x) \text{ pointwise;}$$

(2) $$\lim_{\gamma \to 0} c_\gamma = c,\ c > \min_{x \in G} f(x) \quad \text{and} \quad c_\gamma > \bar{c}_{\epsilon\delta} = \min_{x \in G_\delta} f_\epsilon(x);$$

(3) $$H_c^o = \{ x \mid f(x) < c \} \quad \text{and} \quad H_c = \{ x \mid f(x) \leq c \};$$

(4) $$G^o = \{ x \mid g(x) < 0 \} \quad \text{and} \quad G = \{ x \mid g(x) \leq 0 \};$$

(5) $$G_\delta = \{ x \mid g_\delta(x) \leq 0 \};$$

(6) $$\underline{A}_c^o = \bigcup_{k=1}^{\infty} \bigcap_{m=k}^{\infty} \{ x \mid f_{\epsilon_m}(x) < c_{\gamma_m},\ g_{\delta_m}(x) < 0 \};$$

(7) $$\bar{A}_c^o = \bigcap_{k=1}^{\infty} \bigcup_{m=k}^{\infty} \{ x \mid f_{\epsilon_m}(x) < c_{\gamma_m},\ g_{\delta_m}(x) < 0 \};$$

(8) $$\underline{A}_c = \bigcup_{k=1}^{\infty} \bigcap_{m=k}^{\infty} \{ x \mid f_{\epsilon_m}(x) \leq c_{\gamma_m},\ g_{\delta_m}(x) \leq 0 \};$$

(9) $$\bar{A}_c = \bigcap_{k=1}^{\infty} \bigcup_{m=k}^{\infty} \{ x \mid f_{\epsilon_m}(x) \leq c_{\gamma_m},\ g_{\delta_m}(x) \leq 0 \};$$

for some $\epsilon_m \to 0$, $\delta_m \to 0$, and $\gamma_m \to 0$.

<u>Lemma 6.1</u>: Under conditions (1) - (2) and definitions (3) - (9), we have

$$H_c^o \cap G^o \subset \underline{A}_c^o \subset \bar{A}_c^o, \tag{6.1}$$

and

$$\underline{A}_c \subset \bar{A}_c \subset H_c \cap G. \tag{6.2}$$

<u>Proof</u>: Suppose $\hat{x} \notin \underline{A}_c^o$, i.e., $\hat{x} \notin \bigcap_{m=k}^{\infty} \{x \mid f_{\epsilon_m}(x) < c_{\gamma_m},\ g_{\delta_m}(x) < 0 \}\ \forall\ k$. Then, $\exists$ a subsequence $\{m_j\}$ such that $f_{\epsilon_{m_j}}(\hat{x}) \geq c_{\gamma_{n_j}}$ or $g_{\delta_{m_j}}(\hat{x}) \geq 0$. Letting $m_j \to \infty$, we have $f(\hat{x}) \geq c$ or $g(\hat{x}) \geq 0$. Hence, $\hat{x} \notin H_c^o \cap G^o$ so that (6.1) holds.

Suppose $\hat{x} \in \bar{A}_c$, i.e., $\hat{x} \in \bigcup_{m=k}^{\infty} \{x \mid f_{\epsilon_m}(x) \geq c_{\gamma_m},\ g_{\delta_m}(x) \geq 0\}\ \forall\ k$. We also find a subsequence $\{m_j\}$ such that $f_{\epsilon_{m_j}}(\hat{x}) \geq c_{\gamma_{n_j}}$ and $g_{\delta_{m_j}}(\hat{x}) \leq 0$. Letting $m_j \to \infty$, we have $f(\hat{x}) \leq c$ and $g(\hat{x}) \leq 0$. Hence, $\hat{x} \in H_c \cap G$, so that (6.2) also holds. ∎

Lemma 6.2: Let $c > \bar{c} = \min_{x \in G} f(x)$. Assume that

$$\mu(H_c \cap G \setminus H_c^o \setminus G^o) = 0. \tag{6.3}$$

Under the assumptions of Lemma 6.1, we have

$$\lim_{\substack{\epsilon \to 0 \;\delta \to 0 \\ \gamma \to 0}} \mu\left[(H_{c_\gamma}(\epsilon)) \cap G_\delta\right]) = \mu(H_c \cap G), \tag{6.4}$$

where

$$H_{c_\gamma}(\epsilon) = \{ x \mid f_\epsilon(x) \le c_\gamma \}. \tag{6.5}$$

Proof: By Lemma 6.1, we have

$$H_c^o \cap G^o \subset \underline{A}_c^o \begin{matrix} \subset \bar{A}_c^o \\ \subset \underline{A}_c \end{matrix} \subset \bar{A}_c \subset H_c \cap G, \tag{6.6}$$

for any $\epsilon_m \to 0$, $\gamma_m \to 0$ and $\delta_m \to 0$. Hence,

$$\mu(H_c^o \cap G^o) \le \mu(\underline{A}_c) \le \mu(\bar{A}_c) \le \mu(H_c \cap G). \tag{6.7}$$

Given (6.3), it is easy to see that (6.4) holds. ∎

Theorem 6.3: Suppose $\lim_{\epsilon \to 0} f_\epsilon(x) = f(x)$ uniformly on $\bar{G} = \bigcup_{\delta \ge 0} G_\delta$. Under the assumptions of Lemma 6.2, we have

$$\lim_{\substack{\epsilon \to 0 \;\delta \to 0 \\ \gamma \to 0}} M(f_\epsilon, c_\gamma; G_\delta) = M(f, c; G), \tag{6.8}$$

$$\lim_{\substack{\epsilon \to 0 \;\delta \to 0 \\ \gamma \to 0}} V(f_\epsilon, c_\gamma; G_\delta) = V(f, c; G), \tag{6.9}$$

and

$$\lim_{\substack{\epsilon \to 0 \;\delta \to 0 \\ \gamma \to 0}} M_m(f_\epsilon, a; c_\gamma; G_\delta) = M_m(f, a; c; G) \text{ for some } m \in I^+. \tag{6.10}$$

Proof: We will only prove (6.8) since the proofs of (6.9) and (6.10) are similar. We have

$$|M(f_\epsilon, c_\gamma; G_\delta) - M(f, c; G)| \le I_1 + I_2 + I_3,$$

where

$$I_1 = \left|\frac{1}{\mu(H_{c_\gamma}(\epsilon) \cap G_\delta)} \int_{H_{c_\gamma}(\epsilon) \cap G_\delta} f_\epsilon(x) d\mu - \frac{1}{\mu(H_c \cap G)} \int_{H_{c_\gamma}(\epsilon) \cap G_\delta} f_\epsilon(x) d\mu\right|,$$

$$I_2 = \left|\frac{1}{\mu(H_c \cap G)}\int_{H_{c_\gamma}(\epsilon)\cap G_\delta} f_\epsilon(x)d\mu - \frac{1}{\mu(H_c \cap G)}\int_{H_{c_\gamma}(\epsilon)\cap G_\delta} f(x)d\mu\right|,$$

and

$$I_3 = \left|\frac{1}{\mu(H_c \cap G)}\int_{H_{c_\gamma}(\epsilon)\cap G_\delta} f(x)d\mu - \frac{1}{\mu(H_c \cap G)}\int_{H_c \cap G} f(x)d\mu\right|.$$

Observe that

$$|I_1| \le \left|\frac{1}{\mu(H_{c_\gamma}(\epsilon)\cap G_\delta)} - \frac{1}{\mu(H_c \cap G)}\right|\cdot(M+1)[\mu(H_c \cap G)+1] \quad \to \quad 0 \qquad (\epsilon,\ \gamma,\ \delta \to 0)$$

by Lemma 6.2, and we know that $|f(x)| \le M$ for some M on the compact set $H_c \cap G$. Also,

$$I_2 \le \max |f_\epsilon(x)-f(x)|\left[\mu(H_{c_\gamma}(\epsilon)\cap G_\delta)/\mu(H_c \cap G)\right] \quad \to \quad 0 \qquad (\epsilon,\ \gamma,\ \delta \to 0)$$

because $f_\epsilon(x)$ converges to $f(x)$ uniformly.

Finally

$$I_3 \le [\mu((H_{c_\gamma}(\epsilon)\cap G_\delta)\Delta(H_c \cap G))/\mu(H_c \cap G)]\cdot M \quad \to \quad 0 \qquad (\epsilon,\ \gamma,\ \delta \to 0)$$

by Lemma 6.2. ∎

6.2 Stability of Global Minima

In this section, the stability of the global minimum value and the corresponding global minima will be examined. In addition to the notation given just before the statement of Lemma 6.1 in the preceding subsection, we have

(10) $$\bar{G} = \bigcup_{\delta \ge 0} G_\delta,$$

(11) $$\bar{c} = \min_{x \in G} f(x),$$

(12) $$\bar{c}_{\epsilon,\delta} = \min_{x \in G_\delta} f_\epsilon(x).$$

<u>Theorem 6.4</u>: Suppose Assumptions A1 and A2 are satisfied. If $f_\epsilon(x) \to f(x)$ uniformly as $\epsilon \to 0$ and $g_\delta(x) \to g(x)$ as $\delta \to 0$ for $x \in \bar{G}$. Then

$$\lim_{\substack{\epsilon\to 0\\ \delta\to 0}} \bar{c}_{\epsilon,\delta} = \bar{c}. \tag{6.11}$$

Proof: Since $f_\epsilon(x) \to f(x)$ uniformly on $\bar{G}$, for any $\alpha > 0$ $\exists$ $\epsilon_0 > 0$ such that

$$|f_\epsilon(x)-f(x)| < \alpha, \quad \forall\ x \in \bar{G},$$

whenever $|\epsilon| \le \epsilon_0$, or

$$f_\epsilon(x) \le f(x) + \alpha, \quad \forall\ x \in \bar{G}.$$

Therefore,

$$\bar{c}_{\epsilon,\delta} = \min_{x\in G_\delta} f(x) \le f(x) + \alpha, \quad \text{for } x \in G_\delta \text{ and } |\epsilon| \le \epsilon_0. \tag{6.12}$$

Taking limit superior as $\epsilon \to 0$ and $\delta \to 0$, we have

$$\limsup_{\substack{\epsilon\to 0\\ \delta\to 0}} \bar{c}_{\epsilon,\delta} \le f(x) + \alpha, \tag{6.13}$$

for $x \in \bigcap_{k=1}^{\infty} \bigcup_{m=k}^{\infty} \{x \mid g_{\delta_m}(x) \le 0\} \supset G_o = \{x \mid g(x) < 0\}$, where $\{\delta_n\}$ is a sequence which tends to 0 as $n \to \infty$. Hence, (6.13) holds for all $x \in G = cl(G_o)$ due to the continuity of $f(x)$. Since the left-hand side of (6.13) does not depend on $x \in G$,

$$\limsup_{\substack{\epsilon\to 0\\ \delta\to 0}} \bar{c}_{\epsilon,\delta} \le \bar{c} + \alpha,$$

i.e.,

$$\limsup_{\substack{\epsilon\to 0\\ \delta\to 0}} \bar{c}_{\epsilon,\delta} \le \bar{c}. \tag{6.14}$$

To complete the proof, we show that

$$\liminf_{\substack{\epsilon\to 0\\ \delta\to 0}} \bar{c}_{\epsilon,\delta} \ge \bar{c}. \tag{6.15}$$

Assume the contrary that

$$\liminf_{\substack{\epsilon\to 0\\ \delta\to 0}} \bar{c}_{\epsilon,\delta} < \bar{c} - \beta \tag{6.16}$$

for some $\beta > 0$. Then $\exists$ $\{\epsilon_n\}$ and $\{\delta_m\}$ ($\epsilon_n \to 0$, $\delta_m \to 0$), and N_o, M_o such that

$$\bar{c}_{\epsilon_n,\delta_m} < \bar{c} - \frac{\beta}{2}, \quad \text{for } n > N_o \text{ and } m > M_o.$$

According to the optimality condition and the definitions of constrained mean value in Chapter II,

$$\bar{c}_{\epsilon_n,\delta_m} = \lim_{k\to\infty} \frac{1}{\mu(H_{d_k} \cap G_{\delta_m})} \int_{H_{d_k} \cap G_{\delta_m}} f_{\epsilon_n}(x) d\mu,$$

where $\{d_k\}$ is a decreasing sequence which tends to $\bar{c}_{\epsilon_n,\delta_m}$. It follows that $\exists$ a $K_0(n,m)$ corresponding to each (n,m) such that

$$\frac{1}{\mu(H_{d_k} \cap G_{\delta_m})} \int_{H_{d_k} \cap G_{\delta_m}} f_{\epsilon_n}(x) d\mu < \bar{c} - \frac{\beta}{4}, \tag{6.17}$$

for $k > K_0(n,m)$, $n > N_0$ and $m > M_0$. From (6.17) there exists at least a point $x_{n,m,k} \in H_{d_k} \cap G_{\delta_m}$ such that

$$f_{\epsilon_n}(x_{n,m,k}) < \bar{c} - \frac{\beta}{4}. \tag{6.18}$$

For any pair (n,m), we can find a sequence $\{x_{n,m,k}\}$ such that (6.18) holds for $n \to \infty$, $m \to \infty$, $k(n,m) \to \infty$. Now the sequence $\{x_{n,m,k}\}$ forms a subset of a compact set due to Assumption A2. We can, without losing generality, regard it as a convergent sequence, say, $x_{n,m,k} \to \hat{x}$. Obviously, $\hat{x} \in G$. But for n sufficiently large,

$$|f_{\epsilon_n}(x_{n,m,k}) - f(\hat{x})| \le |f_{\epsilon_n}(x_{n,m,k}) - f(x_{n,m,k})| + |f(x_{n,m,k}) - f(\hat{x})| < \frac{\beta}{16} + \frac{\beta}{16} \tag{6.19}$$

because the first term in the middle can be made arbitrarily small by the uniform convergence of f_ϵ and the second term can also be made samll using the continuity of f. Thus, from (6.18) and (6.19), we have

$$f(\hat{x}) < \bar{c} - \frac{\beta}{8}, \tag{6.20}$$

which contradicts the hypothesis that $\bar{c} = \min_{x\in G} f(x)$. ∎

We now consider the stability of the set of global minima. Let

$$\bar{H} = \{ x \mid f(x) = \bar{c},\ x \in G \}, \tag{6.21}$$

and

$$\bar{H}_{\epsilon,\delta} = \{ x \mid f(x) = \bar{c}_{\epsilon,\delta},\ x \in G_\delta \}. \tag{6.22}$$

Suppose $f_\epsilon(x)$ converges to $f(x)$ uniformly as $\epsilon \to 0$ and $g_\delta(x)$ converges to $g(x)$ as $\delta \to 0$ for $x \in \bar{G}$. Let

$$\bar{A} = \{ x \mid \exists x_k \in \bar{H}_{\epsilon_{n_k}, \delta_{n_k}} \text{ for some } \{\epsilon_{n_k}\} \text{ and } \{\delta_{n_k}\} \text{ such that } x = \lim_{k\to\infty} x_k \}$$

$$= \bigcap_{k=1}^{\infty} \mathrm{cl}\big(\bigcup_{n=k}^{\infty} \bar{H}_{\epsilon_n, \delta_n} \big),$$

for given $\{\epsilon_n\}$ and $\{\delta_n\}$, $\epsilon_n \to 0$ and $\delta_n \to 0$. It is easy (based on a nested-interval type argument) to see that $\bar{A} \neq \emptyset$. If $\hat{x} \in \bar{A}$, then $\exists\, x_k \in \bar{H}_{\epsilon_{n_k}, \delta_{n_k}}$ such that $\hat{x} = \lim_{k\to\infty} x_k$ and

$$\bar{c}_{\epsilon_{n_k}, \delta_{n_k}} = f_{\epsilon_{n_k}}(x_k) \to \bar{c} \quad \text{and} \quad f_{\epsilon_{n_k}}(x_k) \to f(\hat{x}).$$

Hence,

Theorem 6.5: Under the assumptions in Theorem 6.4, $\emptyset \neq \bar{A} \subset \bar{H}$.

§7 Lower Dimensional Approximation

Suppose X is a normed linear space and $X_n \subset X$ such that $X_n \subset X_{n+1}$, n = 1, 2,•••, is a lower dimensional subspace of X and

$$X = \mathrm{cl}\big(\bigcup_{n=1}^{\infty} X_n \big). \tag{7.1}$$

Then, we say that X_n is a lower dimensional approximation of X.

In minimization problems of infinite dimensions, one is normally satisfied with a finite dimensional approximation. It is therefore important to examine whether the approximate solution will converge to the exact one. In this section, we will first discuss the lower dimensional approximation of the global minimum value and the set of global minima and then consider the degree of approximation.

7.1 Approximation of Global Minimum

Let

$$\bar{c} = \min_{x \in X} f(x) \tag{7.2}$$

and

$$\bar{c}_n = \min_{x \in X_n} f(x). \tag{7.3}$$

Let $\bar{H}$ and $\bar{H}_n$ be the respective sets of global minima of f over X and X_n.

Theorem 7.1: Under Assumptions A1 and A2, we have

$$\bar{c} = \lim_{n \to \infty} \bar{c}_n \tag{7.4}$$

and

$$\emptyset \neq B \subset \bar{H}, \tag{7.5}$$

where

$$B = \{ x \mid \exists \text{ a sequence } \{x_{n_k}\},\ x_{n_k} \in \bar{H}_{n_k} \text{ such that } x = \lim_{n_k \to \infty} x_{n_k} \}. \tag{7.6}$$

Proof: Since $X_n \subset X_{n+1} \subset X$, $n = 1,2,\cdots$, we have

$$\bar{c}_n \geq \bar{c}_{n+1} \geq \cdots \geq \bar{c}. \tag{7.7}$$

Clearly,

$$\hat{c} = \lim_{n \to \infty} \bar{c}_n \geq \bar{c}.$$

Suppose $\bar{x} \in \bar{H}$ is a global minimum of f over X. Then there exists a sequence $\{x_{n_k}\}$ such that $x_{n_k} \in X_{n_k}$ and $\bar{x} = \lim_{n_k \to \infty} x_{n_k}$. Note that

$$f(x_{n_k}) \geq \bar{c}_{n_k}. \tag{7.8}$$

Letting $n_k \to \infty$ in (7.8), we obtain

$$\bar{c} = f(\bar{x}) = \lim_{n_k \to \infty} f(x_{n_k}) \geq \lim_{n_k \to \infty} \bar{c}_{n_k} \geq \bar{c}. \tag{7.9}$$

Hence,

$$\bar{c} = \lim_{n \to \infty} \bar{c}_n.$$

Let $x \in B$. Then for each convergent sequence $\{x_{n_k}\}$ with $x_{n_k} \in \bar{H}_{n_k}$,

$$\lim_{n_k\to\infty} x_{n_k} = x \in X.$$

But $\bar{c}_{n_k} = f(x_{n_k})$ and $\lim_{n_k\to\infty} \bar{c}_{n_k} = \bar{c}$. Thus,

$$f(x) = \lim_{n_k\to\infty} f(x_{n_k}) = \bar{c} \text{ and } x \in \bar{H}. \tag{7.10}$$

This means $B \subset \bar{H}$. From Lemma 3.1,

$$B = \bigcap_{m=1}^{\infty} \mathrm{cl}\left(\bigcup_{k=m}^{\infty} \bar{H}_k\right) \neq \emptyset \tag{7.11}$$

since $\bar{H}$ is compact under Assumption A1. ∎

7.2 Estimation of Degree of Approximation

For a fixed vector $x \in X$, let

$$d_n(x) = \inf_{x_n \in X_n} \|x_n - x\|. \tag{7.12}$$

Then,

$$\lim_{n\to\infty} d_n(x) = 0 \tag{7.13}$$

since $X = \mathrm{cl}(\bigcup_{n=1}^{\infty} X_n)$. In general, the sequence

$$\rho_n = \sup_{x\in X} d_n(x), \quad n = 1,2,\cdots, \tag{7.14}$$

tends to 0 as $n \to \infty$, and has information about the approximation of $\{X_n\}$ to X.

Theorem 7.2: Suppose $\exists\ \Delta \geq \delta > 0$ such that

$$\delta\|x-y\| \leq |f(x)-f(y)| \leq \Delta\|x-y\| \tag{7.15}$$

for $x, y \in X$. Then, for $n = 1,2,\cdots$,

$$|\bar{c}_n - \bar{c}| \leq (\Delta^2/\delta)\rho_n \tag{7.16}$$

and

$$\|\bar{x}_n - \bar{x}\| \leq (\Delta/\delta)\rho_n, \tag{7.17}$$

$\forall\ \bar{x} \in \bar{H}$ and $\bar{x}_n \in \bar{H}_n$.

Proof: According to the definitions of $\bar{H}_n$ and $\bar{H}$, for $n = 1,2,\cdots$,

$$f(x_n) \geq f(\bar{x}_n) \geq f(\bar{x}),$$

$\forall\ \bar{x} \in \bar{H}$, $\bar{x}_n \in \bar{H}_n$ and $x_n \in X_n$. Therefore,

$$|f(\bar{x}_n)-f(\bar{x})| \leq |f(x_n)-f(\bar{x})|. \tag{7.18}$$

By (7.15), we have

$$\delta\|\bar{x}_n-\bar{x}\| \leq |f(\bar{x}_n)-f(\bar{x})| \leq |f(x_n)-f(\bar{x})| \leq \Delta\|x_n-\bar{x}\|,$$

or

$$\|\bar{x}_n-\bar{x}\| \leq (\Delta/\delta)\|x_n-\bar{x}\|,$$

$\forall\ x_n \in X_n$. Thus,

$$\|\bar{x}_n-\bar{x}\| \leq (\Delta/\delta)\rho_n.$$

Also,

$$|\bar{c}_n-\bar{c}| \leq |f(\bar{x}_n)-f(\bar{x})| \leq \Delta\|\bar{x}_n-\bar{x}\| \leq (\Delta^2/\delta)\rho_n.$$

∎

CHAPTER IV

MONTE CARLO IMPLEMENTATION

From Chapter III, it is clear that each method of finding the global minimum requires the computation of a sequence of mean values $\{c_k\}$ and a sequence of level sets $\{H_{c_k}\}$. Finding a mean value is tantamount to computing an integral of a function with several variables. The determination of level sets is in general more involved. But accuracy is not generally required from the earlier discussion of the influence of errors. This suggests that a Monte Carlo based technique of finding the global minimum will be appropriate.

In this chapter, we will discuss the Monte Carlo implementation of the optimality conditions and the theoretical algorithms. In Section 1, the implementation of the simple model, which deals with problems with unique global minimum in the initial search domain, is given. In Section 2, the asymptotic behavior of the amount of computation is estimated by statistical means. We show that there is no complexity difficulty in our method. Strategies of adaptive change of search domains will be examined in Section 3. In Section 4, we deal with additional techniques for more complicated models including the multi-solution model and integer and mixed programming models. Six examples are given in Section 5 to compare the actual numerical performance of our methods with that of some standard ones. Problems considered in these examples range from unconstrained minimization to those allowing discontinuity. The results of these computations are compatible with our asymptotic estimation of the growth in the amount of computation being slower than the square of precision.

§1 A Simple Model of Implementation

1.1 The Model

Suppose D is a "cuboid" in $\mathbb{R}^n$ given by

$$D = \{ x \mid a^i \le x^i \le b^i,\ i = 1,\cdots,n \} \tag{1.1}$$

and f is a function with a unique global minimum $\bar{x}$ in D. In other words, for a decreasing sequence $\{c_k\}$ which converges to the global minimum value $\bar{c}$, the size of the level sets satisfies:

$$\rho_k = \rho(H_{c_k}) = \max_{x,y \in H_{c_k}} \|x-y\| \to 0 \quad \text{as } k \to \infty. \tag{1.2}$$

We have

$$\bar{c} = \min_{x \in D} f(x) = \min_{x \in H_{c_k} \cap D} f(x) = \min_{x \in D_k} f(x), \tag{1.3}$$

where D_k is the smallest "cuboid" containing the level set $H_{c_k} \cap D$.

Lemma 1.1: $\{\bar{x}\} = \bigcap_{k=1}^{\infty} D_k$, where $\bar{x}$ is the unique global minimum.

Proof: It is clear that

$$\bar{x} \in \bigcap_{k=1}^{\infty} \left[H_{c_k} \cap D \right] \subset \bigcap_{k=1}^{\infty} D_k. \tag{1.4}$$

Suppose $\{\bar{x}\} \ne \bigcap_{k=1}^{\infty} D_k$, i.e., $\exists\, x_1 \in \bigcap_{k=1}^{\infty} D_k$ such that $x_1 \ne \bar{x}$ and $f(x_1) = d > \bar{c}$. Let D_o be the smallest "cuboid" in $\mathbb{R}^n$ containing $\bar{x}$ and x_1. Then

$$D_o \subset D_k, \quad k = 1,2,\cdots, \tag{1.5}$$

where

$$D_o = \{ x \mid a_o^i \le x^i \le b_o^i,\ i = 1,\cdots,n \} \tag{1.6}$$

and $b_o^i - a_o^i > 0$ for at least one i. From the definition,

$$D_k = \{ x \mid a_k^i \le x^i \le b_k^i,\ i = 1,\cdots,n \},$$

where

$$a_k^i = \min \{ x^i \mid (x^1,\cdots,x^i,\cdots,x^n) \in H_{c_k} \},$$

$$b_k^i = \max \{ x^i \mid (x^1,\cdots,x^i,\cdots,x^n) \in H_{c_k} \}.$$

Now, $\exists\, x_{\alpha_i}, x_{\beta_i} \in H_{c_k}$ such that $a_k^i = x_{\alpha_i}^i$ and $b_k^i = x_{\beta_i}^i$, $i = 1,\cdots,n$. Since

$$\|x_{\alpha_i} - x_{\beta_i}\| = \left[(x_{\alpha_i}^1 - x_{\beta_i}^1)^2 + \cdots + (x_{\alpha_i}^n - x_{\beta_i}^n)^2\right]^{1/2} \geq \left[(x_{\beta_i}^i - x_{\alpha_i}^i)^2\right]^{1/2} = b_k^i - a_k^i,$$

we have, for $i = 1,\cdots,n$,

$$b_k^i - a_k^i \leq \|x_{\alpha_i} - x_{\beta_i}\| \leq \rho(H_{c_k}) \to 0 \quad \text{as } k \to \infty,$$

which contradicts (1.6). ∎

The following is an algorithm for this model.

Step 0: Take $c_o > \bar{c} = \min f(x)$. Give a small positive ϵ. Let $D_o = D$ be an initial cuboid. Let $k = 0$.

Step 1: Compute the mean value

$$c_{k+1} = M(f,c_k;D_k).$$

Let D_{k+1} be the smallest cuboid containing the level set

$$H_{c_{k+1}} = \{ x \mid f(x) \leq c_{k+1} \}.$$

Step 2: Compute the modified variance

$$VF = V_1(f,c_k;D_k).$$

Step 3: If $VF \geq \epsilon$, set $k = k+1$ and go to Step 1. Otherwise, go to Step 4.

Step 4: Set $\bar{c} = c_{k+1}$ and $\{\bar{x}\} \subset D_{k+1}$. Stop.

We try to find D_k instead of H_{c_k} at each iteration because it is easier. Also, computing $M(f,c_k;D_k)$ and $V_1(f,c_k;D_k)$ instead of $M(f,c_k)$ and $V_1(f,c_k)$ gives rise to greater accuracy because $\rho(D_k) \to 0$ as $k \to \infty$.

1.2 Monte Carlo Implementation

Now, the implementation of the model can be described as follows:

(1) Approximating H_{c_o} and $M(f,c_o)$:

Let $\xi = (\xi^1,\cdots,\xi^n)$ be an independent n-triple random number which is uniformly distributed on $[0,1]^n$. Let

$$x^i = a^i + (b^i-a^i)\cdot\xi^i, \quad i = 1,\cdots,n. \tag{1.7}$$

Then, $x = (x^1,\cdots,x^n)$ is uniformly distributed on D.

Take km samples and compute functions $f(x_j)$, $j = 1,\cdots,km$. Comparing the values of the function f at each point, we obtain a set of sample points W which contains t points corresponding to the t smallest function values FV(j), $j = 1,2,\cdots,t$, ordered by their values, i.e., $FV(1) \geq FV(2) \geq \cdots \geq FV(t)$.

The set W is called the acceptance set which can be regarded as an approximation of the level set H_{c_o} with $c_o = FV(1)$, the largest value of $\{FV(j)\}$. Clearly, $f(x) \leq c_o$ for $x \in W$. Also, the mean value of f over the level set H_{c_o} can be approximated by the mean value of $\{FV(j)\}$,

$$c_1 = \left[FV(1) + \cdots + FV(t)\right]/t. \tag{1.8}$$

(2) Generating a new domain:

The new "cuboid" domain of dimension n

$$D_1 = \{ x \mid a_1^i \leq x^i \leq b_1^i,\ i = 1,\cdots,n \} \subset D \tag{1.9}$$

can be generated statistically. We describe one heuristic rule. Suppose the random numbers giving rise to W are $\xi_1, \xi_2, \cdots, \xi_t$. Let

$$\eta_o = \min(\xi_1,\cdots,\xi_t) \tag{1.10}$$

and

$$\eta_1 = \max(\xi_1,\cdots,\xi_t). \tag{1.11}$$

We use vectors

$$\zeta_o = \eta_o - (\eta_1-\eta_o)/(t-1) \tag{1.12}$$

$$\zeta_1 = \eta_1 + (\eta_1-\eta_o)/(t-1) \tag{1.13}$$

as estimators to generate a_1 and b_1.

(3) Continuing the iterative process:

The samples are now taken in the new domain D_1. Consider a random point x_α, where

$$x_\alpha^i = a_1^i + (b_1^i-a_1^i)\cdot\xi^i, \quad i = 1,\cdots,n.$$

Compute $f(x_\alpha)$. If $f(x_\alpha) \geq FV(1)$, drop this point. Otherwise, reconstruct $\{FV(j)\}$ and W such that the new $\{FV(j)\}$ is made up of the best function values so far. The acceptance set W is modified accordingly. Repeating this procedure until $FV(1) \leq c_1$. We obtain new FV and W.

Continuing this process gives a decreasing sequence of mean value $\{c_k\}$ and a decreasing sequence of cuboids of dimension n, $\{D_k\}$.

(4) Iterative solutions:

At each, say the k<u>th</u>, iteration, the smallest value FV(t) in the set $\{FV(j)\}$ and the corresponding point in W can be regarded as iterative solutions to the minimization problem over D_k.

(5) Convergence criterion:

The modified variance VF of the function values $\{FV(j)\}$ is given by

$$VF = \frac{1}{t-1}\Sigma_{j=2}^{t}[FV(j)-FV(1)]^2, \tag{1.14}$$

which can be regarded as an approximation of the modified variance of f over level set H_{c_k}. If VF is less than the given precision parameter ϵ, then the iterative process terminates, and the current iterative solutions in Step 4 can serve as estimates of the global minimum value and the global minimum point.

1.3 The Flow Chart

The flow chart of the above procedure is given in Figure IV.1.

Figure IV.1: Monte Carlo Implementation Flow Chart

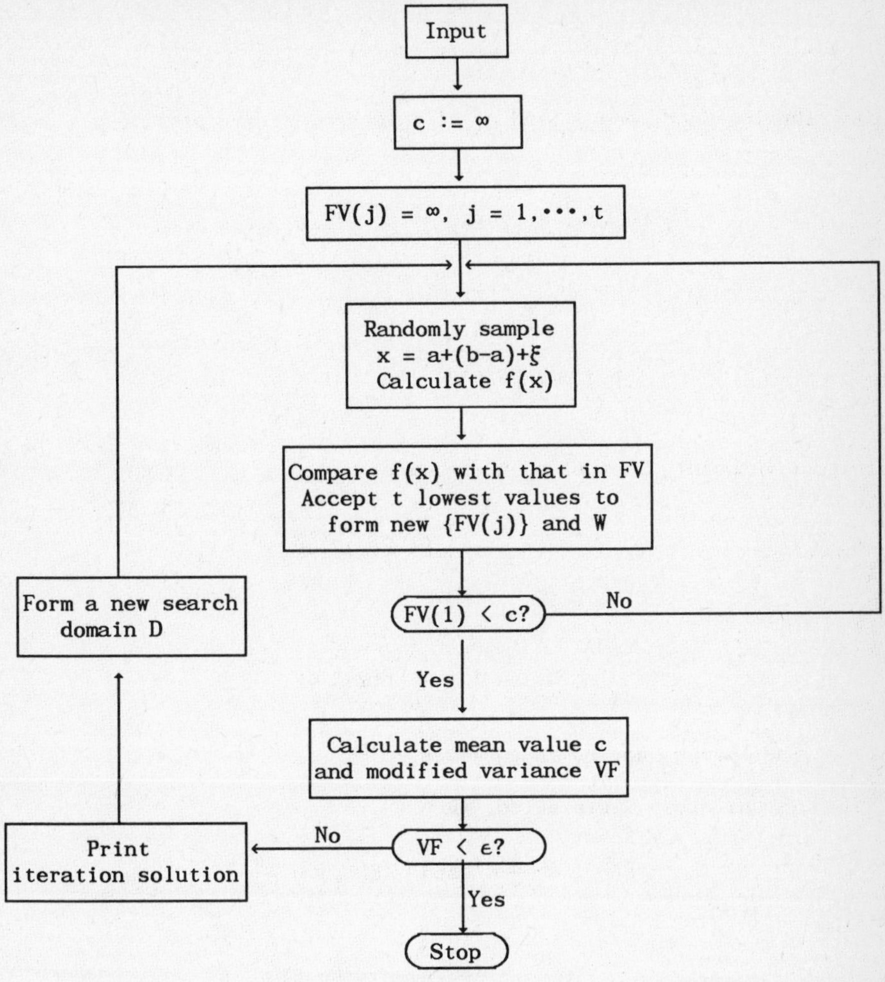

§2 Statistical Analysis of the Simple Model

2.1 Estimators of the Search Domains

Let ξ be a random variable on (a,b) with distribution function F. Given t sample points $\xi_1,\cdots,\xi_t$, we consider the estimation of a and b. Suppose without loss of generality that a = 0 and b = 1, and denote

$$\eta_o = \min\{\xi_1, \xi_2, \cdots, \xi_t\} \tag{2.1}$$

and

$$\eta_1 = \max\{\xi_1, \xi_2, \cdots, \xi_t\} \tag{2.2}$$

The distribution functions ϕ_o and ϕ_1 of η_o and η_1 are respectively

$$\phi_o(y) = \begin{cases} 0, & y \leq 0, \\ 1-[1-F(y)]^t & 0 < y < 1, \\ 1, & 1 \leq y, \end{cases} \tag{2.3}$$

and

$$\phi_1(y) = \begin{cases} 0 & y \leq 0, \\ [F(y)]^t & 0 < y < 1, \\ 1 & 1 \leq y. \end{cases} \tag{2.4}$$

The respective mean values of η_o and η_1 are

$$E(\eta_o) = \int_0^1 [1-F(y)]^t dy \tag{2.5}$$

and

$$E(\eta_1) = 1 - \int_0^1 [F(y)]^t dy. \tag{2.6}$$

Therefore, neither η_o nor η_1 is unbiased.

If ξ is uniformly distributed, then

$$E(\eta_o) = \frac{1}{t+1} \quad \text{and} \quad E(\eta_1) = \frac{t}{t+1}.$$

Thus,

$$\zeta_o = \eta_o - (\eta_1 - \eta_o)/(t-1) \tag{2.7}$$

and

$$\zeta_1 = \eta_1 + (\eta_1 - \eta_o)/(t-1) \tag{2.8}$$

are unbiased estimators of the end-points. The variance of η_o as well as η_1 is given by

$$V(\eta_o) = V(\eta_1) = t/[(t+1)^2(t+2)], \tag{2.9}$$

so that the statistical errors of these estimators approximate $1/t$.

2.2 The Probability of Escape and the Sample Size

In determining a new search domain D_1, we need to ensure that the global minimum $\bar{x}$ does not escape from it. The probability of escape depends on the construction of the function f and is inversely related to the sample size t.

For further analysis, we introduce the concept of the skew rate of a function in a coordinate direction to describe an asymmetry related to the global minimum on a level set. Consider, for convenience, a one-dimensional problem. Suppose the unique global minimum is $\bar{x}$. Let

$$\delta = [2\bar{x}-(a+b)]/(b-a). \tag{2.10}$$

The value of δ varies between -1 (when $\bar{x} = a$) and $+1$ (when $\bar{x} = b$), and is equal to 0 when $\bar{x}$ is in the middle. If the global minimum $\bar{x}$ is skewed towards the right, then the probability of escape on the right is given by

$$P_r = \mathrm{Prob}\left[\zeta_1 < [(a+b)+\delta(b-a)]/2\right]. \tag{2.11}$$

The computation of P_r is too complicated. We will instead consider its asymptotic estimation. If ξ is uniformly distributed, the probabilities are given in the following tableau:

$\delta = 0.3$

t	7	10	12	15	20	30
prob	6.16×10^{-3}	2.06×10^{-3}	9.33×10^{-4}	2.73×10^{-4}	3.35×10^{-5}	4.76×10^{-7}

$\delta = 0.9$

t	7	10	12	15	20	30
prob	0.181	0.173	0.162	0.143	0.115	0.0708

From (2.4), the probability of escape on the right is less than γ_r^t, where

$$\gamma_r^t = F\left[[(a+b)+\delta(b-a)]/2\right]. \tag{2.12}$$

Since the probability of escape on the left is, in this case, less than γ_r^t, the total probability of escape, P_e, satisfies

$$P_e \leq 2\gamma_r^t. \tag{2.13}$$

If the global minimum $\bar{x}$ is skewed towards the left, then the probability of escape on the left is

$$P_\ell = \text{Prob}\Big[\zeta_o > [(a+b)+\delta(b-a)]/2\Big] = 1 - \text{Prob}\Big[\zeta_o \leq [(a+b)+\delta(b-a)]/2\Big]. \tag{2.14}$$

We can estimate P_ℓ from (2.3) to be less than γ_ℓ^t, where

$$\gamma_\ell^t = 1 - F\Big[[(a+b)+\delta(b-a)]/2\Big]. \tag{2.15}$$

Again, since the probability of escape on the right is less than that on the left, the total probability of escape when $\bar{x}$ is skewed to the left is less than $2\gamma_\ell^t$, i.e.,

$$P_e \leq 2\gamma_\ell^t. \tag{2.16}$$

We assume the following:

<u>Assumption C1</u>: $\exists$ constants γ_o and γ_1 such that

$$\gamma_o \leq F_k^i\Big[[a_k^i + b_k^i + \delta_k^i(b_k^i - a_k^i)]/2\Big] \leq \gamma_1, \quad \text{for } i = 1,2,\cdots,n \text{ and } k = 1,2,\cdots,$$

where F_k^i is the sample distribution function of the <u>kth</u> iteration in the <u>ith</u> coordinate. Let $\gamma = \max\{\gamma_1, 1-\gamma_o\}$. Then, after k iterations, P_e, the probability of escape of the global minimum, is given by

$$P_e \leq q_o = 1 - (1-2\gamma^t)^{nk}, \tag{2.17}$$

where n is the dimension of the domain. We label the probability of capturing the global minimum $\bar{x}$ in D_k after k iterations the "probability of capture", denoted by P_c.

2.3 <u>Asymptotic Estimation of the Amount of Computation</u>

Suppose the volume of the initial search domain D_o (cuboid) is V_o and the volume of the new search domain D_1 (which contains H_{c_1}) generated by the interative process is V_1. We label the following ratio the "volume contraction rate":

$$\alpha_1 = V_o/V_1. \tag{2.18}$$

Let V_{H_1} be the volume of level set H_{c_1}. Then,

$$\beta_1 = V_{H_1}/V_1 \tag{2.19}$$

is called the "efficiency ratio".

Suppose km_1 random points are taken in D_o uniformly and t points are accepted in the level set H_{c_1}, we have

$$km_1/V_o \cong t/V_{H_1} \tag{2.20}$$

or

$$km_1 \cong (V_o/V_{H_1})t = (\alpha_1/\beta_1)t. \tag{2.21}$$

Thus, after k iterations, the volume of the k<u>th</u> search domain is given by

$$V_k = V_o/\left[\Pi_{j=1}^{k}\alpha_j\right], \tag{2.22}$$

where α_j $(j = 1,2,\cdots,k)$ is the volume contraction rate at the j<u>th</u> iteration. Suppose the amount of computation at the j<u>th</u> iteration is km_j, then the total amount of computation N is given by

$$N = km_1 + km_2 + \cdots + km_k = \Sigma_{j=1}^{k}(\alpha_j/\beta_j)t. \tag{2.23}$$

We further impose

<u>Assumption C2</u>: $\exists\ \alpha_o$ and α such that

$$1 < \alpha_o \le \alpha_j \le \alpha, \quad j = 1,2,\cdots$$

and

<u>Assumption C3</u>: $\exists\ \beta_o > 0$ such that

$$0 < \beta_o \le \beta_j, \quad j = 1,2,\cdots.$$

Consequently,

$$N \le k\cdot(\alpha/\beta_o)\cdot t, \tag{2.24}$$

where k, the required number of iterations, is determined by the desired accuracy and t by the probability of escape.

Suppose the volume V_o of the initial search domain is unity and we want to find the global minimum $\bar{x}$ in a domain with volume $V_\epsilon = \epsilon$, then the resulting contraction rate is

$$V_o/V_\epsilon = 1/\epsilon = \Pi_{j=1}^{k}\alpha_j \leq \alpha^k. \tag{2.25}$$

If we take

$$k \geq [\frac{\ln(1/\epsilon)}{\ln\alpha_o}] \cong [\frac{\ln(1/\epsilon)}{\ln\alpha_o}] + 1, \tag{2.26}$$

then,

$$V_o/V_\epsilon \geq 1/\epsilon. \tag{2.27}$$

We are now prepared to establish a theorem of asymptotic estimation.

Theorem 2.1: Suppose Assumptions C1, C2 and C3 are satisfied. Then the expected amount of computation N_f needed to ensure a greater than p_o probability of capture of the global minimum within a cuboid of volume ϵ from an initial cuboid of unit volume satisfies the following inequality:

$$N_f \leq \frac{\alpha}{\beta_o}\,\frac{\ln(1/\epsilon)}{\ln\alpha_o}\,\frac{\ln[1-p_o^{\ln\alpha_o/(n\ln(1/\epsilon))}] - \ln 2}{\ln\gamma} \tag{2.28}$$

Proof: Take

$$t = \frac{\ln(1-p_o^{\frac{1}{nk}}) - \ln 2}{\ln\gamma}. \tag{2.29}$$

Then, from (2.17), the probability of escape is less than q_o. We call $p_o = 1-q_o$ the confidence probability which is given in advance.

Substituting (2.26) and (2.29) into (2.24), we obtain (2.28). ∎

Theorem 2.2: Under the hypotheses of Theorem 2.1, the expected amount of computation N_f for capturing the global minimum in a cuboid of volume ϵ from an initial cuboid of unit volume has the following asymptotic bound:

$$N_f \leq c\cdot\ln(1/\epsilon)\cdot\ln[\ln(1/\epsilon)] \quad \text{as } \epsilon \to 0, \tag{2.30}$$

where

$$c = \frac{\alpha}{\beta_o\cdot\ln\alpha_o\cdot\ln(1/\gamma)}. \tag{2.31}$$

Proof: Since

$$\lim_{\epsilon\to 0} \frac{\ln\left[1-p_o^{\frac{\ln\alpha_o}{n\ln(1/\epsilon)}}\right] - \ln 2}{\ln[\ln(1/\epsilon)]} = -1, \tag{2.32}$$

from (2.28), we have (2.30) and (2.31).

Comparing the above with the grid or pure random search method, which has the estimate

$$N_f \leq c_1(1/\epsilon), \tag{2.33}$$

we can see that our method is far superior. In general, however, the constant c in expression (2.31) is greater than c_1 in expression (2.33). In Section 3, where X is assumed to be a metric space, we will develop a few techniques to circumvent this disadvantage.

§3 Strategies of Adaptive Change of Search Domains

3.1 Strategies

As we have mentioned in Section III.5, the initial domain G_0 needs to be small so that the amount of computation would not be very large. In many cases, the choice of the initial domain may leave out the global minimum from G_0. It is also possible for the global minimum to be situated on the boundary of the domain so that the skew rate becomes 1 or -1. This results in the probability being unity. Consequently, we may fail to capture the global minimum by a Monte Carlo search process. This especially applies to the constrained case with a monotone objective function.

We consider four cases:

Case 1: A trivial case is given by $G_k = G_0$, $k = 1,2,\cdots$, so that $G_L = cl(\bigcup_{k=1}^{\infty} G_k) = G_0$. This is the no-change case.

Case 2: Take a search domain $\tilde{G}_{k+1}$ such that

$$G_k \cap H_{c_{k+1}} \subset \tilde{G}_{k+1}, \quad k = 0,1,2,\cdots. \tag{3.1}$$

Then let

$$G_{k+1} = \tilde{G}_{k+1} \cap G_0, \qquad k = 0,1,2,\cdots. \tag{3.2}$$

We have, due to Theorem III.5.1, that $\bar{c} = \lim_{k\to\infty} c_k$ is the global minimum value of f over G_L, where

$$G_L = cl(\bigcup_{k=1}^{\infty} G_k) = cl\left[(\bigcup_{k=1}^{\infty} \tilde{G}_k) \cap G_0\right] \subset G_0. \tag{3.3}$$

Thus, $\bar{c} = \min_{x\in G_L} f(x) \geq \min_{x\in G_0} f(x)$. Nevertheless, we have from (3.1) and (3.2),

$$G_0 \cap G_k \cap H_{c_{k+1}} \subset G_{k+1},$$

i.e.,

$$G_0 \cap \left[G_0 \cap G_{k-1} \cap H_{c_k}\right] \cap H_{c_{k+1}} \subset G_{k+1}$$

or

$$G_0 \cap G_{k-1} \cap H_{c_{k+1}} \subset G_{k+1}$$

so that

$$G_0 \cap H_{c_{k+1}} \subset G_{k+1}, \qquad \text{for } k = 0,1,2,\cdots. \tag{3.4}$$

It follows that

$$\min_{G_0} f(x) = \min_{G_0 \cap H_{c_{k+1}}} f(x) \geq \min_{G_{k+1}} f(x) = c_{k+1}.$$

Letting $k \to \infty$, we obtain

$$\min_{G_0} f(x) \geq \bar{c}.$$

Hence,

$$\min_{G_L} f(x) = \min_{G_0} f(x) = \bar{c}. \tag{3.5}$$

The above strategy is useful in finding the global minimum of f over the constrained set $S = G_0$.

Case 3: $\qquad G_L = cl(\bigcup_{k=1}^{\infty} G_k)$ and $G_0 \subset G_L$.

This strategy is useful when the initial search domain G_0 is not suitably chosen. In other words, the minimum of f found in G_0 lies on its boundary, suggesting the possibility of the global minimum being outside of G_0. In this case, we can change the search domains sequentially until the level set at the $m\underline{th}$ step, H_{c_m}, is contained in G_m. Let $G_k = G_m$, $k \geq m$. Then

$$H_{c_k} \subset H_{c_m} \subset G_m = G_k, \quad k \geq m$$

and

$$G_L = \bigcup_{k=0}^{m} G_k \supset G_0. \tag{3.6}$$

In this case, we may have

$$\min_{G_0} f(x) > \min_{G_L} f(x). \tag{3.7}$$

In Section 1 of Chapter V, we will present an application of this strategy in the automatic design of a thin film system. This strategy gives rise to a better design parameter than what is previously known and widely accepted.

Case 4: $\lim_{k\to\infty} G_k = G_L$ and $G_L \subset G_0$.

With prior knowledge about the objective function , we can adopt this strategy to reduce the amount of computation.

3.2 The Change of Domain Theorem

In this subsection, we will prove a theorem which is useful in treating change-of-domain strategies.

Theorem 3.1: Suppose $\{G_i\}$ is a sequence of compact subsets of a compact set K. Let

$$G_L = \mathrm{cl}\left[\bigcup_{i=1}^{\infty} G_i\right], \tag{3.8}$$

$$G_M = \bigcap_{m=1}^{\infty} \mathrm{cl}\left[\bigcup_{i=m}^{\infty} G_i\right], \tag{3.9}$$

and

$$\min_{G_i} f(x) = t_i, \quad i = 1,2,\cdots. \tag{3.10}$$

If $\{t_i\}$ is a decreasing sequence which tends to t as $i \to \infty$, then

$$\min_{G_L} f(x) = \min_{G_M} f(x) = t. \tag{3.11}$$

<u>Proof</u>: Since $G_i \subset G_L$ and $\min_{G_i} f(x) = t_i$, then

$$\min_{x \in G_L} f(x) \leq t_i, \quad \text{for } i = 1,2,\cdots,$$

so that

$$\min_{x \in G_L} f(x) \leq t. \tag{3.12}$$

If $\min_{x \in G_L} f(x) = t_L < t$, then $\exists$ a point $\hat{x} \in G_L$ such that

$$f(\hat{x}) = t_L < t.$$

Since $\hat{x} \in \mathrm{cl}\left[\bigcup_{i=1}^{\infty} G_i\right]$, there exists a sequence $\{x_r\} \subset \bigcup_{i=1}^{\infty} G_i$ such that $x_r \to \hat{x}$. We have $x_r \in G_{i_r}$ for some i_r. However,

$$f(x_r) \geq \min_{G_{i_r}} f(x) = t_r \geq t,$$

so that

$$\lim_{r\to\infty} f(x_r) = f(\hat{x}) \geq t,$$

which is a contradiction. Hence,

$$\min_{G_L} f(x) = t.$$

It is obvious that

$$\min_{G_M} f(x) \geq \min_{G_L} f(x) = t$$

since $G_M \subset G_L$. Suppose $\hat{x}_i$ is a global minimum of f over G_i, for $i = 1,2,\cdots$, i.e.,

$$f(\hat{x}_i) = t_i, \quad i = 1,2,\cdots.$$

Since $\{\hat{x}_i\}$ is contained in the compact set K, there exists a convergent subsequence $\{\hat{x}_{i_m}\}$ such that $\hat{x}_{i_m} \to \hat{x}$. Moreover,

$$\hat{x}_i \in \bigcup_{i=m}^{\infty} G_i, \quad \text{for } i \geq m,$$

so that

$$\hat{x} \in cl\left(\bigcup_{i=m}^{\infty} G_i \right) \quad \forall\, m.$$

This implies that

$$\hat{x} \in \bigcap_{m=1}^{\infty} cl\left(\bigcup_{i=m}^{\infty} G_i \right) = G_M.$$

Hence,

$$\min_{G_M} f(x) \leq f(\hat{x}) = \lim_{i_m \to \infty} f(\hat{x}_{i_m}) = \lim_{i_m \to \infty} t_{i_m} = t. \quad \blacksquare$$

This theorem gives us the following principle to select strategies for change of search domains:

$$\min_{G_k} f(x) \geq \min_{G_{k+1}} f(x), \quad \text{for } k = 0,1,2,\cdots. \tag{3.13}$$

In this manner, we can find the same global minimum of f over either G_L or G_M.

3.3 Reduction of the Skew Rate

We have seen that the reduction of the skew rate

$$\delta = \frac{2\bar{x}-(a+b)}{b-a} \tag{3.14}$$

can bring down the amount of computation. To this end, we can adopt the following change-of-domain strategy -- to move the search domains in such directions as to reduce the skew rate.

Take three constant $\delta_0 \geq 0$, $\delta_1 > \delta_2 \geq 0$. The skew rate δ is considered not too large if $|\delta| \leq \delta_0$. In this case, the search domain need not be changed. If $\delta > \delta_0$, then, instead of (2.7) and (2.8), we use

$$\zeta_1' = \zeta_1 + \delta_1\delta(\zeta_1-\zeta_0) \tag{3.15}$$

and

$$\zeta_0' = \zeta_0 + \delta_2\delta(\zeta_1-\zeta_0) \tag{3.16}$$

as the estimators of the end-points of the new search domain. Otherwise, if $\delta < -\delta_0$, the following will be used instead:

$$\zeta_1' = \zeta_1 + \delta_2\delta(\zeta_1-\zeta_0), \tag{3.17}$$

$$\zeta_o' = \zeta_o + \delta_1\delta(\zeta_1-\zeta_o). \tag{3.18}$$

The fact remains that the skew rate is unknown because we would otherwise need to know the global minimum $\bar{x}$ in advance. Suppose ξ is a random variable with probability density $p(x) > 0$ on $[a,b]$ and $\xi_1, \cdots, \xi_N$ are samples of ξ. Let $\eta_N = \min_{1\leq i\leq N} f(\xi_i)$. It is not difficult to see that if f is continuous on $[a,b]$, then η_N will tend to $f(\bar{x}) = \min_{a\leq x\leq b} f(x)$ as $N \to \infty$. Moreover, if $f(x)$ has a unique global minimum $\bar{x}$ on $[a,b]$, then $\bar{\xi}_N \to \bar{x}$ as $N \to \infty$, where $\bar{\xi}_N$ is given by $f(\bar{\xi}_N) = \eta_N$. The above discussion suggests taking

$$\hat{\delta} = \frac{2\bar{\xi}_N - (\zeta_1+\zeta_o)}{\zeta_1 - \zeta_o} \tag{3.19}$$

as an estimator for the skew rate δ (Zheng, 1981b).

§4 Remarks on Other Models

In this section, we will discuss the use of techniques specific to the models in question. In subsection 4.1, we consider the rejection and the reduction models. This is followed by the consideration of integer and mixed programming problems. We end the section with some comments on multi-solution techniques which can be used to treat problems with multiple global minima.

4.1 Rejection and Reduction Models

Suppose the constrained set S of a minimization problem is nonempty and robust. Then $\mu(S) > 0$. Let D_k denote the search cuboid at the kth iteration. Then, the ratio

$$\sigma_k = \frac{\mu(S \cap D_k)}{\mu(D_k)} \tag{4.1}$$

measures the efficiency of the search technique at the k<u>th</u> iteration.

The rejection technique is used to generate a probability density on $S \cap D_k$. For instance,

$$\rho_k(x) = \begin{cases} 0, & x \notin S \cap D_k, \\ 1/[\mu(S \cap D_k)], & x \in S \cap D_k, \end{cases} \tag{4.2}$$

which is a uniform density on $S \cap D_k$.

It is very easy to generate on a computer a random variable with probability density $\rho_k(x)$ using the rejection technique:

Step 1: Generate a uniformly distributed random variable in D_k by:

$$\xi = \{ (\xi^1, \cdots, \xi^n) \mid \xi^i = a_k^i + r^i(b_k^i - a_k^i), \ i = 1, \cdots, n \},$$

where r^i $(i = 1, \cdots, n)$ is uniformly distributed in $[0,1]$.

Step 2: If $\xi \notin S$, then (reject it and) go to Step 1. Else go to Step 3.

Step 3: $\eta = \xi$. Stop.

The number η in Step 3 will have the probability density distribution given by (4.2). The efficiency of generating η by the rejection technique is given by σ_k, which is positive due to the robustness of set S.

If the condition "$x \notin S$" is easy to verify and the efficiency is not too low, then the rejection technique is convenient for finding constrained global minima. Otherwise, the nonsequential penalty method is better.

The reduction technique is usually used in equality-constrained problems. Suppose the vector-valued constraint is given by

$$\ell(x) = 0.$$

Then, one can select a variable $y \in X_r$ and $\varphi : X_r \to X$ so that, $\forall\, x \in L = \{x \mid \ell(x) = 0\}$,

$$x = \varphi(y) \text{ for some } y \in D \subset X_r \quad \text{and} \quad \ell(\varphi(y)) = 0, \ \forall\, y \in D,$$

where X_r is a subspace of X and D is nonempty and robust in X.

<u>Example 4.1</u>: Suppose $L = \{x \in \mathbb{R}^n \mid \ell_i(x) = 0, \ i = 1, \cdots, r\}$, $\ell_i \in C^1$, i =

$1,\cdots,r$, and the Jacobian $\partial(\ell_1,\cdots,\ell_r)/\partial(x_1,\cdots,x_r) > 0$. Then, $\forall\ x = (x^1,\cdots, x^r,x^{r+1},\cdots,x^n) \in L$, there are functions $\varphi^1, \cdots, \varphi^m \in C^1$ $(m = n-r)$ such that

$$x^{r+i} = \varphi^i(x^1,\cdots,x^r), \quad i = 1,\cdots,m.$$

For $y = (x^1,\cdots,x^r) \in X_r$, we have

$$x^i = x^i,\ i = 1,\cdots,r \quad \text{and} \quad x^{r+i} = \varphi^i(x^1,\cdots,x^r), \quad i = 1,\cdots,m$$

and

$$\ell_i(\varphi(y)) = \ell_i(x^1,\cdots,x^r,\varphi^1,\cdots,\varphi^m) = \ell_i(x) = 0, \quad i = 1,\cdots,r.$$

Example 4.2: Suppose $\ell(x) = \dot{x}-g(x,t)$ with $x(0) = x^o$ and the objective function is $F(x,x^o)$. For a given x^o, one can solve, under additional hypotheses on g, the differential equation $\ell(x) = 0$ with $x(0) = x^o$. The objective function becomes

$$f(x^o) = F(x(x^o),x^o).$$

Example 4.3 (Optimal Control): Suppose $\ell(x,u) = \dot{x}-g(x,u,t)$ with $x(0) = x^o$ given. The objective function is $F(x,u)$. For a given u within some control set U, the differential equation $\ell(x,u) = 0$ can be solved: $x = x(u)$ and the objective function is $f(u) = F(x(u),u)$.

By the reduction technique, one can reduce an equality-constrained minimization problem to an unconstrained one of a lower dimension which is easier to solve.

4.2 Integer and Mixed Programming

It is not difficult to generate a random number γ_o with the following distribution:

γ_o	x_1	x_2	$\cdots$	x_N
prob	1/N	1/N	$\cdots$	1/N

In fact, let $j = [N\xi_0]+1$, where ξ_0 is uniformly distributed in [0,1]. Then $\gamma = x_j$ is the desired discrete uniform random number. Similarly, $x_{[N\xi]+1}$ is the random number with distribution

γ	x_k	x_{k+1}	...	x_{k+M}
prob	1/(M+1)	1/(M+1)	...	1/(M+1)

where $\xi = a+\xi_0(b-a)$ $((a,b) \subset (0,1))$, $a = (k-1)/N$ and $b = (k+M)/N$.

Note that, uniformity of the random number is convenient but not necessary in our framework. It is generally easier to generate a uniformly distributed random number than others.

For integer programming with countably infinite values, we can use $\gamma = x_{[1/\epsilon_0]}$ as a random number with the following probability distribution:

γ	x_1	x_2	...	x_n	...
prob	$1 - \frac{1}{2}$	$\frac{1}{2} - \frac{1}{3}$	...	$\frac{1}{n} - \frac{1}{n+1}$	...

Observe that

$$\text{Prob}(\gamma = x_n) = \frac{1}{n(n+1)} > 0, \quad \forall\, n,$$

which satisfies the requirement for our theory.

4.3 The Multi-Solution Model

The method in Section 1 can be extended to the case where the function has multiple global minima. The search domain D_k at the kth iteration can be decomposed into a union of several small cuboids of dimension n:

$$D_k = \bigcup_{j=k}^{\gamma_k} D_k^j,$$

so that each smaller cuboid D_k^j can be treated individually as in Section 1. Usually, we assume that $\gamma_k \leq m$ for each k with m as an integer given in advance.

The crucial features of this model are decomposition and combination. At the kth iteration, we may decompose the search domains into more subdomains; certain domains may be combined into one. One of the principles of decomposition and combination is the clustering approach.

§5 Numerical Tests

We consider six numerical test examples here covering the areas of unconstrained minimization, equality constraints, multiple global minima, integer programming and two kinds of discontinuous or noncontinuous minimization.

Example 5.1 (Unconstrained Minimization):

$$\underset{(x_1,x_2) \in D_o}{\text{Minimize}} \ f(x_1,x_2),$$

where f is the Rosenbrock function given by

$$f(x_1,x_2) = 100(x_2-x_1^2) + (1-x_1)^2.$$

Table IV.1 gives a comparison of our method with the LP-searching method. The results are compatible with the estimation of the amount of computation N_f derived in Section 2. There are two realized N_f's, N_I and N_{II}, for our method. The latter is obtained with an improved algorithm.

Example 5.2 (Equality Constraints):

$$\text{Minmize } f(x_1,x_2)$$

Table IV.1

	D_o	V_{D_o}	V_ε	$\bar{x}$	N_f
our method	$-5 \leq x_1 \leq 5$ $-5 \leq x_2 \leq 5$	100	10^{-10}	$x_1 = 1.00000$ $x_2 = 1.00000$	$N_I = 11250$ $N_{II} = 1420$
LP	$-1.2 \leq x_1 \leq 2$ $-1 \leq x_2 \leq 2$	9.6	$0.4 \cdot 10^{-3}$	$x_1 = 1.0103$ $x_2 = 1.0213$	$N_f = 16384$

$$\text{subject to } g(x_1,x_2) = 0,$$

where f is the Rosenbrock function and

$$g(x_1,x_2) = x_1^2x_2 - x_1x_2 + x_2^2 - 0.9x_2.$$

A unimodal function can become a multimodal one in the presence of constraints. We write g in the multiplication form $g_1 \cdot g_2$, where $g_1(x_1,x_2) = x_1^2 - x_1 + x_2 - 0.9$ and $g_2(x_1,x_2) = x_2$. We have two equality constrained subproblems, each having two local minima. Table IV.2 presents their respective global minima obtained via the reduction method. The overall global minimum value is $\bar{c}$ = 0.001162 and the set of global minima $\bar{H}$ consists of just one point, i.e., $\bar{H}$ = {(0.965932,0.932907)}.

Table IV.2

	no. of local minima	$\bar{x}$ (global minimum point)	min f
I	2	$x_1 = 0.965932$ $x_2 = 0.932907$	0.001162
II	2	$x_1 = 0.161272$ $x_2 = 0.000000$	0.771110

Example 5.3 (Multiple Global Minima): (Refer to Table IV.3.)

Table IV.3 is taken from Zhou (1982) which applies a multi-solution algorithm to certain test functions from Dixon and Szegö (1978). Zhou's results are compared with that of the cluster analysis method developed by Törn (1977; 1978).

Table IV.3

	GOLPPR $n_L = 1$			RCOS $n_L = 3$		
	N_f	min f	$\bar{x}$	N_f	min f	$\bar{x}$
our method	570	3.000000	$\begin{bmatrix}0.0000250\\-1.0000727\end{bmatrix}$	649	0.397891 0.397899 0.397895	$\begin{bmatrix}9.425091\\2.477051\end{bmatrix}$ $\begin{bmatrix}3.140882\\12.27907\end{bmatrix}$ $\begin{bmatrix}-3.143403\\12.27879\end{bmatrix}$
cluster method	2499	3.000010	$\begin{bmatrix}0.000202\\-1.000070\end{bmatrix}$	1558	0.397901	$\begin{bmatrix}3.143\\12.28\end{bmatrix}$

Example 5.4 (Integer Programming): Find the minimum of $f(x_1,x_2)$ over S, where

$$f(x_1,x_2) = [1+(x_1+x_2+1)^2(19-14x_1+3x_1^2-14x_2+6x_1x_2+3x_2^2)] \cdot [30+(2x_1-3x_2)^2(18-32x_1+12x_1^2+48x_2-36x_1x_2+27x_2^2)]$$

and

$$S = \{ (x_1,x_2) \mid x_1, x_2 = 0.01i, i = -200, -199, \cdots, 200 \}.$$

After 12 iterations, the variance VF is reduced from $0.77 \cdot 10^5$ to 0.0 and $\bar{x} = (0.00,-1.00)$, min f = 3.0, $N_f = 621$. (The function has four local minima if we consider values of x_1 and x_2 between -2 and 2.)

Example 5.5 (Lower-Semi-Continuity): Find the minimum of f over S, where

$$f(x,y) = 2(x^2+y^2) - [x^2+y^2],$$

with [z] being the integer part of z, and

$$S = \{ (x,y) \mid -10 \le x \le 10, -10 \le y \le 10\}.$$

This is a discontinuous function with numerous local minima and a unique global minimum at (0,0), where f equals zero. After 30 iterations, $N_f = 1310$, we find $\hat{x} = -3.48 \cdot 10^{-10}$, $\hat{y} = 8.19 \cdot 10^{-11}$, $\hat{f} = 2.56 \cdot 10^{-19}$ and $VF = 6.90 \cdot 10^{-35}$.

Example 5.6 (Essential Discontinuity): Find the minimum of f over S, where

$$f(x) = \begin{cases} 1 + (\Sigma_{i=1}^{n} |x_i|)^{1/2} + \operatorname{sgn}(\sin\left[(\Sigma_{i=1}^{n} |x_i|)^{-1/2} - 0.5\right]), & x \neq 0, \\ 0 & x = 0, \end{cases}$$

and

$$S = \{ x = (x_1, \cdots, x_n) \mid -1 \leq x_i \leq 1, \ i = 1, \cdots, n \}.$$

This is a discontinuous function with countably many discontinuous hypersurfaces as well as local minima. The function f has an essential discontinuity at the origin which is also the unique global minimum. As we have seen in Section II.8, f is robust, so its global minimum is accessible. We compute the global minimum using our method.

With $n = 5$, after 100 iterations and $N_f = 4962$, we estimate the global minimum to be

$$\hat{x} = (-8.93 \cdot 10^{-14}, 7.21 \cdot 10^{-14}, -3.01 \cdot 10^{-13}, 6.57 \cdot 10^{-13}, 3.05 \cdot 10^{-14})$$

and the computing estimate of the global minimum value is given by $\hat{f} = 7.27 \cdot 10^{-6}$. The sample modified variance $VF = 3.57 \cdot 10^{-12}$.

CHAPTER V

APPLICATIONS

§1 Unconstrained Problems

In this section, we present examples for the automatic design of optical thin films and optimal equalizer design for transmission lines to illustrate actual applications of global optimization to unconstrained problems.

1.1 Automatic Design of Optical Thin Films

A multi-layer thin film system or filter consists of a number of thin films deposited on a substrate and has the property of reflecting and transmitting to different degrees light of different wavelengths. The range of wavelengths for which a thin film system or filter is highly reflecting or transmitting depends on certain parameters of the component films. We will formulate the problem after stating the relevant notations and relations.

The reflectance $R[\lambda]$ at a wavelength λ of an m-layer film system is given by

$$R[\lambda] = \left|\frac{\eta_o - Y}{\eta_o + Y}\right|, \qquad Y = C/B, \tag{1.1}$$

$$\begin{bmatrix} B \\ C \end{bmatrix} = \left\{\Pi_{r=1}^{m} \begin{bmatrix} \cos\delta_r & i\cdot(\sin\delta_r)/\eta_r \\ i\cdot(\sin\delta_r)\cdot\eta_r & \cos\delta_r \end{bmatrix}\right\} \begin{bmatrix} 1 \\ \eta_m \end{bmatrix}, \tag{1.2}$$

$$\delta_r = \frac{2\pi d_r n_r \cos\theta_r}{\lambda} \tag{1.3}$$

$$\eta_r = \begin{cases} n_r \cos\theta_r, & \text{for s-component of polarization,} \\ n_r/\cos\theta_r, & \text{for p-component of polarization,} \end{cases}$$

where n_r $(r = 1,\cdots,m)$, n_o and n_s $(= n_{m+1})$ are respectively the refractive indices of the r<u>th</u> layer, the medium of incidence, and the substrate; θ_r is the angle in thr r<u>th</u> layer, related to the angle of incidence in the medium of incidence θ_o via Snell's law:

$$n_o \sin\theta_o = n_r \sin\theta_r, \quad r = 1,2,\cdots,m,m+1,$$

and d_r $(r = 1,\cdots,m)$ is the physical thickness of the r<u>th</u> layer.

The purpose of the automatic design of optical thin films is to determine the construction parameters of the film system so that the spectral reflectance $R[\lambda]$ of the system is as close as possible to some required reflectance $RD[\lambda]$. One criterion for closeness is given by the following objective function:

$$F = \|R[\lambda]-RD[\lambda]\|, \tag{1.4}$$

where $\|\cdot\|$ is a distance measure chosen in practice (one frequently chosen measure is the sum of squares of deviations). Therefore, the automatic design of the thin film system is reduced to a minimization problem. In general, the objective function is a very complicated, multimodal function of its parameters. We describe below several instances of applying global optimization to the minimization of F.

<u>Example 1.1</u>: Design a 3-layer anti-reflection coating in the 400mμ ~ 700mμ visible region, with the refractive index of the substrate $n_s = 1.75$, and the refractive index of air $n_o = 1.00$.

If we take initial search domain $D_o = [1.35, 1.35, 1.35, 50, 150, 50; 2.35, 2.35, 2.35, 200, 350, 200]$, where the first three components are refractive indices of the material and the latter three are optical thickness $n_r d_r$, then we have the minimum F curve of reflectance (with $\bar{\bar{F}} = 0.3\times10^{-3}$) shown as curve (1) in Figure V.1. If we take $D_o = [1.35, 1.35, 1.35, 50, 50, 50; 2.35, 2.35, 2.35, 400, 400, 400]$, then the computed curve of reflectance (with $\bar{\bar{F}} = 0.44\times10^{-4}$) is shown as curve (2) in Figure V.1. Design (1) has the traditional structure λ/4 - λ/2 - λ/4 whereas design (2) has λ/4 - λ/2 - λ/2 instead. The structure of design (2) is new and superior to that of design (1).

Figure V.1: 3-Layer Anti-Reflectance Films

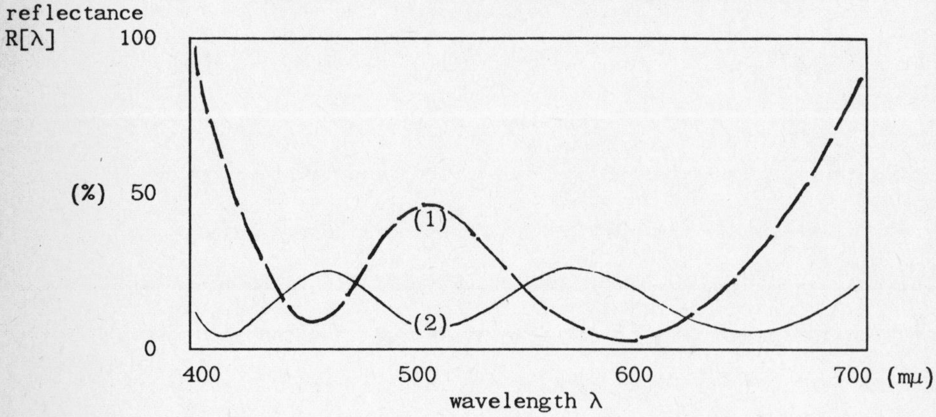

(1) $n_1 = 1.38$, $n_2 = 1.90$, $n_3 = 1.70$,
$n_1d_1 = 126.9$, $n_2d_2 = 251.3$, $n_3d_3 = 152.3$

(2) $n_1 = 1.35$, $n_2 = 1.95$, $n_3 = 1.60$,
$n_1d_1 = 126.9$, $n_2d_2 = 252.6$, $n_3d_3 = 257.6$

Figure V.2: 6-Layer Achromatic Beam Splitter

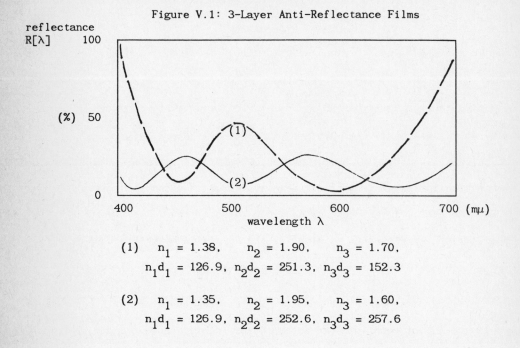

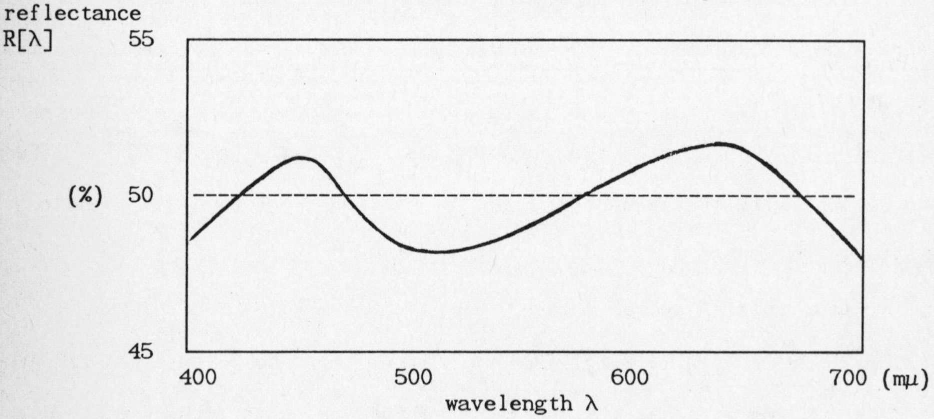

$n_o = n_s = 1.52$, $n_1 = n_3 = n_5 = 1.35$, $n_2 = n_4 = n_6 = 2.35$

$n_1d_1 = 278.49$, $n_2d_2 = 210.18$, $n_3d_3 = 176.16$

$n_4d_4 = 129.43$, $n_5d_5 = 184.56$, $n_6d_6 = 314.04$

<u>Example 1.2</u>: Design a 6-layer achromatic beam splitter over the 400mμ ~ 700mμ visible region with approximately equal reflectance and transmittance at 45° angle of incidence.

We take the maximum norm:

$$F = \max_{400 \le \lambda \le 700} |R[\lambda]-0.5| \tag{1.5}$$

and arrive at the reflectance curve shown in Figure V.2 (with $\bar{F} = 0.0139$).

Using the method suggested by Heavens and Liddell (1968) gave a similar design which is inferior to ours.

<u>Example 1.3</u>: Design a wide-band low-pass optical filter having high reflectance in the 400mμ ~ 700mμ visible region and high transmittance in the 700mμ ~ 1000mμ region, $n_o = 1.00$, $\theta_o = 0°$.

The design uses 23-layer films with refractive indices given by $n_1 = n_3 = \cdots = n_{23} = 2.35$, $n_2 = n_4 = \cdots = n_{22} = 1.35$ and $n_s = 1.52$.

In the computation, the initial region is $D_o = [a_1,\cdots,a_{23};b_1,\cdots,b_{23}]$, where $a_1 = \cdots = a_{14} = 80$mμ; $a_{15} = \cdots = a_{23} = 100$mμ; $b_1 = \cdots = b_9 = 140$mμ; $b_{10} = \cdots = b_{23} = 180$mμ. The resulting reflectance curve is shown in Figure V.3 as curve (1) with a subpeak of about 5%. This is much better than the traditional design with an approximately 15% subpeak. Using the change-of-domain algorithm, we obtain a curve of reflectance (2) with only a 1.5% subpeak.

Figure V.3: A 23-Layer Low-Pass Optical Filter

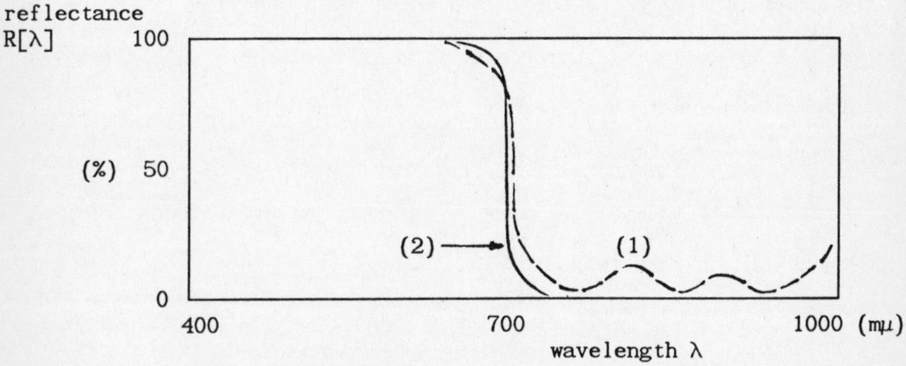

$n_i d_i$ = 48.84, 122.01, 111.88, 61.80, 117.20, 119.87, 120.91, 80.89, 102.46, 61.49, 122.66, 134.15, 128.08, 151.51, 131.35, 147.18, 146.98, 144.20, 124.34, 151.74, 147.95, 106.00, 120.92 (mμ)

1.2 Optimal Design of an Equalizer Network

We consider an equalizer network consisting of m type-T networks connected in cascade. The kth ($k = 1,\cdots,m$) type-T network is displayed in Figure V.4.

Figure V.4: A Type-T Network

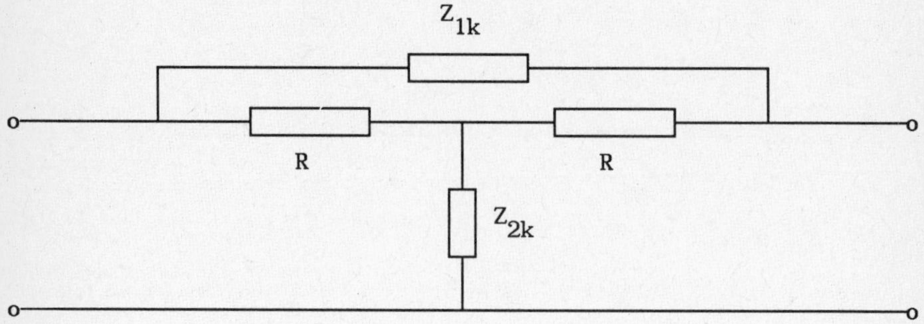

The impedance Z_{1k} is made up of certain combinations of resistance, inductance and capacitance. The impedance Z_{2k} is the conjugate inverse of Z_{1k}. The attenuation coefficient b_{sk} of the kth network is given by

$$b_{sk} = \frac{1}{2} \ln|1 + Z_{1k}/R|^2. \tag{1.6}$$

The total attenuation is $b_s = \Sigma_{k=1}^{m} b_{sk}$. Suppose there are n parameters $x_1, \cdots,$ x_n corresponding to the resistance, inductance, and capacitance component values in the impedance Z_{1k} (Z_{2k}) for the m networks in addition to the common resistance value R. Then the frequency attenuation characteristic b_s of the equalizer network is a function of $(f,R,x_1,\cdots,x_n)$, where f denotes the frequency. Given a desired frequency attenuation characteristic $\hat{b}(f)$, the problem is to find component values to minimize some "distance" measure between the realized response and the desired response. That is,

$$\underset{(R,x_1,\cdots,x_n)}{\text{Minimize}} \ \|b_s(f)-\hat{b}(f)\|, \tag{1.7}$$

where $\|\cdot\|$ denotes the distance measure used. This is a least-square procedure if we adopt the frequently used sum-of-squares norm.

<u>Example 1.4</u>: The desired frequency response $\hat{b}$ is given by

$$\hat{b}(f) = \beta_0 + 0.69(f-740)/(1290-740), \tag{1.8}$$

for $f \in [740,1290]$. The base attenuation β_0 is chosen to be $0.09N_p$.

In this example, two networks (i.e., m = 2) are employed. The corresponding impedances Z_{11} and Z_{12} are of the "parallel R-L-C" and "series L-C shunted with a resistance R" configurations, respectively. The least-square design values, with 16-point partition of the frequencey interval using global minimization, are given by R = 78.778, (R,L,C) = (103.743, 13.609, 4515.505) for the parallel impedance, and (R,L,C) = (56.101, 2.265, 3993.072) for the series-parallel impedance. The realized frequency attenuation b_s is within $0.001N_p \sim 0.002N_p$ of the ideal response $\hat{b}$ over the design frequency domain [740,1290]. This far exceeds the performance of corresponding analytic designs reported in the literature.

§2 Applications of the Rejection Method

The rejection method provides a convenient setting for implementing constrained global optimization using uniformly generated random (vector-) variable by standard random numbers generated within the computer. This technique is very effective when the efficiency σ_k (cf. expression (IV.4.1)) is not too small.

In this section, examples for optimal design of optical phase filters and automatic transmission line attenuation compensation networks will be used to illustrate the application of global optimization to inequality constrained problems.

2.1 Optimal Design of Optical Phase Filters

The Strehl Intensity (S.D.), defined as the ratio of maximum brightness with aberration to the maximum brightness of an ideal system, is a frequently used index of performance for an optical system. Suppose the aperture of an optical system is a circle of unit radius. Its S.D. is given by

$$\text{S.D.} = \frac{1}{\pi^2}\left|\int_0^{2\pi}\int_0^1 \exp(ikW)\rho d\rho d\theta\right|^2, \tag{2.1}$$

where $k = 2\pi/\lambda$ (λ is the wavelength), $W = W(\rho,\theta)$ is the wave aberration of the system. For an ideal system without aberration, S.D. = 1. In practice, the aberration of a system can be improved using a technique called apodization.

After a pupil function $F(\rho,\theta)$ is introduced, the S.D. of the system will be given by

$$\text{S.D.} = \frac{1}{\pi^2}\left|\int_0^{2\pi}\int_0^1 \exp[ik(W+F)]\rho d\rho d\theta\right|^2. \tag{2.2}$$

Obviously, if $F \equiv W$, then S.D. = 1, which is the ideal case. This has yet to be realized in actual manufacturing of optical systems. A more accessible pupil function, called the ring pupil function, is given below:

$$F(\rho,\theta) = \begin{cases} c & a_{2i-2} \le \rho < a_{2i-1} \\ 0 & a_{2i-1} \le \rho < a_{2i} \end{cases} \qquad i = 1,\cdots,m, \tag{2.3}$$

where the phase change alternates between a constant c and zero for different radii $\{a_i\}$. Consequently, the S.D. of the system with the above ring pupil function is a function $\varphi(c,a_o,\cdots,a_{2m})$ of the design parameter c and $(a_o,\cdots,a_{2m})$. The corresponding optimal design problem is stated below as an inequality constrained maximization problem:

$$\begin{aligned} &\text{Maximize} \quad \varphi(c,a_o,\cdots,a_{2m}) \\ &\text{subject to} \quad a_o = 0, \quad a_{2m} = 1, \\ &\text{and} \qquad a_{i-1} \le a_i, \quad i = 1,\cdots,2m. \end{aligned} \tag{2.4}$$

The following is a numerical example of the above problem solved by the rejection method.

Example 2.1: Suppose the wave aberration W of an optical system is given by $W(\rho) = -2\rho^2+4\rho^4$. The uncompensated S.D. of the system is 0.19474. With c = $\lambda/4$ and m = 3, the radii for the optical ring pupil function design are given by

$$a_o = 0,\ a_1 = 0.020,\ a_2 = 0.411 = a_3,\ a_4 = 0.429,\ a_5 = 0.904,\ a_6 = 1.$$

The optimally compensated S.D. of the system is 0.81346. Since the optimization approach to optical phase filter design described here is novel, we are not able to report any related works of others for the purpose of comparison.

2.2 Optimal Design of an Automatic Transmission Line Attenuation Compensation Network

Transmitting pulse-code modulation (PCM) pulse trains through audio cables is a typical method of base-band transmission. The combination of the rich harmonic content of pulse signals with the frequency-sensitive attenuation characteristics of the transmission line leads to significant attenuation and distortion after some length. This necessitates the installation at regular intervals of repeaters, each of which equalizes, amplifies and reshapes (regenerates) the attenuated and distorted pulse signals from a preceding repeater so that the receiver at the other end can eventually decode the original PCM pulse signals.

We are concerned with the optimal design of a passive automatic transmission line compensation network. The specific design considered is a Bode adaptive equalizer. Its attenuation characteristics approximate relatively closely the actual attenuation characteristics of a transmission line section. Varying the voltage applied to a certain diode (providing a dynamic resistance) in the adaptive equalizer leads to different attenuation characteristics which mimic the attenuation characteristics for transmission lines of different lengths. The control voltage may be obtained through feedback from D.C. amplifier after peak detection of the equalized and amplified pulse train. Appropriately calibrating this control voltage, which reflects the degree of attenuation and in turn the length of the intervening transmission line, the automatic compensation function of the adaptive euqalizer is realized.

In this design, we specify the range of attenuation compensation to be ±15dB at 1.024MHz. This range takes into consideration attenuation variations caused by actual variations in the length and diameter of the transmission line (±0.4km and ±0.01mm for a 1.4km, 0.6mm cable) and changes in the underground temperature (-10°C ~ +40°C). The Bode adaptive equalizer, displayed in Figure V.5, is made up of a source resistor R_g, a load resistor R_L, a series resistor R_s and an auxiliary fourport T bridge network. The characteristic resistance of the auxiliary network is R_o and its variable load resistor is R_T. The input impedance Z_1 of the auxiliary network in series with R_s is connected to the voltage divider formed by R_g and R_L.

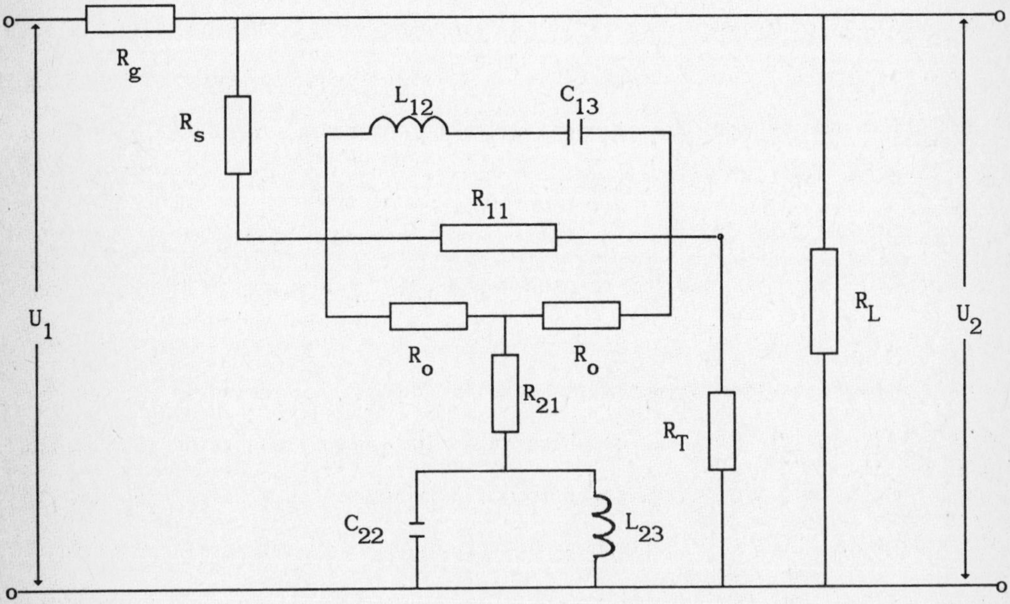

Figure V.5: A Bode Adaptive Equalizer

We can vary the attenuation characteristics of the Bode adaptive equalizer by changing R_T. The attenuation characteristic B_n of the adaptive equalizer is defined, in units of N_p ($1N_p = 8.686dB$), to be

$$B_n = \ln(U_2/U_1).$$

When $R_T = R_o$, the reactance in the auxiliary network does not play any role so that the attenuation is given by some constant B_c as shown in Figure V.6.

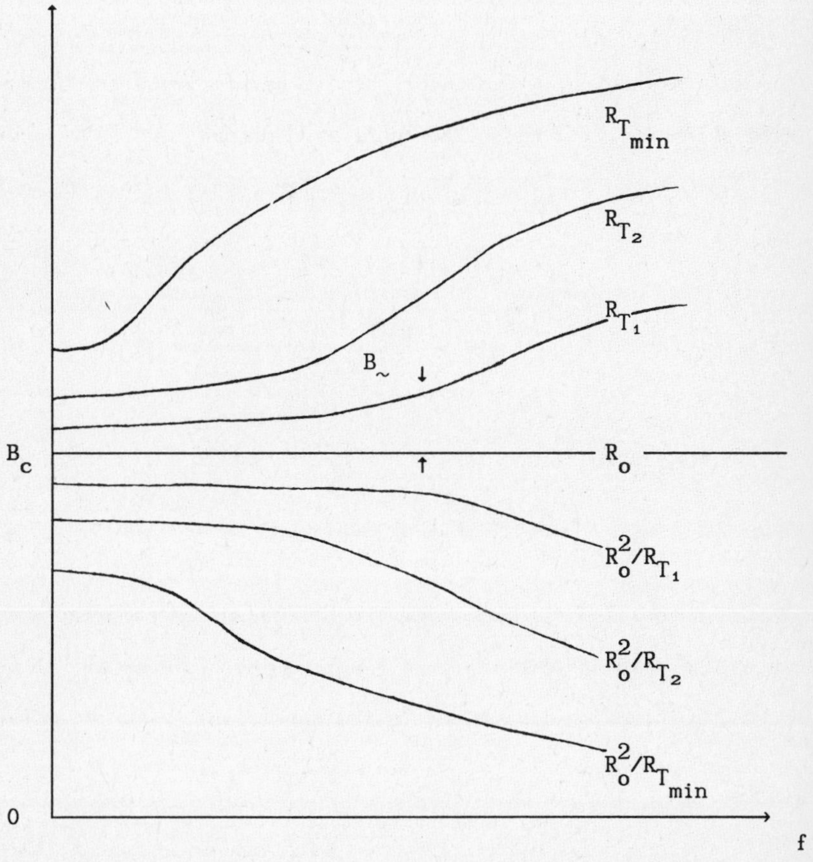

Figure V.6: Attenuation Characteristic of An Adaptive Bode Equalizer

Depending on whether $R_T > R_o$ or $R_T < R_o$, the resulting attenuation characteristic lies below or above the flat response B_c. The difference between B_n and B_c is the additional attenuation denoted by $B_\sim$. The expression for B_c as well as $B_\sim$ is given below:

$$B_c = \frac{1}{2} \ln\left[[1+(R_g/R_L)+(R_g/R_s)][1+(R_g/R_L)]\right],$$

$$B_\sim = \frac{1}{2} \ln\left[\frac{1+2\eta F+\eta^2 e^{-4b}}{1-2\eta F+\eta^2 e^{-4b}}\right].$$

where

$$\eta = \rho' \tanh(\Delta G/2),$$

$$\rho' = [1-(R_T/R_o)]/[1+(R_T/R_o)],$$

$$\Delta G = \ln(R_o/R_s),$$

$$F = e^{-2b}\cos(2a).$$

The parameters a and b, given below, denote respectively the attenuation and the phase-shift coefficient of the auxiliary network.

$$b = \frac{1}{2}\ln\left[[1+Y^2(1+(R_{11}/R_o))^2]/[1+Y^2]\right],$$

$$Y = (2\pi L_{12}/R_{11})f - 1/(2\pi R_{11}C_{13}f),$$

$$\cos(2a) = [1-\cosh(b_m)+\cosh(b_m-2b)]/[1+\cosh(b_m)],$$

$$b_m = \ln\left[1+(R_{11}/R_o)\right].$$

Furthermore, we have a relation between R_g, R_L, R_s and R_o:

$$R_s^2 + \left[\frac{R_g R_L}{R_g+R_L}\right]R_s - R_o^2 = 0.$$

The design objective is to minimize the difference between the additional attenuation $B_{\sim}$ and some desired response B which, in this example, is given in Table V.1. The minimization is subject to the constraint:

$$B_c < 3N_p \quad (\sim 26\text{dB}),$$

which reflects the need of not having B_c too small so as to reduce the possible instability caused by very high amplification subsequently required.

The component values and the initial search domain for implementing the rejection method for this problem are given below:

$$R_o = 200\Omega, \quad R_{T_{min}} = 10\Omega, \quad R_{T_{max}} = 4000\Omega,$$

$$R_g = 1k \sim 10k, \quad R_s = 1\Omega \sim 100\Omega, \quad R_L = 1k \sim 5k, \quad R_{11} = 10\Omega \sim 1k,$$

$$L_{12} = 0.5\mu H \sim 10\mu H, \quad C_{13} = 1000PF \sim 10000PF.$$

The results of our computation are presented in Table V.1. The component values corresponding to our solution are:

$$R_g = 3693\Omega, \quad R_s = 18.75\Omega, \quad R_L = 4946\Omega, \quad R_{11} = 166.7\Omega,$$

$$R_{T_{min}} = 10\Omega, \quad R_{T_{max}} = 4000\Omega,$$

$$L_{12} = 1.00\mu H, \quad C_{13} = 6300PF.$$

Table V.1: $B_{\sim}(f)$

f(kHz)	10	20	30	50	100	200	300	500	772	900	1024	1300	1500	1800	2048
$B_{\sim}$(dB)	3.9	3.9	3.9	4.0	4.5	5.6	7.3	10.3	13.2	14.1	14.8	15.9	16.3	16.4	16.5
B(dB)	3.7	3.7	3.8	3.9	4.7	6.2	7.6	10.0	12.8	13.9	14.9	17.1	18.5	20.6	22.2

The optimal design of the Bode adaptive equalizer described above is being used in the PCM 30/32 regenerative repeaters of the Shanghai Municipality Telephone Company in China.

§3 Applications of the Reduction Method

The typical problem examined here has the following form:

$$\text{Minimize } f(x) \tag{3.1}$$
$$\text{subject to } \ell(x) = 0,$$

where $\ell(x) = 0$ is a functional equation, a differential equation, or an integral equation. Suppose the variable x can be decomposed into $x = (y,u)$ such that $\ell(x) = \ell(y,u) = 0$ can be solved with y as a function of u, i.e.,

$$y = y(u). \tag{3.2}$$

Then, the minimization problem (3.1) becomes the following unconstrained one:

$$\min_u f(y(u),u). \tag{3.3}$$

Examples in the optimal design of a turbine wheel and the identification problem in dynamic systems will be discussed here.

3.1 Optimal Design of a Turbine Wheel

In the design of a turbine wheel, it is desirable under operating conditions that the entire body remains in the elastic state. Meanwhile, for efficiency in material utilization, it is best to achieve a so-called "constant strength" design, yielding equal and constant biaxial stress at every point of the main body of the wheel. Consider a circular rotating disk of variable thickness h(r) and radial temperature gradient dT/dr. The equilibrium equation is given by:

$$\frac{d}{dr}(rh\sigma_r) - h\sigma_\theta + \rho\omega^2 hr^2 = 0, \tag{3.4}$$

where σ_r and σ_θ are the radial and tangential stress, and ρ is the mass density. The condition for compatibility can be expressed in terms of the stress components as:

$$\left[\frac{d\sigma_\theta}{dr} - \upsilon\frac{d\sigma_r}{dr}\right] + \frac{1+\upsilon}{r}(\sigma_\theta-\sigma_r) + E\alpha\frac{dT}{dr} = 0, \tag{3.5}$$

where υ is the Poisson's ratio and E is the Young's modulus.

The following are candidates for the objective function of the alternative turbine wheel designs in terms of their closeness to the desired "constant stress" state:

$$F_1 = \|\sigma_r - c_1\| + \|\sigma_\theta - c_2\|, \tag{3.6}$$

$$F_2 = \|\Delta\sigma_r\| + \|\Delta\sigma_\theta\|, \tag{3.7}$$

$$F_3 = |\Delta\sigma_r| + |\Delta\sigma_\theta| + |\sigma_\theta|, \tag{3.8}$$

$$F_4 = \max\{|\sigma_r|_\infty, |\sigma_\theta|_\infty\}, \tag{3.9}$$

and

$$F_5 = F_3 + |\sigma_r - \sigma_\theta|_\infty, \tag{3.10}$$

where $\|\cdot\|$ is the L^2 norm and $|\cdot|_\infty$ is the L^∞ norm.

To facilitate the optimization of the disk profile design, we reduce the basic equations (3.4) and (3.5) to

$$\frac{d^2k}{dr^2} + A\frac{dk}{dr} + Bk = C, \tag{3.11}$$

where

$$k(r) = \gamma h\sigma_r/\sigma_o, \tag{3.12}$$

$$A(r) = \frac{1}{r} - \frac{1}{h}\frac{dh}{dr}, \tag{3.13}$$

$$B(r) = \frac{\upsilon}{rh}\frac{dh}{dr} - \frac{1}{r^2}, \tag{3.14}$$

and

$$C(r) = -\frac{1}{\sigma_o}\left[(3+\upsilon)\rho\omega^2 rh + E\alpha h\frac{dT}{dr}\right]. \tag{3.15}$$

We have, in addition,

$$\sigma_\theta = \frac{\sigma_o}{h}\left[\frac{dk}{dr} + \frac{\rho\omega^2 r^2 h}{\sigma_o}\right], \tag{3.16}$$

where ω is the angular velocity and σ_o is a constant equal to the radial stress on the outer boundary due to the "dead" rim load. The boundary conditions can be expressed as

$$k_1 = r\left[\frac{dk}{dr} + \frac{\rho\omega^2 r^2 h}{\sigma_o}\right], \quad \text{at } r = r_1, \tag{3.17}$$

and

$$k_o = r_o h_r, \quad \text{at } r = r_o.$$

By dividing the radius into n-1 equal intervals, the finite difference representation of (3.11) for the ith station is given below:

$$k_i - [2 + A_{i+1}\Delta r - B_{i+1}(\Delta r)^2]k_{i+1} + (1 + A_{i+1}\Delta r)k_{i+2} = C_{i+1}(\Delta r)^2, \tag{3.18}$$

with boundary conditions

$$k_1 = r_1\left[\frac{k_2-k_1}{r} + \frac{h_1\rho\omega^2 r_1^2}{\sigma_o}\right]$$

and

$$k_n = r_n h_n.$$

Given h_i, $i = 1,\cdots,n$, one can find σ_r and σ_θ. Therefore the objective function is reduced to a function of h_i, $i = 1,2,\cdots,n$.

There is no essential improvement after applying standard local optimization methods. Using the reduction global method, however, Hu and Pan (1982) have obtained finer solutions.

Table V.2 tabulates the ratio of the volume of the optimal design disk to that of the optimal flat disk for the various objective functions.

Table V.2: Comparison of Ratios of Volumes

objective functions	F_1	F_2	F_3	F_4	F_5
ratio	0.564	0.760	0.578	0.627	0.670

3.2 Nonlinear Observation and Identification

Consider a dynamic system

$$\frac{dx}{dt} = f(x,t,c,u), \quad t \geq t_o, \tag{3.19}$$

where x is the n-vector state, c is an unknown vector parameter, u is a known control and t is the time variable. The known function satisfies standard conditions for the existence and uniqueness of solution x(t), given initial data $x(t_o) = x_o$ which is unknown.

On the trajectories of the system (3.19) are the measured output r-vector given by

$$y = h(x,t,p,u), \quad t \geq t_o, \tag{3.20}$$

where $p \in \mathbb{R}^m$ is an unknown parameter. The equation (3.20) is not generally solvable for x, e.g., whenever $r < n$.

The problem is to find an operation to determine the vectors $x(t_o)$, c, p, given the output (3.20) on a small interval of a real trajectory of the system

(3.19). We assume that the control is piecewise continuous.

Take $t_o \geq 0$ and positive values θ, $\alpha_s \leq 1$ $(s = 1,\cdots,q)$. Define:

Computed Vector	Generating Function	
$Y(t_o) = y(t_o)$	$F_o(x_o,t_o,p) = h(x_o,t_o,p)$	(3.21)
$Y_s(t_o) = \int_{t_o}^{t_s} y(w)dw,$	$F_s(x_o,t_o,p,c) = \int_{t_o}^{t_s} h[G(x_o,t_o,c,w),w,p]dw,$	(3.22)

$$s = 1,\cdots,q; \quad t_s = t_o+\theta\alpha_s,$$

where G is the integration operator for the system (3.19) by which we mean a method to determine the coordinates $x_i(t)$ given c, u(t) and the initial data $x_o = x(t_o)$:

$$x(t) = G(x_o,t_o,c,t), \quad t \geq t_o \geq 0. \tag{3.23}$$

Denoting $(x_o^\tau,p^\tau,c^\tau) = z^\tau$ ("τ" indicates transpose), we construct the following objective function:

$$S(z,t_o) = \|Y(t_o)-F(z,t_o)\|,$$

where $F^\tau = (F_o^\tau,F_1^\tau,\cdots,F_q^\tau)$, $Y^\tau = (Y_o^\tau,Y_1^\tau,\cdots,Y_q^\tau)$, and $\|\cdot\|$ is an appropriately chosen norm. The problem reduces to finding the global minimum of $S(z,t_o)$.

Observability condition can rule out the possibility of an infinite set of solutions with $S(z,t_o) = 0$. In the nonlinear case, however, the set of global minima may be finite. Galperin (1972) discussed two ways of discriminating among extraneous solutions.

Example 3.1: Let us consider the small oscillation of a simple pendulum

$$\ddot{x} + \omega^2 x = 0, \tag{3.24}$$

where ω is the angular velocity. The observation is taken to be

$$y(t) = \dot{x}^2. \tag{3.25}$$

The general solution of (3.24) is

$$x(t) = a\cos(\omega t+\alpha), \tag{3.26}$$

and the initial data $x(t_o)$ and $\dot{x}(t_o)$ are expressed uniquely by the arbitrary constants a and α. We shall attempt to determine a and α from the measured signal (3.25).

The component of the vector $Y = \{Y_o, Y_1\}$ are formed by

$$Y_o = y(t_o); \quad Y_1 = \int_{t_o}^{t_o+\theta} y(\tau)d\tau, \quad (\theta > 0).$$

Applying the L^2 norm to the objective function $S(z, t_o)$, we consider the following parameters: $\omega = 1.0$, $\theta = 1.0$, $t_o = 0.0$, 0.2 and 0.5. Table V.3 displays the computation results. The initial search domain for parameters a and α is given by $D_o = [1.5, 0.5; 2.5, 1.5]$.

Table V.3*

ω	1.0	1.0	1.0
θ	1.0	1.0	1.0
t_o	0.0	0.2	0.5
a	2.0	2.0	2.0
$\hat{a}$	2.00000	2.00000	2.00000
α	1.0	1.0	1.0
$\hat{\alpha}$	1.00000	1.00000	1.00000
Y_1	2.83229	3.47479	3.97999
$\hat{Y}_1 - Y_1$	$5.00679 \cdot 10^{-6}$	$1.66893 \cdot 10^{-6}$	$-0.953674 \cdot 10^{-7}$
Y_2	3.66610	3.62707	3.10005
$\hat{Y}_2 - Y_2$	$3.8147 \cdot 10^{-6}$	$4.29153 \cdot 10^{-6}$	$-1.90735 \cdot 10^{-6}$
S_{min}	$3.96199 \cdot 10^{-11}$	$2.1206 \cdot 10^{-11}$	$4.54747 \cdot 10^{-12}$
$V_1 f$	$3.64516 \cdot 10^{-19}$	$2.17815 \cdot 10^{-17}$	$1.83110 \cdot 10^{-20}$
N_{it}†	19	14	16

$$S^2 = w_1[Y_1 - \hat{Y}_1]^2 + w_2|Y_2 - \hat{Y}_2|^2, \quad w_1 = w_2 = 1.$$

† N_{it} = number of iterations

* The computation was done on an Osborne 01.

§4 An Application of the Penalty Method

When a priori knowledge of a constrained minimization problem suggests that the feasible region is highly irregular or constitutes a very small fraction of some reasonable initial search cuboid, the penalty method may be expected to work more efficiently than the rejection method. This will be illustrated by an example of the weight minimization of a speed reducer for small aircraft engines.

4.1 Weight Minimization of a Speed Reducer

In the design of a speed reducer for small aircraft engines, a primary concern is the minimization of its weight. It affects, for instance, the power-rating which is usually stated in terms of horsepower per engine weight as well as the costs of material and operations. Golinski (1970) formulated this problem as a nonlinear minimization problem with constraints on design parameters including power transmission gas bending capacity, contact stress, the deflection and stress of shafts, and various constraints on the dimension of the weight reducer. Golinski's computational results were improved upon by Lee (1977) in a subsequent paper using a heuristic combinational algorithm.

The constrained minimization problem as formulated by Lee is stated below. The reader is referred to the original reference for the meaning of the parameters and the derivation of the objective function.

$$\text{Minimize } 0.7854x_1x_2^2(3.3333x_3^2+14.9334x_3-43.0934) - 1.5080x_1(x_6^2 + x_7^2) + 7.4770(x_6^3+x_7^3) + 0.7854(x_4x_6^2+x_5x_7^2) \quad (4.1)$$

subject to

$$x_1x_2^2x_3 \geq 27, \quad (4.2)$$

$$x_1x_2^2x_3^2 \geq 397.5, \tag{4.3}$$

$$x_2x_3x_6^4/x_4^3 \geq 1.93, \tag{4.4}$$

$$x_2x_3x_7^4/x_5^3 \geq 1.93, \tag{4.5}$$

$$A_1/B_1 \leq 1100, \tag{4.6}$$

where

$$A_1 = \left([\frac{745x_4}{x_2x_3}]^2 + 16.91\cdot10^6\right)^{1/2}, \tag{4.7}$$

$$B_1 = 0.1x_6^3; \tag{4.8}$$

and

$$A_2/B_2 \leq 850, \tag{4.9}$$

where

$$A_2 = \left([\frac{745x_5}{x_2x_3}]^2 + 157.5\cdot10^6\right)^{1/2}, \tag{4.10}$$

$$B_2 = 0.1x_7^3; \tag{4.11}$$

$$x_2x_3 \leq 40, \tag{4.12}$$

$$x_1/x_2 > 5, \tag{4.13}$$

$$x_1/x_2 \leq 12, \tag{4.14}$$

$$1.5x_6 + 1.9 \leq x_4, \tag{4.15}$$

$$1.1x_7 + 1.9 \leq x_5, \tag{4.16}$$

$$2.6 \leq x_1 \leq 3.6, \tag{4.17}$$

$$0.7 \leq x_2 \leq 0.8, \tag{4.18}$$

$$17 \leq x_3 \leq 28, \tag{4.19}$$

$$7.3 \leq x_4 \leq 8.3, \tag{4.20}$$

$$7.3 \leq x_5 \leq 8.3, \tag{4.21}$$

$$2.9 \leq x_6 \leq 3.9, \tag{4.22}$$

$$5.0 \leq x_7 \leq 5.5. \tag{4.23}$$

Lee (1977) reported in his Table 2 the results of two implementations -- the adaptive optimization approach of Golinski (1970) and the heuristic combinational optimization based on Lin's (1965) earlier work with the penalty function equal to zero at their minima where F = 3518 and 2856, respectively. Paradoxically, neither minimum satisfies the given constraints. Applying the nonsequential penalty method, Zheng (1981) identified a feasible minimum point:

$$\bar{x} = (3.5, 0.7, 17, 7.3, 7.71, 3.35, 5287) \text{ with } F_{min} = 2994.47.$$

Relaxing the constraints (4.17), (4.18) and (4.20) (by changing the parameter 3.6 in (4.17) to 4.4; the parameter 0.7 in (4.18) to 0.6 and the parameter 7.3 in (4.20) to 6.6) so as to make Lee's solution feasible, the nonsequential penalty method yields a better minimum with $F_{min} = 2821.76$.

§5 An Application of Integer and Mixed Programming

Many application problems can be formulated as integer or mixed programming problems. Some problems involving continuous variables may become integer or mixed programming ones due to manufacturing or material constraints. The example in subsection 5.1 illustrates an application of the global mixed programming algorithm.

5.1 Optimal Design of an Optical Thin Film System

As we have mentioned in Section 1, the reflectance $R[\lambda]$ of an optical thin film system is a function of the refraction indices and the thickness of the film system. When we can only choose from a finite set of refractive indices corresponding to the available thin film material, the optimal design of the optical thin film system becomes a mixed programming problem.

Example 5.1: Design a 3-layer anti-reflection coating in the 400mμ ~ 700mμ visible region. The refractive index of the substrate is $n_s = 1.75$.

We have six variables. The feasible region S is given by

$$S = \{\ x = (x^1,\cdots,x^6)\ |\ x^1,x^2,x^3 \in I \text{ and } 50m\mu \leq x^4,\ x^5,\ x^6 \leq 400m\mu\ \},$$

where the first three variables take values in the finite set I consisting of the available refractive indices:

$$I = \{1.35,\ 1.38,\ 1.46,\ 1.52,\ 1.59,\ 1.60,\ 1.63,\ 1.75,\ 1.80$$
$$1.92,\ 1.95,\ 2.00,\ 2.04,\ 2.10,\ 2.20,\ 2.30,\ 2.35\}.$$

The following objective functions were used to design this anti-reflection coating. For each objective function F, we use $\bar{F}$ to denote the minimum value obtained by the global optimization algorithm.

(1) Sum-of-squares: $F = \Sigma_{\lambda=1}^{16}(R[\lambda])^2$, $\bar{F} = 0.414 \cdot 10^{-4}$.

(2) Sum-of-absolute values: $F = \Sigma_{\lambda=1}^{16}|R[\lambda]|$, $\bar{F} = 0.210 \cdot 10^{-1}$.

(3) Maximum value: $F = \max_{\lambda} |R[\lambda]|$, $\bar{F} = 0.244 \cdot 10^{-2}$.

Table V.4 gives these designs.

Table V.4: Alternative Designs of A 3-Layer Anti-Reflection Coating

	n_1	n_2	n_3	n_1d_1	n_2d_2	n_3d_3
F_1	1.35	1.95	1.59	126.86mμ	253.49mμ	254.37mμ
F_2	1.35	1.95	1.59	127.53mμ	253.42mμ	254.53mμ
F_3	1.35	1.92	1.59	127.32mμ	254.47mμ	254.72mμ

Bibliography

Basaraa, M.S. and C.M. Shetty, *Foundations of Optimization*, Lecture Notes in Economics and Mathematical Systems, No.161, Springer-Verlag, 1976.

Clarke, F.H., "Generalized Gradient and Applications," *Trans. American Math. Soc.* 205 (1975): 247-262.

Clarke, F.H., "A New Approach to Lagrange Multipliers," *Mathematics of Operations Research 1* (1976): 165-174.

Delano, E., "First-Order Design and the y, $\bar{y}$ Diagram," *Applied Optics* 2 (1963): 1251-1256.

Dixon, L.C.W. and G.P. Szegö, "The Global Optimization Problem," an introduction in *Towards Global Optimization* 2, edited by L.C.W. Dixon and G.P. Szegö, North-Holland, 1978.

Gal'perin, YE.A., "Observation Procedures for Nonlinear Systems," *Engineering Cybernetics 1* (1972): 165-172.

Gal'perin, YE.A. and Zheng Q., "Nonlinear Observation via Global Optimization Methods," *the Proceedings of the 1983 Conference on Information Science and Systems*, March 23-25, 1983.

Girsanov, I.V. *Lecture on Mathematical Theory of Extremum Problems*, Lecture Notes in Economics and Mathematical Systems, No.67, Springer-Verlag, 1972.

Golinski, J., "Optimal Synthesis Problems Solved by Means of Nonlinear Programming and Random Methods," *Journal of Mechanisms* 5 (1970): 287-309.

Heavens, O.S., H.M. Liddell, "Least-Squares Method for the Automatic Design of Multi-Layers," *Optica Acta 15* (1968): 129-138.

Hiriart-Urruty, J.B., "On Optimality Conditions in Nondifferentiable Programming," *Mathematical Programming 14* (1978): 73-86.

Hiriart-Urruty, J.B., "Tangent Cones, Generalized Gradients and Mathematical Programming in Banach Spaces," *Mathematics of Operations Research 4* (1979): 79-97.

Hu L.W. and Pan X.C., "Optimal Design of Rotating Disk with Temperature Gradient," Working Paper, Department of Engineering Science and Mechanics, the Pennsylvania State University, 1982.

Lee L.E., "Weight Minimizations of a Speed Reducer," an ASME publication, 77-DET-163, 1977.

Lin R.J. and Zheng Q., "Autoequilibrium of PCM Transmission Network," *Journal of Shanghai University of Science and Technology* (1978): 57-82.

Lin S., "Computer Solutions of the Travelling Salesman Problems," *the Bell System Technical Journal 44* (1965): 2245-2269.

Mangasarian, O.L., *Nonlinear Programming*, New York: McGraw-Hill, 1969.

Nelder, J.A. and R. Mead, "A Simplex Method for Function Minimization," *Computer Journal 7* (1965): 308-313.

Rockafellar, R.T., *Convex Analysis*, Princeton: Princeton University Press, 1970.

Sobol, J.M. and M.A. Statnikov, "Testing of LP-Searching Method on Some Test Functions," in *Stochastic Searching Problems* 2, edited by L.A. Rastrigin, 1973.

Törn, A.O., "Cluster Analysis Using Seed Points and Density-Determined Hyperspheres with an Applicaton to Global Optimization," *IEEE Transactions on Systems, Man and Cybernetics* (1977): 394-398.

Törn, A.O., "A Search-Clustering Approach to Global Optimization," in *Towards Global Optimization*, edited by L.C.W. Dixon and G.P. Szegö, North-Holland, 1978.

Zhang L.S., "On the Set of Global Minima under Adaptive Change of Search Domain," *Numerical Mathematics*, No.3 (1981): 1-7 (in Chinese).

Zheng Q., "A Method for Searching Global Extrema: Construction and Implementation," *Nature*, No.1 (1978): 1-2 (in Chinese).

Zheng Q., "Problems of Global Optimization with Adaptive Change of Search Domain," *Numerical Mathematics*, No.1 (1979): 143-149 (in Chinese).

Zheng Q., "On Optimality Conditions for Global Extremum Problems," *Numerical Mathematics*, No.3 (1981a): 273-275 (in Chinese).

Zheng Q., "Strategies of Changed Domain for Searching Global Extrema," *Numerical Computation and Applications of Computer*, No.2 (1981b): 257-261 (in Chinese).

Zheng Q., "Higher Moments and Optimality Conditions for Global Extremum Problems," *Chinese Journal of Operations Research*, No.1 (1982a): 73-74 (in Chinese).

Zheng Q., "Rejection and Reduction Methods for Finding Global Minima," *Numerical Mathematics*, No.3 (1982b): 283-287 (in Chinese).

Zheng Q., "Optimality Conditions of Global Minimum with Constraints," *Numerical Mathematics*, No.4 (1982c): 94-95 (in Chinese).

Zheng Q., "Penalty Global Optimality Conditions," *Chinese Journal of Operations Research*, No.1 (1983): 56-58 (in Chinese).

Zheng Q., Tang J.F. and Jiang B.C., "Automatic Design of Optical Thin Films (II): A Numerical Optimization Method and Its Applications," *Journal of Zhejiang University* (1980): 1-14 (in Chinese).

Zheng Q. and Tao Z., "Reduced Methods and Optimality Conditions of Global Extremum Problem with Linear Equality Constraints," Research Report of Department of Mathematics No.8199, Pennsylvania State University, 1981.

Zheng Q., Jiang B.C. and Zhuang S.L., "A Method for Finding Global Extrema," *Acta Mathematicae Applagatae Sinica* No.1 (1978): 161-174 (in Chinese).

Zheng Q. and Zhang L.S., "Penalty Function and Global Optimization Problem with Inequality Constraints," *Computation Mathematics*, No.3 (1980): 146-153 (in Chinese).

Zhou J., "A Modified Method for Finding Global Minimum," Master Degree paper, Department of Mathematics, Shanghai University of Science and Technology, 1982.

Zhuang S.L., Jiang B.C. and Zheng Q., "Real-Time Compensation for the Aberrations of Optical Systems," *Acta Optica Sinica*, No.1 (1981): 59-66 (in Chinese).

Zhuang S.L., Zheng Q. and Yu F.T.S., "Automatic Generation of Prototype Lenses," *Optics Letters* 7 (1982): 581-583.

Vol. 211: P. van den Heuvel, The Stability of a Macroeconomic System with Quantity Constraints. VII, 169 pages. 1983.

Vol. 212: R. Sato and T. Nôno, Invariance Principles and the Structure of Technology. V, 94 pages. 1983.

Vol. 213: Aspiration Levels in Bargaining and Economic Decision Making. Proceedings, 1982. Edited by R. Tietz. VIII, 406 pages. 1983.

Vol. 214: M. Faber, H. Niemes und G. Stephan, Entropie, Umweltschutz und Rohstoffverbrauch. IX, 181 Seiten. 1983.

Vol. 215: Semi-Infinite Programming and Applications. Proceedings, 1981. Edited by A. V. Fiacco and K. O. Kortanek. XI, 322 pages. 1983.

Vol. 216: H. H. Müller, Fiscal Policies in a General Equilibrium Model with Persistent Unemployment. VI, 92 pages. 1983.

Vol. 217: Ch. Grootaert, The Relation Between Final Demand and Income Distribution. XIV, 105 pages. 1983.

Vol. 218: P. van Loon, A Dynamic Theory of the Firm: Production, Finance and Investment. VII, 191 pages. 1983.

Vol. 219: E. van Damme, Refinements of the Nash Equilibrium Concept. VI, 151 pages. 1983.

Vol. 220: M. Aoki, Notes on Economic Time Series Analysis: System Theoretic Perspectives. IX, 249 pages. 1983.

Vol. 221: S. Nakamura, An Inter-Industry Translog Model of Prices and Technical Change for the West German Economy. XIV, 290 pages. 1984.

Vol. 222: P. Meier, Energy Systems Analysis for Developing Countries. VI, 344 pages. 1984.

Vol. 223: W. Trockel, Market Demand. VIII, 205 pages. 1984.

Vol. 224: M. Kiy, Ein disaggregiertes Prognosesystem für die Bundesrepublik Deutschland. XVIII, 276 Seiten. 1984.

Vol. 225: T. R. von Ungern-Sternberg, Zur Analyse von Märkten mit unvollständiger Nachfragerinformation. IX, 125 Seiten. 1984

Vol. 226: Selected Topics in Operations Research and Mathematical Economics. Proceedings, 1983. Edited by G. Hammer and D. Pallaschke. IX, 478 pages. 1984.

Vol. 227: Risk and Capital. Proceedings, 1983. Edited by G. Bamberg and K. Spremann. VII, 306 pages. 1984.

Vol. 228: Nonlinear Models of Fluctuating Growth. Proceedings, 1983. Edited by R. M. Goodwin, M. Krüger and A. Vercelli. XVII, 277 pages. 1984.

Vol. 229: Interactive Decision Analysis. Proceedings, 1983. Edited by M. Grauer and A. P. Wierzbicki. VIII, 269 pages. 1984.

Vol. 230: Macro-Economic Planning with Conflicting Goals. Proceedings, 1982. Edited by M. Despontin, P. Nijkamp and J. Spronk. VI, 297 pages. 1984.

Vol. 231: G. F. Newell, The M/M/∞ Service System with Ranked Servers in Heavy Traffic. XI, 126 pages. 1984.

Vol. 232: L. Bauwens, Bayesian Full Information Analysis of Simultaneous Equation Models Using Integration by Monte Carlo. VI, 114 pages. 1984.

Vol. 233: G. Wagenhals, The World Copper Market. XI, 190 pages. 1984.

Vol. 234: B.C. Eaves, A Course in Triangulations for Solving Equations with Deformations. III, 302 pages. 1984.

Vol. 235: Stochastic Models in Reliability Theory. Proceedings, 1984. Edited by S. Osaki and Y. Hatoyama. VII, 212 pages. 1984.

Vol. 236: G. Gandolfo, P.C. Padoan, A Disequilibrium Model of Real and Financial Accumulation in an Open Economy. VI, 172 pages. 1984.

Vol. 237: Misspecification Analysis. Proceedings, 1983. Edited by T. K. Dijkstra. V, 129 pages. 1984.

Vol. 238: W. Domschke, A. Drexl, Location and Layout Planning. IV, 134 pages. 1985.

Vol. 239: Microeconomic Models of Housing Markets. Edited by K. Stahl. VII, 197 pages. 1985.

Vol. 240: Contributions to Operations Research. Proceedings, 1984. Edited by K. Neumann and D. Pallaschke. V, 190 pages. 1985.

Vol. 241: U. Wittmann, Das Konzept rationaler Preiserwartungen. XI, 310 Seiten. 1985.

Vol. 242: Decision Making with Multiple Objectives. Proceedings, 1984. Edited by Y. Y. Haimes and V. Chankong. XI, 571 pages. 1985.

Vol. 243: Integer Programming and Related Areas. A Classified Bibliography 1981–1984. Edited by R. von Randow. XX, 386 pages. 1985.

Vol. 244: Advances in Equilibrium Theory. Proceedings, 1984. Edited by C. D. Aliprantis, O. Burkinshaw and N. J. Rothman. II, 235 pages. 1985.

Vol. 245: J. E. M. Wilhelm, Arbitrage Theory. VII, 114 pages. 1985.

Vol. 246: P. W. Otter, Dynamic Feature Space Modelling, Filtering and Self-Tuning Control of Stochastic Systems. XIV, 177 pages. 1985.

Vol. 247: Optimization and Discrete Choice in Urban Systems. Proceedings, 1983. Edited by B.G. Hutchinson, P. Nijkamp and M. Batty. VI, 371 pages. 1985.

Vol. 248: Plural Rationality and Interactive Decision Processes. Proceedings, 1984. Edited by M. Grauer, M. Thompson and A.P. Wierzbicki. VI, 354 pages. 1985.

Vol. 249: Spatial Price Equilibrium: Advances in Theory, Computation and Application. Proceedings, 1984. Edited by P. T. Harker. VII, 277 pages. 1985.

Vol. 250: M. Roubens, Ph. Vincke, Preference Modelling. VIII, 94 pages. 1985.

Vol. 251: Input-Output Modeling. Proceedings, 1984. Edited by A. Smyshlyaev. VI, 261 pages. 1985.

Vol. 252: A. Birolini, On the Use of Stochastic Processes in Modeling Reliability Problems. VI, 105 pages. 1985.

Vol. 253: C. Withagen, Economic Theory and International Trade in Natural Exhaustible Resources. VI, 172 pages. 1985.

Vol. 254: S. Müller, Arbitrage Pricing of Contingent Claims. VIII, 151 pages. 1985.

Vol. 255: Nondifferentiable Optimization: Motivations and Applications. Proceedings, 1984. Edited by V.F. Demyanov and D. Pallaschke. VI, 350 pages. 1985.

Vol. 256: Convexity and Duality in Optimization. Proceedings, 1984. Edited by J. Ponstein. V, 142 pages. 1985.

Vol. 257: Dynamics of Macrosystems. Proceedings, 1984. Edited by J.-P. Aubin, D. Saari and K. Sigmund. VI, 280 pages. 1985.

Vol. 258: H. Funke, Eine allgemeine Theorie der Polypol- und Oligopolpreisbildung. III, 237 pages. 1985.

Vol. 259: Infinite Programming. Proceedings, 1984. Edited by E. J. Anderson and A. B. Philpott. XIV, 244 pages. 1985.

Vol. 260: H.-J. Kruse, Degeneracy Graphs and the Neighbourhood Problem. VIII, 128 pages. 1986.

Vol. 261: Th. R. Gulledge, Jr., N. K. Womer, The Economics of Made-to-Order Production. VI, 134 pages. 1986.

Vol. 262: H.U. Buhl, A Neo-Classical Theory of Distribution and Wealth. V, 146 pages. 1986.

Vol. 263: M. Schäfer, Resource Extraction and Market Structure. XI, 154 pages. 1986.

Vol. 264: Models of Economic Dynamics. Proceedings, 1983. Edited by H.F. Sonnenschein. VII, 212 pages. 1986.

Vol. 265: Dynamic Games and Applications in Economics. Edited by T. Başar. IX, 288 pages. 1986.

Vol. 266: Multi-Stage Production Planning and Inventory Control. Edited by S. Axsäter, Ch. Schneeweiss and E. Silver. V, 264 pages. 1986.

Vol. 267: R. Bemelmans, The Capacity Aspect of Inventories. IX, 165 pages. 1986.

Vol. 268: V. Firchau, Information Evaluation in Capital Markets. VII, 103 pages. 1986.

Vol. 269: A. Borglin, H. Keiding, Optimality in Infinite Horizon Economies. VI, 180 pages. 1986.

Vol. 270: Technological Change, Employment and Spatial Dynamics. Proceedings 1985. Edited by P. Nijkamp. VII, 466 pages. 1986.

Vol. 271: C. Hildreth, The Cowles Commission in Chicago, 1939–1955. V, 176 pages. 1986.

Vol. 272: G. Clemenz, Credit Markets with Asymmetric Information. VIII, 212 pages. 1986.

Vol. 273: Large-Scale Modelling and Interactive Decision Analysis. Proceedings, 1985. Edited by G. Fandel, M. Grauer, A. Kurzhanski and A.P. Wierzbicki. VII, 363 pages. 1986.

Vol. 274: W.K. Klein Haneveld, Duality in Stochastic Linear and Dynamic Programming. VII, 295 pages. 1986.

Vol. 275: Competition, Instability, and Nonlinear Cycles. Proceedings, 1985. Edited by W. Semmler. XII, 340 pages. 1986.

Vol. 276: M.R. Baye, D.A. Black, Consumer Behavior, Cost of Living Measures, and the Income Tax. VII, 119 pages. 1986.

Vol. 277: Studies in Austrian Capital Theory, Investment and Time. Edited by M. Faber. VI, 317 pages. 1986.

Vol. 278: W.E. Diewert, The Measurement of the Economic Benefits of Infrastructure Services. V, 202 pages. 1986.

Vol. 279: H.-J. Büttler, G. Frei and B. Schips, Estimation of Disequilibrium Models. VI, 114 pages. 1986.

Vol. 280: H.T. Lau, Combinatorial Heuristic Algorithms with FORTRAN. VII, 126 pages. 1986.

Vol. 281: Ch.-L. Hwang, M.-J. Lin, Group Decision Making under Multiple Criteria. XI, 400 pages. 1987.

Vol. 282: K. Schittkowski, More Test Examples for Nonlinear Programming Codes. V, 261 pages. 1987.

Vol. 283: G. Gabisch, H.-W. Lorenz, Business Cycle Theory. VII, 229 pages. 1987.

Vol. 284: H. Lütkepohl, Forecasting Aggregated Vector ARMA Processes. X, 323 pages. 1987.

Vol. 285: Toward Interactive and Intelligent Decision Support Systems. Volume 1. Proceedings, 1986. Edited by Y. Sawaragi, K. Inoue and H. Nakayama. XII, 445 pages. 1987.

Vol. 286: Toward Interactive and Intelligent Decision Support Systems. Volume 2. Proceedings, 1986. Edited by Y. Sawaragi, K. Inoue and H. Nakayama. XII, 450 pages. 1987.

Vol. 287: Dynamical Systems. Proceedings, 1985. Edited by A.B. Kurzhanski and K. Sigmund. VI, 215 pages. 1987.

Vol. 288: G.D. Rudebusch, The Estimation of Macroeconomic Disequilibrium Models with Regime Classification Information. VII, 128 pages. 1987.

Vol. 289: B.R. Meijboom, Planning in Decentralized Firms. X, 168 pages. 1987.

Vol. 290: D.A. Carlson, A. Haurie, Infinite Horizon Optimal Control. XI, 254 pages. 1987.

Vol. 291: N. Takahashi, Design of Adaptive Organizations. VI, 140 pages. 1987.

Vol. 292: I. Tchijov, L. Tomaszewicz (Eds.), Input-Output Modeling. Proceedings, 1985. VI, 195 pages. 1987.

Vol. 293: D. Batten, J. Casti, B. Johansson (Eds.), Economic Evolu tion and Structural Adjustment. Proceedings, 1985. VI, 382 page 1987.

Vol. 294: J. Jahn, W. Krabs (Eds.), Recent Advances and Historic Development of Vector Optimization. VII, 405 pages. 1987.

Vol. 295: H. Meister, The Purification Problem for Constraine Games with Incomplete Information. X, 127 pages. 1987.

Vol. 296: A. Börsch-Supan, Econometric Analysis of Discre Choice. VIII, 211 pages. 1987.

Vol. 297: V. Fedorov, H. Läuter (Eds.), Model-Oriented Data Ana sis. Proceedings, 1987. VI, 239 pages. 1988.

Vol. 298: S.H. Chew, Q. Zheng, Integral Global Optimization. V 179 pages. 1988.